AMAZON REVIEWS OF CASE IN POINT

★★★★★ **Secret to success — consulting case interviews.** In graduate school I browsed many books on consulting case interview preparation. This was the only book I read. The clear, consistent way of thinking through how to manage case interviews made sense. Rather than focusing on formulas, frameworks (e.g., Porter's Five Forces), or just examples, Cosentino classifies cases into sensible categories and coaches the student through how to think about answering. Additionally, he gives valuable tips on how to get comfortable in the interview.

The true proof, however, was that I interviewed with the two top strategy consulting firms and received offers from both. I would highly recommend this book to anyone considering interviewing with top strategy consulting firms.

★★★★★ **Outstanding prep for case interviews.** *Case in Point* is in my view the best book of its type on the market. The top firms vary their cases from interviewer to interviewer; Cosentino's book provides a good system for tackling any case that you're presented. This book got me extremely well-prepared for my interviews. I just received a summer associate offer from what's arguably the top consulting firm, despite my non-business background.

★★★★★ **This is excellent.** This is probably the best consulting book on the market for undergrads looking to get a job in a top consulting firm after college. I own the *Vault Guide to the Case Interview* and felt this was MUCH better because it gives you a system to follow, not just a bunch of random structures and cases. Cosentino does a great job of putting all these pieces together into a very useful book.

★★★★★ **Great book for consulting preparation.** Cosentino's compilation of cases is a superb way to prepare for management consulting case interviews. Not only does he provide a wide variety of cases (from market-sizing to acquisition opportunity to dipping profits) he also offers several helpful frameworks for approaching consulting cases in general. I would highly recommend this book to anyone planning to do consulting interviews (and they're tough!).

★★★★★ **Having a job interview? Use this book: it's a must.** I used this book as a tool to prepare for interviews, and it really helped me. In this tough period, I followed the Ivy Case Method proposed, and it didn't fail. The book presents in a very readable way what to expect in an interview and how to create your best strategy. I'm usually very skeptical about these kinds of books, but I must say that Cosentino is able to attract the reader and through anecdotes and concrete examples, keep the reader's interest till the last page. Definitely a must.

★★★★★ **Got me a consulting job!** I was VERY nervous about getting a good job after school. I compared several interview guides and found some to be incomplete and others to be too long and confusing. Cosentino's *Case in Point* was easier to understand and covered the key techniques/frameworks behind case interviews. I practiced the sample cases and I eventually got a job in strategy consulting.

Here's what's new in the 8th edition

- Revised Ivy Case System
- More Case Starts with Notes
- 4 Strategy Cases
- Anatomy of an "Entering a New Market" Case

Also by Marc P. Cosentino

The Harvard College Guide to Consulting Case Questions

The Harvard College Guide to Consulting

The Harvard College Guide to Investment Banking

Churchill Must Die

Marketing Case Interviews

Case In Point

Complete Case Interview Preparation

EIGHTH EDITION

Marc P. Cosentino

MBA Analytica

CASEQUESTIONS.COM

Published by Burgee Press, Santa Barbara, CA

Acknowledgments

Special thanks are due to Brett Deware, Cullen Hilkene, Lynda Knoll Cotter, and Semil Shah, who contributed cases.

Thanks are also owed to all the students from around the world who contributed thoughts and case questions, especially Max Lund, Kevin Bittner, Colin Cosentino, Oliver Higgs, Aditi Bhargava, Basil Waite, Deepa Gupta, Emily Cosentino, Eric Edwards, Gonzolo Zubieta, Javier Luzarraga, John Loken, Memphis Gator, Mukund Jain, Sebastien Desreux, and Sinjin Brooks.

Many thanks to an unsung hero, my book designer, Jean Hammond, whose patience and sense of humor made many hours of toil great fun.

Burgee Press
P.O. Box 60137
Santa Barbara, CA 93160

As with all case questions, we assume facts not in evidence, as well as generous assumptions. Familiar companies are used as examples because of the power of their brand and their familiarity to the general public. Information concerning the actual companies cited as examples may not be accurate. This information was based on research but should not be used as reliable, up-to-date data.

Edited by Joan Oleck

ISBN 978-0-9710158-8-3
Library of Congress Cataloging-in-Publication Data:
Case in Point: Complete Case Interview Preparation / Marc P. Cosentino — 8th ed.
Library of Congress Card Number 2001117521

First Printing, 1999
Printed in the United States of America
Second Edition 2001
Third Edition 2004
Fourth Edition 2005
Fifth Edition 2007
Sixth Edition 2009
Seventh Edition 2011
Eighth Edition 2013

The mind is wondrous. It starts working the second you're born and doesn't stop until you get a case question.

Dedication

To Leisa — for sticking with me and loving me in a way I thought I'd never be loved, and to our new life together.

Contents

In Q4, the number-three US wireless carrier slipped further behind its rivals in its number of customers, even as profits rose 35%. What do you think is going on?

Consulting firms are in the business of renting out brains. Consultants get paid to synthesize massive quantities of foreign data, toss out the irrelevant information, structure an approach to a given client issue and hypothesize logically and creatively before people of power and influence (like bigwigs at the wireless company). That's why consulting firms put so much weight on the case question — because it allows them to judge how logically and persuasively a potential consultant (i.e., you) can present a case. In essence, a case interview is a role-playing exercise.

In order to nail a case interview, you need to know both how to prepare and how to perform. This book will help you do both. It walks you through the overall consulting interview, teaches you how to conduct your research, tells you what the consulting firms are looking for in a candidate, explores the various types of case questions and then introduces you to the Ivy Case System©.

As a career officer at Harvard University for over eighteen years, I've helped more than ten thousand of the nation's top students prepare for case interviews. During this time, students have tirelessly memorized individual frameworks and then struggled to decide which one(s) to apply. All the while, the case questions given by consulting firms, as well as by a growing number of companies in various industries, have become increasingly complex. The standard frameworks of the past, while still valuable, aren't enough to solve these sophisticated cases. I've developed The Ivy Case System© in order to simplify things. This system will allow you to make an impressive start (without a long and awkward pause) and ensure that you approach the answer in an organized and logical way. The difference between a framework and a system is that a framework is a tool; a system is a process with all the tools built in. The Ivy Case System© is the most sensible and comprehensive case interview strategy you can learn.

Keep in mind that case questions help educate you during your job search by acting as a self-imposed screening device. Is this the type of work you want to be doing? Is this the type of environment in which you can learn and flourish? You need to ask yourself, "Do I enjoy problem solving? Do I enjoy these types of questions and issues?" Case questions can and should be fun.

The best way to prepare is to hunker down and (i) read this book and don't skip any pages; (ii) attend all case question workshops sponsored by consulting firms or your career services office; (iii) practice with your econ professor, roommates, friends and anyone you know who worked or is currently working in consulting; and (iv) read this book again and don't skip any pages.

Sounds like you had better start reading . . .

Relax, it's worse than you think. If you figure the odds of getting chosen for an interview, having all the interviewers like you and making it through seven to ten cases, you'll be spending next semester's tuition on lottery tickets. But you know what? You faced much tougher odds when you applied to a top school. Not only were you accepted, you thrived. So forget about the odds and concentrate on *you*. If there was ever a time for tunnel vision, this is it. Besides, the recruiters don't know about the time you ... well, they don't know and we're certainly not going to tell them. So head into your interview with a clean slate.

This chapter will walk you through a first-round interview and show you how to prepare properly for each step. Some firms set up two back-to-back 45-minute interviews for the first round. In these interviews, one interviewer spends more time questioning you about yourself and then gives a short case question, while the other interviewer spends less time on you and more time on the case.

FIRST-ROUND INTERVIEW

Usually two 45-minute back-to-back interviews

The first person spends 25 minutes talking to you about you (why consulting?), asking for examples of leadership, persuasion, failure and team experience. Next, a small case, either a market-sizing, factor case, or more likely small-business problem. She then ends with your questions for the company.

The second person spends 10 minutes breaking the ice and then gives you a full case, taking up 25 to 30 minutes and often including charts for analysis. The last few minutes are taken up with your questions.

Introduction

You get called, offer your clammy hand then lie and say, "It's great to be here." Nothing to it; you did it the last time you had a blind date. (Let's hope this goes a little better.)

Cliché time: You never get a second chance to make a first impression. Eye contact, a pleasant smile and a firm handshake are paramount.

Questions About You

The first part of the interview is all about "getting to know you." McKinsey calls it a PEI, which stands for Personal Experience Interview. They will ask you to come up with several examples of times when you influenced or persuaded a group, about your relationship-building style and about goals that you set for yourself and were successful in meeting. Interviewers will ask you several questions drawn from your résumé (anything on your résumé is fair game). They may even ask, "Your life is a newspaper article. What's the headline?"

What they are looking for:

- a confident, comfortable demeanor and strong communication skills (Are you a nervous wreck?)
- leadership ability and initiative (Forget about the time you organized that keg party.)
- ability to be a team player (Do you play well with others?)
- drive, aspirations, energy, morals, and ethics (Do you have any?)

In this part of the interview you should be responding, not thinking. During the case questions you're going to do enough thinking to last you for a week. You need to research yourself beforehand. Look at the list of the most commonly asked questions in a consulting interview (see sidebar). You may not be asked any of these questions, but if you take the time to *write out the answers* or, better yet, bullet-point the answers, you will be forced to think about things you haven't thought about in years (or ever). Don't be surprised if the interviewer asks, "Tell me about a time you persuaded a group to do something they didn't want to do." You give her your answer and she replies, "Great, give me another example." It is common for interviewers to ask for two or three examples for the same question. When thinking through your answers, go three stories deep. Remember to bullet-point your answers instead of writing passages. People try to memorize passages, but unless you're Gwyneth Paltrow, there is no way you're going to deliver your answer and make it seem real.

COMMONLY ASKED CONSULTING INTERVIEW QUESTIONS

If you take the time to answer these questions before the interview, you will be more articulate and focused when it comes time to perform.

- Tell me about yourself.
- What are you doing here?
- Why consulting?
- Why did you pick your school?
- What do you think consultants do?
- What do you know about this job and our firm?
- Why would you choose our firm over our competitors?
- How are your quantitative skills?
- What percentage is 7 of 63?
- Tell me of a time you showed leadership skills.
- Tell me of a time you were a team player.
- Give me an example of a time you influenced or persuaded a group.
- Tell me about a recent crisis you handled.
- Have you ever failed at anything?
- Tell me about a time you took the initiative to start something.
- What type of work do you like to do best?
- With which other firms are you interviewing?
- Which other industries are you looking into?
- What accomplishments have given you the greatest satisfaction?
- What experiences/skills do you feel are particularly transferable to our organization?
- Why should I hire you?

Interviewers remember stories and accomplishments more than common answers ▶ ▶ ▶

You want to get labeled. If you tell the interviewer your captivating tale about windsurfing across the English Channel, then at the end of the day when the interviewer sees your name on her list, she'll remember you as "the windsurfer." Everything you spoke about will come back to her. If she sees your name and thinks, "Which one was he?" your candidacy is over.

So dig into the old treasure chest and come up with memorable stories and accomplishments that substantiate the skills needed to make you a strong candidate.

How do I answer? ▶ ▶ ▶

Three of the most problematic interview questions are:

- **Have you ever failed at anything?**
- **With which other firms are you interviewing?**
- **With which other industries are you interviewing?**

How do you answer these truthfully?

A DOZEN REASONS TO ENTER CONSULTING

Just in case you're not sure, below are 13 (a baker's dozen) of the most popular reasons students go into consulting:

1. You'll work and learn from very intelligent and articulate people.
2. You'll develop a vast array of marketable skills in a prestigious environment.
3. The learning curve never ends.
4. You'll receive exposure to the corporate elite: the way they think, act and analyze their problems.
5. You'll be exposed to many industries.
6. You'll work as part of a team.
7. You'll solve problems.
8. You'll make organizations more efficient.
9. You'll work on multiple projects.
10. You'll travel.
11. You'll improve your chances of being accepted into a top business school.
12. It will always look great on your résumé.
13. The money's good.

Q : 1 Have you ever failed at anything?

Say yes! Everybody has failed at something. People fail all the time. That's how you learn.

• **Dos:** Do talk about a failure and what you learned from that failure. Better yet, talk about how you failed, what you learned from that mistake, then how you turned it into a success. A perfect example comes from Michael Jordan. He failed to make his high school basketball team his freshman year, persevered and became a basketball legend. Have a story to tell; make it memorable.

• **Don'ts:** Don't talk about a personal failure. Stay away from anything that is going to make the interviewer feel uncomfortable (i.e., "I never got to straighten things out with my dad before he passed away," or, "My girlfriend dumped me ..." or, "I couldn't outrun that police car when I was seventeen."). Interviewers don't want to hear it. The other thing they don't want to hear about is an academic failure. I can't tell you how many Harvard students have told me in mock interviews, "I took an upper-level science class, worked like a dog, but I failed." "What did you get in the class?" I'd ask. "B minus." That's not failing. If you really did fail a course, they would know about it and ask why it happened.

Q : 2 With which other firms are you interviewing?

It's okay to tell them that you're interviewing with other consulting firms. Competition's tough; you'd be foolish to put all your energy into just one firm. However, you must be able to tell them why they're your first choice and what makes them better in your mind than the other firms.

Q : 3 With which other industries are you interviewing?

Consulting goes hand-in-hand with two other industries. While interviewing for a consulting position, it's okay to mention that you are looking at investment banking and/or strategic planning. These positions look for the same qualities in a candidate and require similar job skills. In fact, McKinsey's and BCG's biggest competitor is Goldman Sachs — not each other.

+ Why Consulting?

You know the interviewer is going to ask you why you want to be a consultant. Now this is important: not only should your answer be immediate, but you must look the interviewer right in the eye. If you look away, it indicates that you are thinking about the question and that's enough to end the interview right then and there. You should have given this answer a great deal of thought long before you walked into the interview. While I don't want you to memorize your answer, I do want you to memorize bullet points. This makes your answer focused, linear and of an appropriate length. Avoid talking aimlessly. Having several good reasons why you want to be a consultant isn't enough. It's not always what you say but how you say it and, most important, what they hear. Your voice should carry sincerity and enthusiasm.

+ Possible Math Question

They may ask you about your quantitative skills. This could be followed by a small math question such as, "What's 100 divided by 7?" Or, "9 is what percentage of 72?" The questions aren't hard, but they might take you by surprise. It may be time to break out the flash cards.

During the first part of the interview, you're being judged. The interviewer is asking herself whether or not she'd like to work and travel with you. Are you interesting? Engaging? Do you have a sense of humor and like to have fun? This is better known as the "airport test." The name comes from the question, "How would I feel if I were snowed in with this candidate for nine hours at the Buffalo airport? Would we have a lot to talk about, or would I have to pretend that I was in a coma so I wouldn't have to talk?"

The interviewer is also measuring your maturity, poise and communication skills, while thinking, "Would I feel comfortable bringing this candidate in front of a client?"

An important component of the "maturity test" is to determine whether you think before you speak. I had a Harvard student who, when asked what percentage 3 of 17 is, he blurted out "80%." (I don't know how he got into Harvard, either.) For him that interview was over. He might as well have gotten up and walked out because nothing was going to save him. Not because he got the wrong answer, but because it was clear that he didn't think before he spoke. If he does something like that in an interview, what is he going to do in front of a client? I couldn't trust him, and if I can't trust him, I am not going to hire him.

+ Case Questions

The second part of the interview is the case question. These questions carry a tremendous amount of weight. You can pass the airport test and be as poised and articulate as John F. Kennedy, but if you fumble the case, that's it. Alternatively, if you hit a home run on the case but have the social skills of Napoleon Dynamite, then you have bigger problems than getting a job. We'll cover the case questions in depth in Chapter Three.

+ Your Questions

The last part of the interview requires a good deal of research about both the industry and the company. In addition, if you can find out who will be interviewing you, you should be Googling them to see what articles they have written or issues they are involved with. You can bet that they will be Googling you. In your research, you should be looking for answers to the pre-interview questions (see sidebar, next page). Questions for which you can't locate answers become excellent questions to pose to your interviewer.

PRE-INTERVIEW QUESTIONS

1. What type of consulting does the firm do?
2. In what industries does the firm specialize?
3. How big is the firm?
   - How many domestic and international offices does the firm have?
   - How many professionals are in the firm?
4. What kinds of training programs does the firm offer?
5. What type of work does an entry-level consultant do?
6. How much client contact does an entry-level consultant have the first year?
7. Does the firm have a mentor program?
8. How often do first-years sleep in their own beds? What's their travel schedule like?
9. How many hours make up a typical work day?
10. How is a case team picked?
11. How often do consultants get reviewed?
12. How many consultants does the firm expect to hire this year?
13. How does that compare to last year?
14. Where do the consultants go when they leave the firm?
15. Is it possible to transfer to other offices, even international offices?

However, before you ask your first question, if there is anything critical that you didn't get a chance to bring up in the interview, now is the time. Simply state, "Before I ask my first question, I just want to make sure you understand ..." Get it out before you leave the room. If you don't, you're going to kick yourself all the way home, and even worse, you'll never know if that statement could have turned the tide.

The best ways to collect these answers are to: ▶ ▶ ▶

❑ **Attend career fairs and speak to the firm representatives.** Pull out your list of questions and ask three or four. Make sure that you try to turn this meeting into a conversation. At the end, thank the reps for their time, ask them for their business cards and inquire whether it would be all right if you called or e-mailed them with further questions. At this point, no one is going to judge you on your level of company knowledge. They are there to provide information and hype the firm.

❑ **Scour the company's website.** This will let you know how the firm sees itself and the image that it's trying to project.

❑ **Talk to alumni and graduate school students who used to work for the companies that you're interviewing with.** Often, career services offices will be able to match you up with alumni who are working in a specific industry. Interviewing past employees can be very enlightening. They will tell you more about their old firm in half an hour than you'll learn by spending two hours on the Internet. Plus, they'll tell you things that you'll never find on the Internet. They can be completely objective; they don't have to try to sell the firm.

❑ **Attend company information meetings.** Get your name and face in front of firm representatives so that they can associate your face with your résumé. While these people don't have the power to hire you, they do have the power to get you on the interview list. Top-tier firms often get 400 résumés for 100 first-round interview slots. Snag that interview slot by networking and schmoozing with firm representatives every chance you get. One of the best kept secrets of company presentations is to go early. If a company presentation is scheduled to start at 6 pm, show up at 5:45. Most students won't arrive until 6 pm or a little after, but the firm's representatives show up at around 5:30 to make sure that the room is set up correctly and the cheese table is laid out nicely. If you show up early, not only will it impress the consultants, but it will allow you to get at least five minutes of quality face time with one of them. They are more likely to remember you if you talk for five minutes at the beginning of the night than if you hang around until the end hoping for 45 seconds of their time. They are also more likely to have their business cards with them. Remember to ask for those business cards and send a follow-up e-mail.

❑ **Search *The Wall Street Journal* and the Internet for articles and information on the firm.** This allows you to be current on any firm's news.

Have your list of questions with any specific facts or figures you've dug up written out when you walk into the interview. This shows that you have done your homework and have given this interview a great deal of thought. Besides, if you freeze up, it's all right there in front of you.

✢ The Grand Finale: Why Should I Hire You?

This is your opportunity to shine and market yourself. But before you launch into a laundry list of skills and attributes, you may want to simply state that they should hire you because you want to be a consultant. Then, reiterate all the reasons that you brought up earlier when they asked you, "Why consulting?"

Consulting firms look for "low-risk" hires. You're a low-risk hire if you've worked in consulting, liked it and want to return, or have done your homework. Consulting firms' biggest fear is that they will spend a lot of time and money recruiting, hiring and training you, only to have you bail out after six months because consulting isn't what you expected it to be.

If they aren't convinced that this is what you want to do, then it doesn't matter how talented you are; it's not worth it for them to extend you an offer. Think of it this way: How would you feel if someone accepted your dinner invitation because his first choice fell through? If your heart's not in it, they don't want you.

Students who receive job offers in consulting do so for four reasons: ▶ ▶ ▶

1. They are able to convince the interviewer that they are committed to consulting and know what they're getting into (i.e., type of work, lifestyle, travel).
2. They can demonstrate success-oriented behavior.
3. They exhibit good analytical skills when answering case questions. (That's where we come in.)
4. They are able to articulate their thoughts, create a positive presence and defend themselves without being defensive.

Now that you understand the structure of the interview for the first round, the subsequent rounds are not all that different. The second round is often held at a nearby hotel and usually consists of two interviews, both 60 minutes in length, each with a heavy focus on case questions. The third round is typically held in the firm's offices where there are five interviews, 60 minutes each, again with a heavy emphasis on case questions. During all the final rounds you can expect to analyze many charts. In addition, some firms give written cases requiring you not only to analyze the information but to design charts to back up your recommendations.

There are other kinds of first-round interviews. Some firms conduct phone interviews while others conduct group case interviews.

First-Round Telephone Interviews

There will be times when your first-round interview will be conducted over the phone. Sometimes this is a screening interview; other times you'll get a case question as well. There are several things to remember: if possible, go to a quiet and private place. Turn off the television and lock the door so your roommate doesn't barge in and interrupt you.

Most importantly, **you are your voice**. That is the only thing the person on the other end of the line has to go on. Your voice should be upbeat and enthusiastic; so speak clearly and with confidence, but not arrogance.

Finally, lose the calculator. I know that it is tempting to have it right there, but if you get the answer too quickly, or the interviewer can hear buttons being pushed, you're sunk.

First-Round Telephone and Skype Interviews

In addition to all that, for a Skyping interview you will need to dress up as you would for a regular interview. I've heard stories where the interviewee was dressed up above the waist, but had on pajama bottoms, shorts or sweat pants. Normally this wouldn't be a problem but they had to get up and retrieve something. Also, be aware of your background. What can the person on the other side of the computer see? If you have a poster of a bikini-clad Sports Illustrated swimsuit model hanging on your wall you might want to remove it or angle the camera away from the poster. I Skype with students from around the world and I'm always interested in the background – what their apartment or dorm room looks like. It gives me additional information on their personalities and organizational skills.

First-Round Group Case Interviews

McKinsey and other firms have started holding group interviews for non-MBA graduate students as part of their first-round interviews. During a group interview, consultants look more at the group dynamics than how the group answers the question. Does this candidate have the ability to build relationships, empathy and teamwork? On one hand, you are a competitor to the other people in the group, but on the other hand, for this moment in time you are teammates. People who are aggressive and try to dominate the conversation are the ones that don't get called back. Remember, consultants work in teams, and if you're not willing to be a team player, then you're out.

In my Harvard Business School classes, the professor rarely called on anyone who had his hand raised while someone else was speaking. This indicated that the hand-raising student wasn't listening to his classmate and had his own agenda. Like a business school case class, you are expected to build on what others have said, and move the discussion forward, not take it off on a tangent, or move the discussion back because you had a point you wanted to make.

+ Stress Interviews

Well, they're back. Stress interviews. They usually come in one of two forms. The first type is the two-on-one (you're the one). The interviewers ask you question after question without giving you much of a chance to answer. They'll make unfavorable comments to each other about your answers, dismissing your answers as amateurish or ridiculous. They may even turn rude and snappish.

Why do the interviewers do this? They put you through this to see how you react. Can you defend yourself and your answers without getting defensive? Can you maintain your cool and your professionalism? Can you handle it if someone snaps at you or will you crumble and cry?

The second type is the silent treatment. The interviewer doesn't smile; he usually sits in silence waiting to see if you start talking. If you ask the interviewer a question, he'll usually shoot back a one-word answer. He might question many of your statements, making you explain even the simplest of answers.

Why do they do this? They'll tell you that silence leads to stupid statements, where interviewees will blurt out irrelevant conversation just to fill the silence, and it's important to know how you would react in a situation like this with a client.

Sometimes during a case you'll be asked to make a decision. You will be forced to choose between A and B. If you choose A, the interviewer will look you right in the eye and say, "Let me tell you why you are wrong." If you had chosen B, he would have looked you right in the eye and said, "Let me tell you why you are wrong." It doesn't matter which one you choose, He is going to tell you why you are wrong. Again, he does this to see how you react. Do you turn red? Does your jaw tighten or do your eyebrows shoot up? Clients are going to challenge your findings and ideas all the time. He wants to make sure you can handle criticism when someone gets in your face.

While he is telling you why you are wrong, if you don't find his answer very persuasive, then simply say, "That was an interesting argument, but I didn't find it compelling enough. I'm sticking with answer A." That's what he wants you to do: Stick with your answer if you think you are right. Defend your answer without getting defensive.

If in his argument he brings up something that you didn't think about and now that you're thinking about it, it changes everything, admit that you were wrong. Simply say, "That was a very persuasive argument, and to be honest, I didn't think about the inventory issue. I think you're right; I think B is the right answer." There is no shame in changing your answer if you were wrong. It shows that you are still objective and open to reason. Remember, one of the main reasons corporations hire consulting firms is because of their objectivity. If you can remain objective about your answer, then you are one step closer to being a consultant. What the interviewer doesn't want you to do is change your answer just because he said you were wrong.

Rules for stress interviews:

- Don't take it personally.
- Try not to get flustered.
- Roll with the punches .
- Watch what you say; make sure that it is relevant to the interview.
- Remain confident.

Confidence

To add to the fun, while all this is going on, you need to sound confident even if you don't feel it. If your confidence level is too low, they're going to question everything you say. There is an old saying about Harvard professors: they're often wrong, but never uncertain. You need to carry that same mindset into your interview. Even if you are uncertain, you need to remain confident.

Advice for International Students

Having spent 18 years at Harvard, I've advised thousands of international students pursuing a career in consulting. Most of these students wanted to work initially in the United States before returning to their home countries. While many were successful, like their American classmates, the majority were not. Consulting jobs are very competitive and highly sought after. I offer three additional pieces of advice for international students.

1. Be honest about your communication skills.
Much of the interview process is driven by communication skills. Are you truly fluent in English? Do you have an accent? How pronounced is it? A couple of years ago, I worked with a brilliant Chinese student at Harvard. He did very well in the mock case interviews I gave him; however, his language skills, particularly his presentation skills, were poor. While his understanding of English was excellent, his verbal and written skills left much to be desired. Against my advice he applied to the Boston offices of all the top firms. While he received a number of first-round interviews, he didn't get a single second-round interview. He found himself competing against American Harvard students and he didn't stand a chance.

2. Think long-term and play to your strengths.
I met several times with a Russian student. Her English was excellent, she could articulate her thoughts and she even had a good command of "business English." While she had an Eastern European accent, she was easy to understand. Her grades, work experience and extracurricular activities were just okay, but nothing great, so she faced some pretty stiff competition from her American classmates. She wanted to work in New York. Her problem was getting the first-round interview. We talked about thinking long-term. If she applied to the Moscow office of these firms, she would have a significantly better chance of getting hired than if she focused on New York. She knew the language, the culture and the economics of the region, and she had a degree from a prestigious American university. She could work in Moscow for two years, then transfer back to the United States, which is exactly what she did.

3. Come back to campus in case-fighting form.
Summer internships are tough to get, so don't get discouraged if you don't land one. I have pockets full of stories about students who didn't get a summer internship but landed a full-time consulting job upon graduation. There are many more full-time opportunities than summer positions, but they are still very competitive. Don't waste your summer; use it to become a better candidate in the autumn. The first step is to secure a summer job where you will be developing some of the same skills you would if you worked in a consulting firm. The sec-

ond is to practice your cases over the summer. I had a brilliant student from the Caribbean who had no business experience but plenty of great leadership experience. He received four first-round summer internship interviews. He made it to the second round with two firms but didn't get an offer. He spent the summer working for a large international financial agency in Washington, DC, where he wanted to settle. He spent the summer contacting alumni who worked in the DC offices of the two major consulting firms and invited them out for lunch, coffee and beer. He learned about their firms, and he made great connections within those offices. Every time he sipped a coffee or drank a beer with them, he asked them to give him a case question. This went on all summer long. When he returned to campus in September, he was in case-fighting form and had many supporters within each firm. He ended up with full-time offers from both McKinsey and BCG.

To summarize:

- Strengthen your communication skills.
- Think long-term and play to your strengths.
- Come back to campus in fighting form.

✢ Advice for Industry Hires

If you are applying as an industry hire, there are a few things you need to know. While most of the hires made by the big consulting firms are university hires, the number of industry hires has been increasing, although it is still around an 80/20 breakdown, university over industry. Having years of experience in a particular industry isn't always a good thing. For example, if you have ten years' experience in the health-care industry, some firms might be reluctant to hire you for your industry experience because you come with certain prejudices or beliefs about an industry. The firms are worried that if you see a problem with a client, you are going to solve it the same way you solved it when you worked in health care. They like people who can look at a problem objectively, with no preconceived notions. They will, however, draw on your industry knowledge when building industry files. So don't be surprised if you are assigned to new industries at first.

The interview process is somewhat the same. If you are applying to McKinsey, you'll probably be asked to take the written exercise that most non-MBAs have to take. The first round might consist of three one-hour interviews, which will have both a personal experience component to it as well as a case. I'd be surprised if the cases you get touch on your old industry. They want to test your thought structure, not your industry knowledge.

They will expect you to be more confident than a university candidate, more professional in your demeanor. Another thing to remember is that you will enter the firm at the same level as a newly minted MBA (unless you bring a host of clients with you). You may be reporting to someone years younger. Keep in mind that these firms are meritocracies and you can move up as quickly as your talents allow. In fact, you want to enter at that level; it will give you time to get your sea legs and establish yourself.

And now, at last, it's time for...

A case question is a fun, intriguing and active interviewing tool used to evaluate the multi-dimensional aspects of a candidate.

WHAT FIRMS LOOK FOR

Consultants spend a great deal of their time on the road at the client's site. They work in small teams and are sometimes put in charge of groups of the client's employees. Often, consultants work under great pressure in turbulent environments while dealing with seemingly unmanageable problems. It takes a certain type of personality to remain cool under pressure, to influence the client without being condescending and to be both articulate and analytical at the same time.

As we said earlier, the business of consulting is really the renting of brains, packaged and delivered with an engaging and confident personality. So as you work through the case, the interviewer is asking herself: Is the candidate...

- relaxed, confident and mature?
- a good listener?
- engaging and enthusiastic?
- exhibiting strong social and presentation skills?
- asking insightful and probing questions?
- able to determine what's truly relevant?
- organizing the information effectively and developing a logical framework for analysis?
- stating assumptions clearly?
- comfortable discussing the multifunctional aspects of the case?
- trying to quantify his response at every opportunity?
- displaying both business sense & common sense?
- thinking creatively?
- rolling with the punches?
- defending himself without being defensive?

+ Purpose of the Case Question

Interviewers don't ask case questions to embarrass and humiliate you. They don't ask case questions to see you sweat and squirm (although some might consider it a side perk). They do ask case questions...

- to probe your intellectual curiosity
- to test your analytical ability
- to test your ability to think logically and organize your answer
- to observe your thought process
- to probe your tolerance for ambiguity and data overload
- to assess your poise, self-confidence and communication skills under pressure
- to discover your personality
- to see if you're genuinely intrigued by problem-solving
- to determine if consulting is a good "fit" for you

+ Case Preparation

Case questions can be made simple through preparation and practice. I never like to equate an interview with a test, but they are similar in that the more you prepare, the better you'll do. Maybe you've experienced the feeling of being so prepared for an exam that you can't wait for the professor to hand it out so you can rip right through it. Case questions are the same way. Firms look to see if you have that "rip right through it" look in your eyes. It's called confidence.

Some of my students, even after they got the job, would come into my office and ask me to give them a case. They loved doing cases. To them it was no different than working a crossword puzzle. They loved the intellectual challenge, and they learned something new every time they did one.

Before we look at some cases, it is best to understand The Case Commandments. Follow these rules and your case interviewing life will become much easier.

✛ The Case Commandments

[1. Listen to the Question.]

Listening is the most important skill a consultant has. The case isn't about you or the consultant; it's about the client. What are they really asking for? Pay particular attention to the last sentence — one word can change the entire case.

[2. Take Notes.]

Taking notes during the case interview allows you to check back with the facts of the case. As someone once said, "The palest ink is stronger than the best memory." If you blank out, all the information is right in front of you.

[3. Summarize the Question.]

After you are given the question, take a moment to summarize the highlights out loud:

- It shows the interviewer that you listened.
- It allows you to hear the information a second time.
- It keeps you from answering the wrong question.
- It fills that otherwise awkward pause when you're trying to think of something intelligent to say.

[4. Verify the Objectives.]

Professional consultants always ask their clients to verify their objectives. Even if the objective seems obvious, there could be an additional, underlying objective. When the objective seems apparent, phrase the question differently: "One objective is to increase sales. Are there any other objectives I should know about?"

[5. Ask Clarifying Questions.]

You ask questions for three main reasons:

- to get additional information that will help you identify and label the question
- to demonstrate to the interviewer that you are not shy about asking probing questions under difficult circumstances (something you'll be doing on a regular basis as a consultant)
- to turn the question into a conversation (nothing turns off an interviewer more quickly than a five-minute monologue)

In the beginning of the case, you have more latitude in your questioning. You should ask basic questions about the company, the industry, the competition, external market factors and the product. The further you get into the case, the more your questions should switch from open-ended questions to closed-ended questions. You start to get into trouble when you ask broad, sweeping questions that are hard for the interviewer to answer. These kinds of questions give the impression that you're trying to get the interviewer to answer the case for you. You'll know that you crossed that line when the interviewer says to you, "What do you think?" When this happens, substitute assumptions for questions.

[6. Organize Your Answer.]

Identify and label your case, then lay out your structure. This is the hardest part of a case, and the most crucial. It drives your case and is often the major reason behind whether you get called back. We will spend more time on this in Chapter Four.

[7. Hold That Thought for "One Alligator."]

The interviewer wants you to think out loud, but also to think before you speak. If you make a statement that is way off base in an interview, the recruiter will wonder if he can trust you in front of a client. If he thinks he can't trust you, the interview is over.

[8. Manage Your Time.]

Your answer should be as linear as possible. Don't get bogged down in the details. Answer from a macro level and move the answer forward. It's easy to lose your way by going off on a tangent. Stay focused on the original question asked. Finally, don't lose track of the question, the objective or the framework. Go back to the original question and objectives during the case to make sure you haven't lost your way.

[9. Work the Numbers.]

If possible, try to work numbers into the problem. Demonstrate that you think quantitatively and that you are comfortable with numbers. When doing calculations, explain what you are thinking and how you are going to do it. Take your time. I'd rather have you get it right than rush and make a careless mistake.

[10. Be Coachable.]

Listen to the interviewer's feedback. Is she trying to guide you back on track? Pay attention to her body language. Are you boring her? Is she about to nod off? Is she enthralled?

Being coachable also means asking for help when you need it. If you run into a wall, lose your train of thought or are just in over your head, ask for help. There is no shame in asking for help; it's a sign of maturity. Look at it from the interviewer's point of view. If you were working on an actual project and got stuck, she would much rather that you ask for help than waste time spinning your wheels.

[11. Be Creative and Brainstorm.]

Some of the best experiences you'll have as a consultant will be brainstorming over Chinese food at 10 o'clock at night. *Brainstorming without commitment*, as consultants call it, allows you to toss out uninhibited suggestions without being married to them. It gives you the opportunity to review all the options and eliminate the inappropriate ones. Consulting firms like liberal arts candidates with intellectual curiosity who can "think outside the box" and offer up a new and interesting perspective.

[12. Exude Enthusiasm and a Positive Attitude.]

Earlier we spoke about a "rip right through it" attitude. It's not enough to do well on the case; you have to thrive on the challenge of the case. Recruiters want people who are excited by problem-solving and can carry that enthusiasm throughout the entire interview.

[13. Bring Closure and Summarize.]

If you have done all of the above and you've made it through the analysis, the final action is to create a sense of closure by summarizing the case. Review your findings, restate your suggestions and make a recommendation. You don't need to sum up the whole answer; pick two or three key points and touch on those. Students are often afraid to make a recommendation, thinking that their analysis was faulty, so therefore their answers will be wrong. There are no wrong answers. Just make sure your answer makes good business sense and common sense.

+ Interview Evaluation Forms

Every firm has its own unique evaluation form; however, what they look for is the same. Some are broken down into *analytics* (structure, quant acumen and good use of data), *communication* (eye contact, articulation, listening, asking probing questions, and note layout) and *personal* (enthusiasm, self-confidence, teamwork and original thought and intellectual curiosity).

To use one example, the Bain & Company interview evaluation form is broken down into three areas; *value addition, client/team, reality check* plus *a final summary rating*. You are rated 1 to 5 in several categories under these areas, with 5 being the highest score.

▶ **Value Addition**

Under value addition you have five categories; structured problem solving, business judgment, quant skills, creativity and drive to results (80/20), plus a final overall value addition score.

▶ **Client/Team**

There also five categories plus a summary score. The five areas are, drive/achievement, team skills, communication, professionalism and leadership.

▶ **Reality Check**

Under this heading, the interviewee is asked to answer three questions. Is this person interested in Bain? Would you have this person on your team? (The Pittsburgh Airport test). And, would you pass on/give an offer to this person?

▶ **Summary**

Finally you get an overall interview rating.

In the first two sections there is a space for the interviewer to write comments under two headings, *strengths* and *weaknesses/topics to test in next round.*

+ Types of Case Questions

Case questions generally fall into one of four major categories: brainteasers, back-of-the-envelope questions (which are often called market-sizing questions), factor questions and business case questions. It's quite common to find a market-sizing question enclosed within a larger business case question. Whether fun or frustrating, all case questions are valuable learning experiences.

Brainteasers

Brainteasers are scarce these days, but they still pop up in the occasional first-round interview, so it's important to be aware of them. Brainteasers are basically the same riddles and conundrums that we've all been struggling to solve since fourth grade. Some brainteasers have a definite answer; others are more flexible in their solutions. Interviewers are looking to see not only if you can come up with a good answer, but also whether you can handle the pressure. Do you get frustrated, stressed and upset? The key is to keep your cool and try to break the problem down logically. Just give it your best shot and don't be afraid to laugh at your mistakes or be a bit self-deprecating. It makes you human and more fun to be with.

Below is an example of a brainteaser with a definite answer.

The Bags of Gold

Q : 1 ***There are three bags of gold. One of the bags contains fake gold. All the bags and all the coins look exactly alike. There is the same number of coins in each bag. The real gold coins weigh one ounce each, the fake coins weigh 1.1 oz. apiece. You have a one-pan penny scale and one penny, which means you can weigh something just once. (You load the scale, put the penny in and the scale spits out a piece of paper with the weight.) How can you tell which bag has the fake gold?***

A : 1 *You take one coin from the first bag of gold, two coins from the second bag and three coins from the third bag. Place them all on the scale. If the coins weigh 6.1 oz., then you know that the first bag held the fake gold. If they weigh 6.2 oz., then it is the second bag. If the coins weigh 6.3 oz., then the third bag held the fake gold.*

There are numerous puzzle and brainteaser books to be found in your local bookstore. If you are worried about these types of questions, you may want to pick up one of these books.

Market-sizing Questions

Market-sizing questions surface all the time and can be found during any round of interviewing. Sometimes they're a stand-alone question or they can be embedded in a larger case. When I hear a market-sizing question I like to label it. Is it a population-based question, a household question or a preposterous question? Regardless of the type of market-sizing question, your answer should be based on logic and assumptions.

There are going to be instances when your assumptions are wrong. Sometimes the interviewer will correct you; other times she will let it go. **The interviewer is more interested in your logic and thought process than whether your assumptions are spot–on.** If you are still concerned, you can always say, "I'm not that familiar with this market, so if my assumptions are off, please correct me." Ninety percent of the time, the interviewer will tell you not to worry about it. However, everything you say has the potential to be questioned — be ready to defend your assumptions, as they should be based on some type of logic. If you just pull them out of the air, you're risking the interviewer aggressively challenging your assumptions and your credibility.

During a market-sizing case you don't get a chance to ask questions. You can only ask questions if you don't understand something. If they rattle off a string of initials, industry jargon or slang, and you're not sure what they mean, ask. You don't lose any points for asking clarifying questions. These questions are tough enough to answer even when you understand all the information.

When I go into a market-sizing question I've already memorized several key facts and numbers. I don't want to be caught flatfooted, I don't want to pull numbers out of the air that are going to be difficult to work with, I want numbers that are going to be easy, numbers that I'm familiar with, so I can do calculations with confidence.

Here are some key numbers that you should memorize.

- US population is 320 million
- Life expectancy of an American is 80 years
- Even distribution between the ages (so there is the same number of 2-year-olds as 72-year-olds. We know that this is not true, but in a case like this, it's fine to assume, thus 4 million people per age group.)
- 100 million US households

MARKET-SIZING QUESTIONS

Your answer should be based on logic and assumptions.

Structure

- Listen to the question: then determine the type of case: population based, household, or preposterous?
- Ask clarifying questions only if you don't understand the question or terminology.
- Lay out your structure first and the steps you'll need to answer the question; then go back through it with the numbers.

Assumptions

- Don't worry if your assumptions are off; the interviewer is more interested in your thought process than whether your assumptions are correct.
- If your assumptions are way off, they will tell you; otherwise they'll let it go.
- Base your assumptions on some sort of logic; otherwise the interviewer might press you on how you drew that conclusion.
- You can group several assumptions into one number (i.e., the 20 percent takes into account X, Y and Z.)

Math

- Estimate or round off numbers to make calculation easier.
- Write all numbers down.

Regardless of where you're interviewing you should know these key facts for your country or region. Also, don't use your friends as a sample population. Chances are you're at an elite university and your friends are unlikely to represent the general population. And remember to use easy numbers, numbers that you can divide and multiple without much problem.

As they give you the question, write everything down. Determine and label the question: Is it a population-based, household or preposterous question.? Next, ask questions *only* if you don't understand the questions or terminology. Finally, lay out your structure, then go back through it and fill in the numbers. That way you get a second bite at the apple as you work through the problem again. Base your assumptions on some sort of logic; otherwise the interviewer might press you on how you drew that conclusion. And take advantage of grouping assumptions together. You can say something like, "The 20% takes into account X, Y, and Z."

Population-based questions

❑ How many smartphones were sold in the US last year?

- Make assumptions and break the population down by generation.
- Determine the number of cell phones in each generation.
- Calculate the number or percentage of smartphones out of each generation's number of cell phones.
- You may want to draw a chart to show how well organized you are and how logically you think. It also makes it easier for the interviewer to follow your thought process.

Assumptions: 320 million Americans, life expectancy of 80 years, even distribution among the ages. I'm going to divide it into generations, 0–20, 21–40, 41–60 and 61–80. That means 80 million people per generation.

Kids 0-12 or 52 million American children don't own cell phones. Out of the remaining 28 million kids I'll assume that 20 million have a cell phone. Out of that 20 million I'll assume that 10 million have a smartphone. These are older kids and they're technology driven.

Reason through your numbers for each generation and fill in the chart as you go along.

	Population	No. of Cell Phones	No. of smartphones
0 – 20	80m	20m	10m
21 – 40	80m	60m	40m
41 – 60	80m	60m	40m
61 – 80	80m	60m	10m
		200m	100m

We came up with a 100 million smartphones in the US. However, the question called for the number of smartphones sold in the US last year. The average cell phone contract is two years, new models come out every 18 months. I'll assume 80 percent will upgrade to a new model. That means 50 million are eligible for the upgrade and 80 percent of the 50 million or 40 million will buy a new smartphone. I'll also assume that 20 percent of the 50 million regular cell phone users eligible for an upgrade will switch to a smartphone, which equals 10 million. Thus, 50 million smartphones were sold last year.

Now you may not agree with all my assumptions, but as long as you can follow my logic, I'm fine.

❑ How many gas stations are there in the US?

I live in a town with a population of 30,000. There are six gas stations serving our town (not really, but six divides nicely into 30). Therefore, I'll assume that each gas station serves about 5,000 customers. If the population of the US is 300 million, I'll just divide 300 million by 5,000 and get 60,000 gas stations in the US.

If you had tried to answer this question as a household question, you would quickly find yourself mired in numerous and unnecessary calculations.

Household questions

❑ **How many digital movies get downloaded each year in the US?**

- Determine the US population and break it down by household.
- Estimate the number of households with Internet access.
- Eliminate categories of households that wouldn't download movies.
- Make assumptions about the number of movies downloaded, either rented or purchased each week, and multiply by 50 weeks.

Assumptions: 320 million Americans, 3.2 people per household, thus 100 million households. (You always want to work with 100 million US households and 200 million households in Europe.) 70 percent of US households have access to the Internet.

So, we have 70 million US households with Internet access. From that number I'm going to subtract households with dial-up service (it would take them two weeks to download a movie), households that would never put their credit card on the Internet; households that are happy with cable and network television and would never download a movie; a percentage of Netflix customers that don't mind waiting an extra 30 days to see the new releases; and households with Direct TV or cable that have video-on-demand or pay-per-view.

To that number, I'm going to add people who don't have Internet at home but could go to Starbucks and download a movie while drinking a latté, or download a movie during finance class at school or while at work.

Taking all that into consideration, I'll assume that 50 million out of the 70 million households with access to the Internet will download movies. Now some households with teenagers or a road warrior might download several movies a week, while I think most houses might download one movie a month. So I'll assume that on average those households download 20 movies a year.

That means, 50 million households downloading 20 movies a year equals 1 billion downloads a year.

❑ **How many garden hoses were sold in the US last year?**

- Determine the US population and break it down by household.
- Estimate the number of households in the suburbs and in the rural areas.
- Calculate the number of those households that have a yard and are in need of a garden hose.
- Add in businesses that use garden hoses to get a total.
- Estimate the life of a garden hose.

Assumptions: 320 million Americans, 3.2 people per household, thus 100 million households.

I'm going to estimate that 50 percent of the households are either suburban or rural. That makes 50 million households. I'll assume that 20 percent of those homes are apartments or condos. That narrows us down to 40 million houses that most likely use a garden hose. Garden hoses are relatively inexpensive, so people are likely to have two hoses, a hose in the front yard and a hose in the backyard. That makes 80 million hoses. To that number I'd like to add another 10 million hoses, which can be found in nurseries, zoos and other outdoor facilities. Most of those businesses have at least two hoses.

We are now up to 90 million garden hoses. Hoses aren't replaced every year. I'd say that they are replaced every three years unless they run into the business end of a dog's tooth. So we take 90 million hoses, divide that number by 3 and come up with 30 million garden hoses sold each year.

▶ Worldwide market-sizing

Suppose someone asked you to determine the market-size for the worldwide bulletproof auto glass (bpag) industry. That's a daunting task. You might start off with a list of people and organizations that use bulletproof auto glass, such as the military, Fortune 500 corporations, governments and various organizations such as the mob, drug lords, celebrities and armored trucks. But then you would need to figure how many government vehicles use bulletproof glass for every country in the world! Yikes!

There is an easy and logical way to attack a problem like this. You pick one country, determine its market size and extrapolate out.

❑ What is the worldwide market size for bulletproof auto glass?

- Make a list of possible customers or users.
- State that you are going to figure out the US market and extrapolate.
- Calculate the percentage of US cars that have bpag.
- Estimate the US's percentage of the worldwide market share.
- Determine the US market size by:
  - Breaking the US households down by income levels
  - Estimating the number of cars in each income group
  - Adding non-household cars to the count

Assumptions: 2 percent of all US cars have bulletproof auto glass. The US makes up 10 percent of the market; 100 million US households.

The biggest users of bulletproof auto glass would be militaries, Fortune 500 companies, governments, the mob, drug lords, celebrities and armored trucks.

I'm going to break the US market size down by household incomes: high, middle and low. I'll assume that the high-income households make up 10 percent of the total US households and that they have on average 3 cars per household. That makes 30 million cars.

I think the middle-income households make up 60 percent and that they average two cars; Maybe both spouses work or they have teenagers of driving age. That leaves the low-income households at 30 million. A big percentage of the low-income population lives in the cities and don't need a car. I'm going to estimate .5 cars per household, or 15 million.

Income	HH	# of Cars	Total Cars
High	10m	3	30m
Middle	60m	2	120m
Low	30m	.5	15m

That gives us a total of 165 million cars. To that total I'm going to add 35 million cars representing government cars, military vehicles, taxicabs, limos, university-owned cars and rental cars. We now have a grand total of 200 million cars on the road. If 2 percent of US cars have bpag that means there are 4 million cars. If 4 million is 10 percent of the world wide market then the total world wide market is 40 million cars.

Preposterous cases

Preposterous market-sizing questions are usually stand-alone questions. These are asked not only to test your math skills, but also to see how you handle the absurd. The best advice is to roll with the punches, do the best you can, but have fun with it. They love people who love solving problems so keep a sense of humor and attack it logically. These are questions like, how many jelly doughnuts fit into the leaning Tower of Pisa? Or, how many slices of pizza does it take to reach the moon? Or, how much does a 747 weigh?

❑ How much does a 747 weigh?

Your guess is as good as mine. Ask questions, then break down the elements and make assumptions. Are there passengers on board? No. Any baggage? No. Are the fuel tanks full or empty? Full. Any food or beverages on board? No.

Now, just go ahead and calculate the weight of each part of the plane.

- 8 full fuel tanks: I'll assume the plane can fly 6,000 miles and uses 10 gallons to the mile. So that's 60,000 gallons at 2 pounds a gallon equals 120,000 pounds.
- 18 tires: I'll assume that the tires weigh 200 pounds each — that's 3,600 pounds.
- 4 engines: I'll assume 2,500 pounds each adds another 10,000 pounds.
- 2 wings: 200 feet long by 30 feet wide is 6,000 square feet, times a square foot weight of 5 pounds times 2 wings equals 60,000 pounds.
- Interior: 75 rows of seats times 4 feet per row equals 300 feet. Add on the cockpit, bathrooms, etc., let's say around 400 feet long. I assume that the average weight per foot is 10 pounds, which equals 4,000 pounds.
- The seats: They number, say, 500, and weigh 10 pounds each, so that's 5,000 pounds.
- Air in the cabin: It's captured air so we need to add one ton for the air in the cabin — 2,000 pounds.
- The aluminum exterior: It's pretty thin and lightweight. If the plane is 400 feet long by 25 feet high, then about 10,000 exterior square feet at 1 pound per foot equals 10,000 pounds.
- Miscellaneous materials: The tail, overhead bins, carpet, stairs and bathroom fixtures add on, say, another 2,000 pounds.

Now you add up the pieces:

120,000 + 3,600 + 10,000 + 60,000 + 4,000 + 5,000 + 2,000 + 2,000 + 10,000 = 216,000, or round up to 220,000 pounds, or 110 tons.

It's a little scary to think, after how many years of school, that your job comes down to a question like this — welcome to consulting!

▸ Factor questions

Factor questions usually start with "What factors influence..." or "What factors would you consider..." Factor questions are gaining popularity for when time is short and interviewers can't devote significant time to walking you through an entire case but want to see how you think in broad strokes. They may also pop up in place of stand-alone market-sizing questions during the first-round interviews. Think in broad terms; try not to get too detailed.

❑ **What factors would you consider when marketing a theatrical film?**

First, I'd want to know something about the film, particularly who its target market is. You would have a different marketing strategy for a Baby Boomer film then you would for a Millennial film. Since the majority of films are geared toward Millennials, I'll use that example.

Millennials spend a lot of time online. There are digital marketing agencies that develop social media APIs called "widgets," which often feature a sweepstakes or some call to action and are virally spread across Myspace, Facebook and Meebo. Similarly a great trailer, sometimes "unauthorized" or seemingly user-generated on YouTube, is often seen by more people than the official trailer, which is placed on traditional TV and shown at theaters before current movies.

Second, I'd want to know, is this a studio film with big-name stars attached or an independent film? Is it a branded title, like *American Pie,* or a new indie film without any brand recognition? This is going to determine the number of screens on which it is shown. If it is a studio movie showing on 3,000 screens the first week, then most of the marketing budget will be spent in the two weeks prior to the film's release. Ads will be placed on network TV during shows like *American Idol*. Billboards will be displayed as well as signs on the side of a bus — the more traditional movie marketing efforts. If it is an indie film being shown on 50 screens, then the limited budget has to be allocated toward the more viral online environment. If the film does well and builds a buzz, then the distributor may kick in additional marketing funds as the number of screens increase — think *Slumdog Millionaire* or *The King's Speech*.

Pan-media "takeovers" are becoming more commonplace, as a film's stars and creative team blitz multiple outlets in hopes of achieving a massive opening weekend. In one day, for example, actress Olivia Wilde might appear on *Good Morning America*, cut a ribbon in a ceremony in Central Park with local TV crews, attend a charity luncheon (photographed for the tabloids) and in the evening hit *Letterman* and Jon Stewart's *The Daily Show* — all while the studio is running multiple display ads across Yahoo! and MSN's landing pages. The idea is that "media ubiquity" will grab the attention of an audience whose consumption habits are becoming increasingly fragmented.

In sum, like anything, you need to analyze the market as well as your product and figure where you'll get the best ROI (return on investment). And because technology is changing so quickly, you need to constantly research new ways to get the word out.

Business case questions

Business case questions come in all shapes and sizes, but they usually fall into two categories: (1) number cases and (2) business strategy and operations cases.

❑ **Number Cases:** There are pure number cases that are really just math problems you are expected to do in your head. There are also "case-like" numbers cases, which seem like strategy cases but are not. Case-like number cases are about numbers. They sound simple, but most people get them wrong because they don't listen to the question and try to turn it into a strategy case.

- **Pure number cases to do in your head**

A) The total widget market is $170 million and our sales are $30 million. What percentage of the market share do we hold?

B) Our total manufacturing costs are $20 million. With that we can make 39,379 units. What is our approximate cost per unit?

C) Our total costs are $75,000. Labor costs make up 25 percent of the total costs. How much are our labor costs?

D) You bought a stock for $36 a share. Today it jumped 6 percent. How much is your stock worth?

E) You raised $3.5 million for a start-up. Your commission is 2.5 percent. What's your commission in dollars?

F) What's 7 x 45?

G) The number of current outstanding shares for UKL Inc. was 41,084,000. Institutional investors hold 25,171,000 shares. What is the approximate percentage of shares held by institutions?

	Price	Change	Percentage change
H)	$27.00	$0.54	
I)	$31.00	$0.62	
J)	$40.00	$1.00	
K)	$75.00	%3.00	
L)	$10.00	$1.70	
M)	$50.00	$2.50	

N) Banana Republic® makes 14% of Gap®'s estimated $16 billion in sales. What are BR's sales?
O) Europe's population is approximately 480 million. By 2014, the European Union population is expected to drop to 450 million. What percentage change is that?

Go figure: Try to estimate some of the percentages in your head, and then work out the others without a calculator. Round off the answers as you would during a case question. (Worth noting: these are from a fifth-grade math test.)

P) 60% of 70 = ___ **Q)** 25% of 124 = ___ **R)** 68% of 68 = ___ **S)** 12% of 83 = ___

T) 23% of 60 = ___ **U)** 27% of 54 = ___ **V)** 13% of 19 = ___ **W)** 65% of 80 = ___

X) 78% of 45 = ___ **Y)** 78% of 90 = ___

Answers:
A) about 18% B) about $500 C) $18,750 D) $38.16 E) $87,500 F) 315 G) 60%
H) 2% I) 2% J) 2.5% K) 4% L) 17% M) 5%
N) approximately $2.3 billion O) Europe's population drops by around - 6 percent
P) 42 Q) 31 R)46 S)10 T) 14 U) 15 V) 2 W) 52 X) 35 Y) 70

- **Case-like number cases:**

Every three minutes an American woman is diagnosed with breast cancer. How many American women will be diagnosed this year?

One woman every three minutes equals 20 women an hour. Twenty women diagnosed an hour times 24 hours in a day equals 480 woman a day. 480 women a day times 365 days equals 175,200 American women diagnosed with breast cancer each year.

In Brazil, each airline is allocated a certain number of landing spots: Airline A, 2,000; Airline B, 1,000; Airline C, 500; and Airline D, 100. Airline C goes out of business and its landing spots are distributed proportionally to the other airlines. How many spots does each airline get?

You find the percentage of landing spots each airline has without C. Airline A has 65 percent of 3,100 spots, B has 32 percent and Airline D has 3 percent. Next you figure out what percentage of the 500 spots C used to have. Thus, A has 65 percent of 500, which equals 325; B has 32 percent of 500, which equals 160; and C has 3 percent, which equals 15. Add them up and they total 500.

American Express® is facing stiff competition from a host of new credit cards that have no annual fee and low interest rates. In response, American Express is considering dropping its $50 annual fee. What are the economics of dropping the $50 fee? (This is a popular case and one that has repeatedly turned up in interviews.)

Nine out of 10 students think this case is about competition. They focus their answer on strategy and alternatives to dropping the fee. The first part of this question is not relevant. The real question is **"What are the economics of dropping the $50 fee?"**

In order to answer this question, you need to ask three questions:

- How many card members does Amex have?
- What is the average amount that each card member spends annually?
- What are Amex's revenue streams?

Amex has 10 million card members. Amex card members average $2,000 a year in purchases. Amex makes 2 percent from each purchase.

Amex Revenues:

10 million customers paying a $50 annual fee equals $500 million. Each member spends $2,000 x 2 percent = $40 a year x 10 million customers = $400 million. Total revenues then = $900 million, with 55 percent of that figure coming from fees.

Would card members spend more money if they didn't have to pay the annual fee? Amex card members would have to more than double their purchases to make up for the loss in fee revenues. It seems unlikely that they would go from spending $2,000 a year to spending $4,000 a year because of a dropped $50 fee. Even a modest bump in new members couldn't make up the difference.

How many new customers would Amex have to secure in order to make up the $500 million difference? Amex would have to more than double its card members from 10 million to about 25 million in a short period — say, two years. Is that feasible? It took Amex 25 years to reach the 10 million customer base it currently has. So doubling it in two years seems unrealistic.

My advice to Amex is to keep its fee in place.
That's it. That's the answer. The interviewer doesn't want to hear about reducing the fee to $25 or turning Amex into a credit card. This is a straightforward question. Listen to the question.

❑ **Business Strategy and Operations Cases:** Some business strategy and operations cases should be answered in less than 15 minutes. These are referred to as mini-cases. An example:

- *GE has invented a new light bulb that never burns out. It could burn for more than 500 years and never blink. The director of marketing calls you into her office and asks, "How would you price this?" What do you tell her? (See answer on page 103.)*

A regular case question, like the DuPont case below, could take anywhere from 25 to 35 minutes to answer. It could be a market-sizing question and a strategy question all rolled into one, such as:

- *DuPont has just invented a light-weight, super-absorbent, biodegradable material that would be perfect for disposable diapers. Estimate the size of the diaper market and tell me if Dupont should enter this market and if so, how? (See answer on page 105.)*

✢ Written Group Case and Tests

Over the last couple of years more and more firms have turned to written cases; particularly in the second and third rounds. Monitor was the first to pioneer the written case. Since then firms have added a few new twists to the process. The interview can go something like this:

Scenario 1: You arrive for the interview and are handed a written case (usually about five pages: three pages of text and two of charts). You are given 20 to 30 minutes to read and take notes. When your time is up, a consultant comes into the room and you are expected to "present" the case, much as you would in a business school class. More often than not a discussion ensues. Chances are you will be touching on the same points you would if given a verbal case.

Scenario 2: The interviewer hands you a written case (usually three pages). You are given 30 minutes to read it, takes notes and draw up three PowerPoint™ slides to go along with the case, one of which needs to be a chart. You have no calculator, no computer, which means no PowerPoint™ or Chart Wizard™, just three plain sheets of paper. The consultant comes back in and you present the cases as you would to a client.

Scenario 3: You are sitting in a conference room. A consultant comes in and gives you an 80-page document and tells you to read it and be prepared to discuss it in 30 minutes. In a case like this, what you want to do (besides climb out the window) is to read the executive summary upfront and then spend the rest of the time in the back of the document analyzing the exhibits. You can learn much more by studying the exhibits than by reading as far as you can in 30 minutes.

Group cases are also becoming more and more popular.

Scenario 4: You are sitting around a table with three other candidates all going after the same job. The interviewer throws out a case to the group. How do you respond? The interviewer is most interested in how you interact with your peers. Are you kicking your competition under the table? Elbowing them in the gut? Talking over them to get your point across? If you are, then shame on you. The interviewer wants to see if you play well with others. You are going to be working as part of a team and even though the other candidates are your competition, for this one moment in time they are your teammates and you should treat them with respect. Treat them as you would your classmates when working through a problem set. Don't be dominated by others; get your points across. Build on what others say in a positive and civil manner. Persuade them to look at a different point of view if you think they might be wrong. Don't call them out or embarrass them. It all boils down to fit, communication skills, respect for others, empathy and teamwork.

Scenario 5: You are shown into a conference room where three other candidates join you. The group is given a written case and 60 minutes to design a presentation. There is a computer in the room, but the only program on the computer is PowerPoint™. The recruiter sits in the corner of the room and watches the dynamics unfold. Who becomes the leader and how did they become the leader? Did it happen naturally or was it forced upon the group? Who does the quant stuff? Who does the PowerPoint™ design? Are there discussions, arguments or fist-fights? When your team is ready to present, two other consultants join in and your "team" presents the case. The only requirement is that everyone speak for five minutes.

Now one, two or all of you might get called back for the next round. While you act as part of a team during the presentation of the case, you are all judged individually.

Written exercises

McKinsey now requires that some candidates take a written exercise. "The test is testing problem-solving in a written format; folks will be surprised that the straight 'quant' questions are the minority. It's not like a GRE quant test," explains a senior McKinsey recruiter.

"The bulk of it involves making judgment calls/recommendations based on information available to you at that point," the recruiter adds. "The exercise is supposed to feel like a case interview, but with multiple-choice responses."

Last year the McKinsey Problem Solving Test (McKPST) contained 26 questions and you had an hour to complete it. Candidates received a bit more information about the business, the environment and the problem with each question.

Students can't bring in calculators or scratch paper. The test was developed internally by McKinsey and validated by Applied Psychological Techniques Inc. (APT). "It was fun, now that it's over," recounts a non-MBA Harvard graduate student. "There are some ratios and percentages, a couple of formulas, but nothing too overwhelming. Also, a few charts are used to present some of the information, but again fairly basic, in my opinion."

A McKinsey recruiter states, "You need to be comfortable with calculating some percentages, basic equations, understanding relationships among data, but nothing terribly advanced."

Some international offices have a math section that one student says is more like the GMAT than the GRE. You have 18 questions and 30 minutes to complete them. "You start with probability and it gets harder from there," recounts a Harvard graduate student.

The McKinsey recruiter explains, "The resulting score is used as one more 'data point' on problem-solving for the interviewers to refer to if they have concerns or opposing reads. There is no magic or required score, and performance in face-to-face interviews is of greater importance to us."

Reading Charts and Graphs One of the best ways to shake the dust off your chart and graph reading is to look at the charts and graphs printed in *The Wall Street Journal* and *The Economist* and draw some conclusions. Then read the article and compare your thoughts to the main points of the article.

Making Slides and Graphs There is another twist: making slides and graphs. The recruiter hands you a few pages of data and asks that you create (on paper) three or four PowerPoint® slides. You are then expected to present them during the case as you would during a presentation to a client.

You will be given charts, sometimes at the outset of the case. Sometimes they slip them into the middle of the case, changing the dynamics of the question. You are expected to quickly analyze the charts, extract the most important information and then apply it to your answer. It is easy to get overwhelmed.

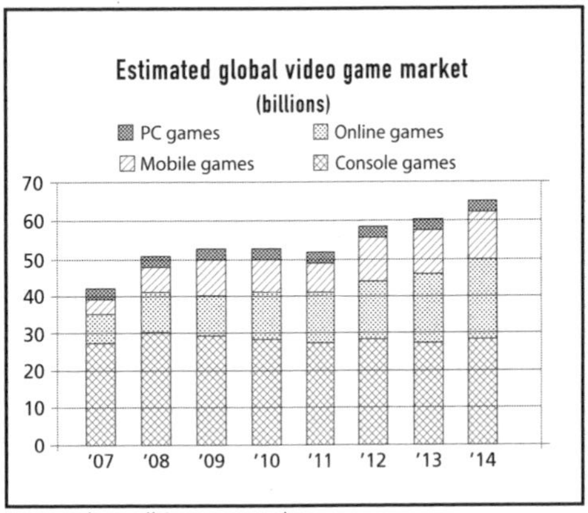

Source: The Wall Street Journal

Candidates tend to get beleaguered by the pressure to perform and don't always see the elegance of the chart or the simplicity of the message.

Therefore, as you look at each chart, I recommend that you eyeball the numbers, round them off and then determine how they are related to one another, what trends you see and what message you derive from what you see.

As you review the charts, there are three easy steps that will help you get your bearings:

1. identify the chart form — is it a bar graph, a line chart or pie chart?
2. determine what comparison each chart calls for
3. summarize the message

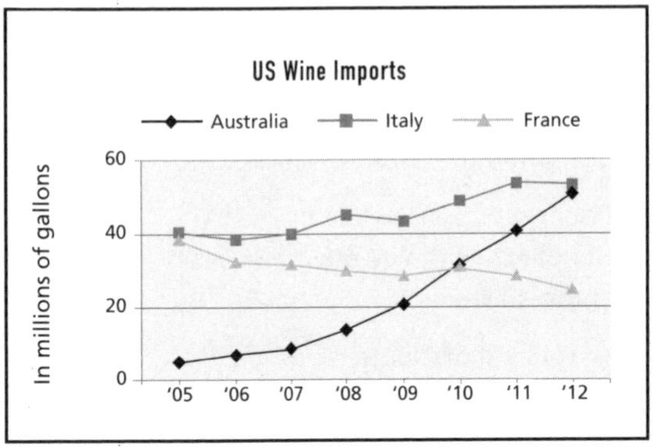

Chances are you will only need to use one of the three basic graph forms: the bar graph, the line graph or the pie chart (BCG doesn't like pie charts). Be sure to give your charts and graphs an appropriate title that explains what the data measure.

Use the bar graph when you want to show relationships among groups. The two items being compared don't need to affect each other. The top chart shows the growth in revenues for the global video game market.

Trends over time are generally shown in line graphs. The line graph plots the rise and fall of one data set or multiple data sets. The line graph is needed when you want to show the effect of an independent variable on a dependent variable. The second chart follows US wine import levels from Australia, Italy and France over an eight-year period.

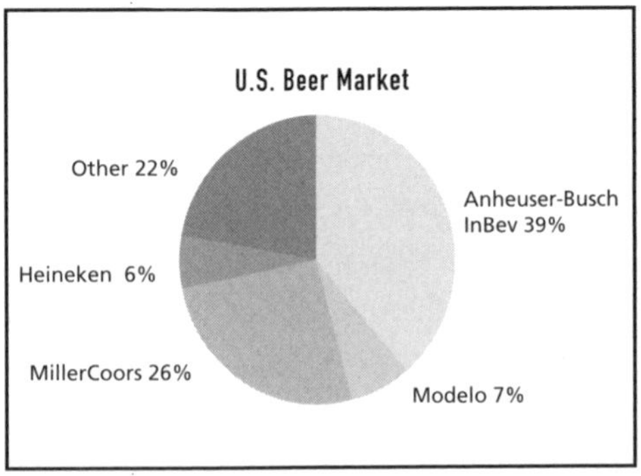

A pie chart is used to show how something relates to the whole. It usually deals with percentages. This last chart shows the market share of the US beer market in 2012.

✣ Irking the Interviewer

Interviewers get easily bored and irked. Let's face it, these guys and gals spend most of their days telling the CEOs of Fortune 1,000,000 companies what to do. Now they've been yanked out of a really important assignment to interview you and a dozen of your closest friends. Yawn..."I postponed my meeting with Mark Zuckerberg for this? Dazzle me!"

The first step toward Case Interview Dazzlement (CID) is to avoid costly and obvious mistakes. Listed below are the most common mistakes that past interviewees (some still unemployed) have made.

❑ **The Leno / Letterman syndrome**
A five-minute monologue will do more to hurt your career than any of the other mistakes. Remember, you ask questions not only to get additional information but to draw the interviewer into the case with you. Make the interviewer feel that he is a stakeholder in your candidacy. Turn the question into a conversation.

❑ **What was the question again?**
Listen to the question, write it down, then repeat it to the interviewer. Candidates are always answering the wrong question because they don't take the time to identify what the interviewer is really asking.

❑ **Explosion of the mouth**
I see it all the time: People can't give me the answer fast enough. Slow down. Don't jump off the mark and give the first answer that pops into your head. Take your time and analyze the information. The interviewer is there to observe the logic and thought process behind your answer.

❑ **Digression city**
You go off on a tangent because it's easy, you're on a roll and it provides you with a false sense of security. You think it hides the fact that you can't move forward in your answer, but it doesn't. Tangents take you off the path and it becomes extremely difficult to get back on the straight and narrow.

A case question is like a long corridor with numerous side doors. Suppose the question was, "How do we increase sales for the local 7-Eleven convenience store?" You start walking down the corridor and you open the first door on the right and yell, "We can raise our prices." Close the door and move on to the next door. Open that door and yell, "We need to get more people in the store." Close the door and move on.

The problem arises when you open the door and yell, "We need to get more people in the store." Then you start walking down the side hall trying to come up with creative ways to get more people in the door. You come up with all sorts of promotions involving your favorite late-night snack food. Hey, this is easy! But that's NOT the question.

❑ **The bull in the consulting china shop**

Don't use terms that you don't fully understand. Throwing out a buzzword or business term in the wrong context highlights the fact that you have a nasty habit of discussing things you know little about. You may be able to get away with that in class, but it doesn't fly in a case interview. If you do that in an interview, will the firm be able to trust you in front of a client?

❑ **Asking open-ended questions**

Open-ended questions that try to get the interviewer to answer the case for you will irk the interviewer, big time. It is far better to make assumptions than to ask the interviewer for the answer. Consider a scenario where you are reviewing labor costs:

Right: Because the economy is strong and there are plenty of jobs, I'll assume that our labor costs have gone up.

Wrong: What has been going on with our labor costs?

❑ **Silence**

One of the questions I get asked most often is about silence. Is it ever okay to be silent? Yes and no. The simple rule to remember is that silence is okay when you are doing something like calculating, writing down your thoughts or drawing a graph or decision tree. You can get up to 40 seconds of silence before the "awkward" clock starts ticking and the interviewer gets restless. It is not okay when you are just thinking while staring out the window or looking down at your shoes, particularly in the beginning of the case. If the interviewer gives you the case and you just sit there thinking, you've lost your momentum, you're sitting dead in the water. (See The First Five Steps and read Summarize the Question on page 35.)

+ If You Get Stuck

If you get stuck during a case and the interviewer doesn't ask you a question to help you along, then there a few things you can do. First, take a moment to recap where you've been. Chances are you've either gone into too much detail and are now stuck in the mud or you went off on a tangent. Recapping pulls you out of the mud and back above the trees. Remember, for the most part you want to view the case from a macro point of view. Many times, as you recap, you can see where you got off track. The second thing to do is to go back and look at the information that the interviewer gave you. Information that was originally irrelevant often becomes relevant as you work through the case. Third, quickly run through the Five C's... (see page 53) in your head to see if there is something obvious that you missed. Finally, if you are still stuck, ask for help. There is no shame in asking for help. If we were working on a project together, I would much rather have you ask me for help than have you waste a lot of time banging your head against a wall. That being said, I wouldn't ask for help more than once.

✢ The Trouble with Math

Do you have trouble doing math in your head? Are you often off by a zero? When I do case interviews with students, the most common problem is basic math. It's the zeros that students have trouble with. From PhDs to undergraduates, it's the zeros. Take a look at the table below, and get to know it very well.

Number Table*

	10	100	1,000	10,000	100,000
10	100	1,000	10,000	100,000	1,000,000
100	1,000	10,000	100,000	1,000,000	10,000,000
1,000	10,000	100,000	1,000,000	10,000,000	100,000,000
10,000	100,000	1,000,000	10,000,000	100,000,000	1,000,000,000
100,000	1,000,000	10,000,000	100,000,000	1,000,000,000	10,000,000,000

* Number Table produced and designed by Maria Teresa Petersen, Harvard MPP '01.

✢ Notes Design

While there is no standard for note taking, the landscape format is becoming the norm. The first page of notes is divided into two sections. The lefthand section is where you write down the question. The problem statement for this case is that the CEO of Coors is thinking of entering the bottled water market. Then you draw a line, put the object across the top then lay out your structure or write down the answers to the questions that you asked them.

The use of plain white paper is fine; however, some consulting firms like it when you use graph paper. There are several reasons why.

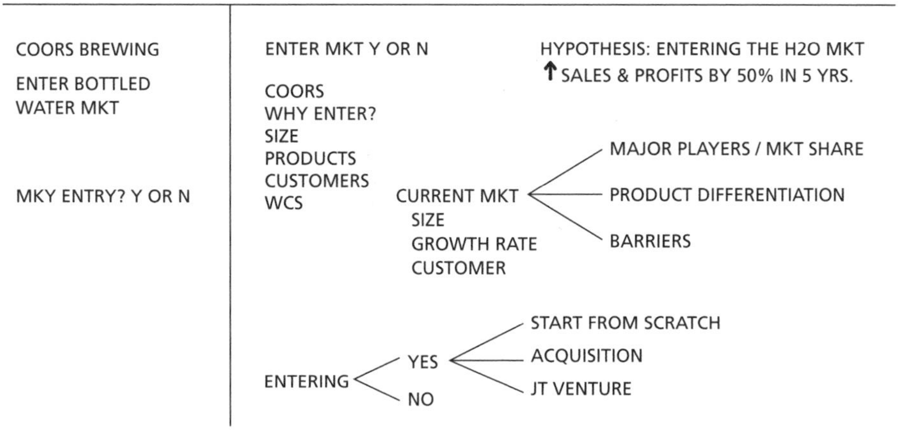

- Graph paper makes it easier to draw your notes.
  - Be visual with your notes. Draw boxes, graphs, arrows, decision trees, value chains and flow charts.
  - When appropriate, turn your notes toward the interviewer to explain your thought process. It makes him feel more like a team member and less like an interviewer.
- Graph paper lines up your zeros. There is a lot of math in these questions and you can't use a calculator. It is not always easy to tell when you are off by a zero when your answer has eight zeros at the end of it.
- Graph paper organizes your notes. Well-organized notes make it easier for the interviewer to follow. When he isn't looking into your eyes, he's looking at your notes to see what you wrote down because he knows what you should be writing down. In addition, there is a good chance that the interviewer will collect your notes at the end of the interview. He uses your notes as one more data point — what did you write down? How did you write it? How did you do your math? And, can he read your handwriting?

When it comes time for the case portion of your interview, rip out five pages of graph paper and number them (you can do this before the interview to save time and look well-organized). Remember to write on just one side of the page. Flipping pages back and forth can be disruptive and make it hard to find important data at a glance. Using bullet points will make your notes seem better organized and make it easier to go back to find information. Star or highlight important points that you think will make the summary. This way those points will jump out at you when it comes time to summarize the case.

As you fill up the pages (while leaving plenty of white space on your notes), spread your notes out in front of you. That way you can see the whole case at a glance. You'll want to check the first page of notes from time to time. There is a lot of important information on that first page. Some of it is immediately relevant; some is smoke put there to throw you off track. Other information will become relevant as you move through the case.

Some students use a separate sheet for their math. That way your main notes stay clean and linear. If you do use a separate sheet, make sure that you label each calculation so you can tie it back into the case and not be left looking at a page full of random calculations.

Oftentimes the interviewer will hand you a chart. Always ask for permission before you write on the chart. As strange as it may seem, sometimes interviewers only show up with one copy of a chart.

▶ Idea box

Oftentimes, after hearing the initial problem statement, candidates will think of an idea, solution, or strategy that's not appropriate to state at the beginning of the case for fear that the interviewer might think that you are "shooting from the hip" and not analyzing the problem. They write it down in their notes and then forget about it during the case even if it becomes relevant. The candidates wind up kicking themselves because they had the solution, but forgot about it. I tell students to draw an "idea box" on the first page of their notes. If anything pops into your head write it in the idea box. That way you know where it is, and you'll get into the habit of checking the box whenever you review your first page of notes (which you should do several times during the case).

+ The Summary and The Final Slide

In most case interviews you will be asked to summarize the case. You need to jump right into this without any down time to collect your thoughts. A good summary is anywhere from 30 seconds to a minute-and-a-half at the most. It is not a rehash of everything you spoke about; it is a short recap of the problem and two or main points or recommendations that you want to remember.

In some cases — particularly those that ask for a list of numbers the interviewer wants you to figure out, i.e., market-size, price, break-even and profit, or those that compare two or more strategies, ideas or options using the same criteria — you can create the "final slide" right at the beginning of the case. No one ever remembers to do this, so if you can think of it, you'll score big points with the interviewer.

On a separate sheet of paper, draw a chart listing the product or markets (whatever it is that you are comparing) and below that, the criteria. As you calculate the numbers, fill them in on the final slide; this keeps all relevant information in one place and makes it easier for the interviewer to follow (think of it as a scorecard). Once all the information is filled out, the student turns the final slide toward the interviewer and walks him through it. This is the best summary. It is similar to the final slide of a deck that a consultant would present to a client. In the Partner Cases section of the book (page 160), there are three great examples of the final slide.

Market-size	
Price	
Breakeven	
Est. Profits	

	Y1	Y2	Y3	Y4	Y5
Option One					
Option Two					

+ Case Journal

I had a student who graduated Phi Beta Kappa from an Ivy League school. She spent her time between undergrad and graduate school working for a non-profit. While at Harvard's Kennedy School, she decided that she wanted to do consulting, but she had no business background. Her first attempt at a mock case interview with me was a disaster. That day she started a journal. For every live case she did with me, her classmates and alumni (she did around 30 live cases) and with every case that she read (about 80 cases), she wrote down the problem, the solution and, most important, what she hadn't thought of. The student constantly reviewed it, so that what she didn't think of naturally soon became second nature to her. She also recorded structures, concepts, ideas and strategies. When she had spare moments between classes or bus rides, she would flip through her journal. When she read articles in *The Wall Street Journal*, *Bloomberg Businessweek* or *McKinsey Quarterly*, she would add to her journal. It never left her side.

She ended up at a top firm and took the journal with her. With every engagement she learned something new and added it to her journal. When she and her co-workers sat around brainstorming problems, she would flip through her journal and throw out ideas, which often sparked discussions and occasionally led to a solution.

I saw her five years after she had graduated and she still had her journal. Although it was as beaten up as Indiana Jones's journal, it held just as many treasures. She was headed to a new job and the journal was the first thing she packed.

Since then, whenever I speak at schools I recommend creating a journal. Besides keeping all your notes in one place, it becomes a single source for case material that is also extremely helpful for your classes. If you are truly serious about case interviewing, then you will continue to read and practice all summer long. Recruiting events start as soon as you get back to campus, so if you take the time over the summer to practice, life is going to be easier in the fall.

✛ Best Case Thinking

In my years of training Harvard students to answer case questions; I've realized that the major problem many of my students had was simply getting started. Sometimes they were overwhelmed, sometimes they were nervous and sometimes they just didn't have a clue. So in 1996, with the help of a student, I developed the Tomensen/Cosentino Case Framework. Over the years it has been successfully tested in thousands of case interviews. After hundreds of debriefings, I have redefined it, simplified it and renamed it. But the biggest change is that I turned it from a framework into a system, The Ivy Case System©.

A framework is a structure that helps you organize your thoughts and analyze the case in a logical manner. Often; however, you have to cut and paste from a number of frameworks in order to answer any single question. As I mentioned, the difference between a framework and a system is that the framework is really a tool, while a system is a process. Instead of memorizing seven individual frameworks and then trying to decide which one(s) to apply, you learn a system, which already has the tools built in.

The Ivy Case System© is a two-part system made up of five easy steps to get you going and four popular case scenarios, each equipped with a collection of ideas and questions that will help you structure the remainder of your response. If you follow through the outline I've given for each scenario, you can be confident that your response will be logical and cohesive. And because it is all based on business sense and common sense, you'll find that there is nothing in there that you don't already know... it is just organized a little differently.

The first five steps will provide you with a quick start (no long awkward pause between question and answer). They will get you five minutes into the question, give you momentum provide you with enough information to decide which of the four scenarios (or whatever combination thereof) is most appropriate to the case question at hand.

You may want to read through the following explanation of the Ivy Case System© and then check out a practice case or two to see how the system can be applied. Then it will be time to revisit the system and learn it.

The interviewer has just finished giving you the case. Here's what you do!

✛ The First Five Steps

1. Summarize the question.
2. Verify the objective(s).
3. Ask clarifying questions.
4. Label the case and lay out your structure.
5. State your hypothesis.

[1. Summarize the Question]

Sometimes the question is short; "How do we increase sales at the campus bookstore?" Other times the question is long and involved and is filled with data that comes at you like a fire hose. It's difficult to capture all that information in your notes, so the first step is to summarize the question. That way, if you missed something or wrote it down wrong, the interviewer will correct you before allowing you to move on. It puts you and the interviewer on the same page from the beginning, thus keeping you from answering the wrong question.

Summarizing the question shows the interviewer that you listened, and it fills the gap of silence between the end of their question and the beginning of your answer.

Also, get into the habit of quantifying related numbers as a percentage, i.e., year-to-year comparisons or a change in stock price. If the interviewer tells you that the stock price jumped from $15 to $18, don't say; "It jumped from $15 to $18." Don't say; "It jumped $3." Tell the interviewer that it jumped 20 percent. This is the way that consultants and senior managers think and it's how they want you to think.

[2. Verify the Objective(s)]

You can bet that when a consultant first meets with a client, she always asks about objectives and goals. What are the client's expectations, and are those expectations realistic? In the client's mind, what constitutes success? Even if the objective of the case seems obvious, there is always the possibility of an additional, underlying objective. So you (the interviewee) should say, "One objective is to raise profits. Are there any other objectives that I should know about?" If the interviewer says, "No, higher profits is the only objective," you just focus on the one objective. If there is an additional objective, you may need to break the case in two and tackle one objective at a time.

[3. Ask Clarifying Questions]

As we've said, you ask questions for three reasons: to get additional information, to show the interviewer that you're not shy about asking questions and to turn the case into a conversation. The key is to ask broad, open-ended questions that help you narrow the information at the start, because as the case progresses, you'll lose your "right" to ask these sweeping questions. (Reason: You may give the impression that you are trying to get the interviewer to answer the case for you.) The case scenarios will guide you in asking these questions.

[4. Label the Case and Lay Out Your Structure]

This is by far the toughest part of the process and you may want to "take a moment" to think about structure at this point. Thirty to 90 seconds of silence now may save wasted time later in the interview. You've decided which case scenario(s) to work with, and you have asked a few broad questions that have given you the information you need to form a logical response. Because you have studied the scenarios, you can quickly go through the bullet points in your mind and decide which are the most relevant to this particular question. You then just need to tell the interviewer how you plan to proceed. Keep in mind that you are not married to your structure. Because new information is constantly added, as well as twists and turns in the case, your structure could either stand through the whole case, or it might become obsolete rather quickly. Basically a structure is, given the limited information you have at this moment in time, what would you analyze and in what order, to solve this problem?

Once you draw your structure, turn your notes toward the interviewer and walk him through your thought process. This brings him into the interview and makes him feel less like an interviewer and more like a client.

[5. State Your Hypothesis]

Some firms want to see you state a hypothesis during the case, preferably toward the beginning of the case. The advantages are that a hypothesis will help you ask the right questions, make your analysis more linear and force you to focus on issues that you can either prove or disprove. It also helps you identify which structure to use, thus defining the starting point. You are most likely to state a hypothesis in an interviewee-driven case. When the interviewer says "Here's my problem, what do I do?", the case is likely very broad and vague. This is where a hypothesis can be most helpful. During an interviewer-driven case, (where the interviewer tells you "Here's my problem, I want you to figure out these four things; market size, profits, price, and breakeven") a hypothesis is not necessary.

In real life, consultants can take up to two days to form their hypothesis, but you have about five minutes. So don't worry if your hypothesis is wrong. It eliminates one possibility and allows you to restate your hypothesis and focus on another aspect of the case. Think of the process as one of elimination.

Steps 3 thru 5 can be flipped around. Sometimes you will get a profit and loss case stating that "sales are up, but profits are down", so your hypothesis then seems obvious: "Rising costs are pulling profits down." In this case, because we will learn the P&L structure, you can layout your structure first, state your hypothesis and then ask questions. However, there will be times when you'll want to ask three to five questions before laying out your structure or stating your hypothesis.

+ The Four Key Case Scenarios, developing your structure

The four key case scenarios are:

1. Profit and loss
2. Entering a new market
3. Pricing
4. Growth and increasing sales

[1. Profit and loss]

Question: Our client manufactures high-end athletic footwear. Sales are up but profits are down in the US. What's going on, and how do we fix it?

Profit-and-loss questions have been the most popular type of question for the last five years. Whenever you hear the words "bottom line," "profits," "costs" or "revenues," you should immediately think: "Profits = (Revenues – Costs)." However, I'm going to change this formula to the framework or structure: **E(P=R-C)M**. The E represents the economy, and M represents the market or the industry. You always want to look at external factors first. You want to know if this is a company problem or an industry-wide problem. But first take a moment and draw your notes.

COMPANY X HIGH-END ATHLETIC FOOTWEAR MANUFACTURER SALES ↑ PROFITS ↓ IN U.S. MARKET WHY? FIX	ANALYZE PROFITS AND FIX E(P=R–C)M HIGH UNEMPLOYMENT MORTGAGE CRISIS LESS DISPOSABLE INCOME HIGH PETRO COSTS COMP X MKT LEADER REVENUES > TRENDS PRODUCT MIX, NEW PRODUCT PRODUCTION LOCATION CUSTOMER SEGMENTATION WCS (What constitutes success?)	 INDUSTRY REV TRENDS (3 YRS) COMPETITORS, SAME ISSUES? Λs IN INDUSTRY, SUPPLY OF RAW MATERIALS REVENUE STREAMS ANY Λ IN REVENUES? NO. OF CUSTOMERS DISTRIBUTION CHANNELS Λ IN PRICES COSTS ANY Λ IN COSTS? TRENDS? NEW MATERIALS ANY COSTS SEEM OUT OF LINE? LABOR OR TRANSPORT?

Your notes should look something like the notes above. Since you know that the structure for a P&L case is E(P=R-C)M, start by spelling out your take on the current economy, especially the parts that would affect the company or the industry overall. This will show the interviewer that you know what's going on outside the classroom. More importantly, it will allow you to define the economic environment in which this case is taking place. This definition step will be a huge advantage because you can then take control of the interview and reduce the number of potential surprises that the interviewer can throw at you. You can probably list off twenty things going on in the economy, but that's not going to help. I like to go into a case with five or six economic factors in the back of my mind: three good factors and three bad. These factors include things like the unemployment rate, interest rates, the dollar's strength in the currency market, petro prices, and consumers' amount of disposable income. Those factors can either be good or bad depending on the economy and the case; however, they are pretty universal, so it's good to know these things before you walk into an interview. Information about the overall economy and the market will help you decide whether the rest of the industry is having similar problems.

The M stands for the market or industry. No one is going expect you to know what's going on in various industries. The interviewer has a lot of information to give you, but he's not going to give it to you unless you ask for it. Ask about industry trends and competitors to determine whether they are facing the same problems as the client. How has our client been doing compared to the rest of the industry? You don't have to go into great detail, but take some time to review the Industry Analysis section in the next chapter.

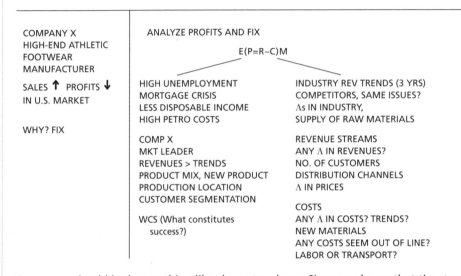

Going inside the parentheses is the same as going inside the company. Start by asking questions about the company:

The company: Who are they? What do they do? What are their products? (Get into the habit of writing these down so they become second nature to you.)

- Market leader?
- Size, in terms of revenues (public or privately-held)?
- Trends in growth? (Always ask for trends, three years is good.)
- Products or services? Product mix? Revenue mix and trends?
- Customer segmentation?
- What constitutes "success"? (WCS?) This is different from "meeting the objective". If the object was to enter a new market, we can come up with a strategy for that. Most companies can enter a new market, but it's always good to "reality test" the objective. What constitutes success? Ten percent of the market in three years might be do-able, while 10 percent of the market in one year is unlikely, but not impossible.

Review the revenue streams. Even if your hypothesis stated that costs are the problem, you need to understand your revenue streams before you can intelligently analyze the situation and cut costs. Ask, "What are the major revenue streams, and how have they changed over time?" Then, when you get to costs: "What are the major costs, both fixed and variable, and how have they changed over time?" Again, it's always good to ask for trends: this is how consultants think, and it's how they want you to think.

The other parts to the profit-and-loss formula are price and volume. Price and volume are interdependent. You need to find the best mix, because changing one isn't always the best answer. If you cut prices to drive up volume, what happens to the profit and next year sales? Do profits increase or decrease? There needs to be a balance. The reason behind the decision needs to make sense.

Once you have an understanding of the market and the company you'll need to come up with some solutions to raise profits – that, after all is the objective. The first thing you want to do is ask for a moment to write down your thoughts. Start with headings, revenue-based strategies and cost-based strategies. You do this for several reasons: It shows the interviewer that you are well-organized and thinking ahead. It's also easier to come up with ideas when you are looking at a heading instead of a blank sheet of paper. And it keeps you from co-mingling your ideas. Dividing ideas into short-term and long-term solutions is also desirable, particularly if there is a time constraint to raising profits. You want to present all the revenue-based ideas first, then all the cost-based ideas. If appropriate, divide your cost-based ideas into production, labor and finance. It will show the interviewer that you are well organized and thinking ahead. For cost-based ideas review **21 Ways to cut costs** on page 59.

Keep in mind that the interviewer has probably given this case ten times. He knows every possible answer you can think of, and he's grown impatient with the answers. There's a good chance that he'll cut you off as soon as he knows where you're headed. This can be tough, because when you are in a pressure situation and you get cut off, it's difficult to drop that thought and come up with something new. Indeed, in my own experience, I know when I cut students off in mid-thought, they tend to pretend that they didn't hear me and keep talking. Then after I cut them off again, they panic, then scramble as their brains shut down.

Don't let that happen to you. If you take the time to write down your answers first, and the interviewer cuts you off, just look at your notes and give him another idea. It takes a lot of the stress out of the situation and makes you look more professional.

Questions to think about:

Revenues:

1. What are the major revenue streams, and what percentage of the total revenue does each stream represent?
2. Does anything seem unusual in the balance of percentages?
3. Have the percentages changed lately? If so, why?

Costs:

1. Any major shifts in costs?
2. Do any costs seem out of line?
3. If we benchmarked our costs against our competitors' costs, what would we find?

Products

1. With new products make sure you ask about the advantages and disadvantages. Everyone forgets to ask about the disadvantages, but oftentimes disadvantages can drive the case more than the advantages.

[2. Entering a New Market]

Question: Your client Company Z manufactures hair products. The company is thinking about entering the sun screen market. Is this a good idea?

Entering-a-new-market questions can be as straightforward as the one above, or they can involve mergers, acquisitions, joint ventures, starting a new business or the development of a new product. So it's not just, "Do we enter?", but "How do we enter and what are the advantages and disadvantages of each strategy?"

Your notes might include something like the following, covering the company, the current market and how best to enter the market.

Step 1: Start off with questions about the company.

Why does the company want to enter this market?
What are their revenue streams and trends?
What is their product mix?
What are their costs and how have they changed over time?
What makes up their customer segmentation?
What constitutes success? (How much market share and in what time frame?)

Step 2: Determine the state of the current and future market

- What is the size of the current market?
- What is the growth rate? (Ask for trends.)

- Where is the industry in its life cycle? (Stage of development: Emerging? Mature? Declining?)
- Who are the customers and how are they segmented?
- What role does technology play in the industry and how quickly will it change?
- How will the competition respond?

Step 3: Investigate the market to determine whether entry makes good business sense.

- Who are our competitors, and what size market share do they have?
- How do their products differ from ours?
- How will we price our products or services?
- Are substitutions available?
- Are there any barriers to entry? Examples might include capital requirements, access to raw materials, access to distribution channels, and government policy.
- Are there barriers to an exit? How would we exit if this market sours?
- What are the risks? (For example, market regulations or technology.)

Step 4: If we decide to enter this market, we need to figure out the best way to become a player. There are three major ways to enter a market.

- Start from scratch and grow organically.
- Acquire an existing player from within the industry.
- Form a joint venture/strategic alliance with another player with a similar interest. What can both sides bring to the venture?

Analyze the pros and cons of each strategy. This is sometimes called a cost benefit analysis. You can use this whenever you are trying to decide whether to proceed with a decision.

Your notes might look something like this.

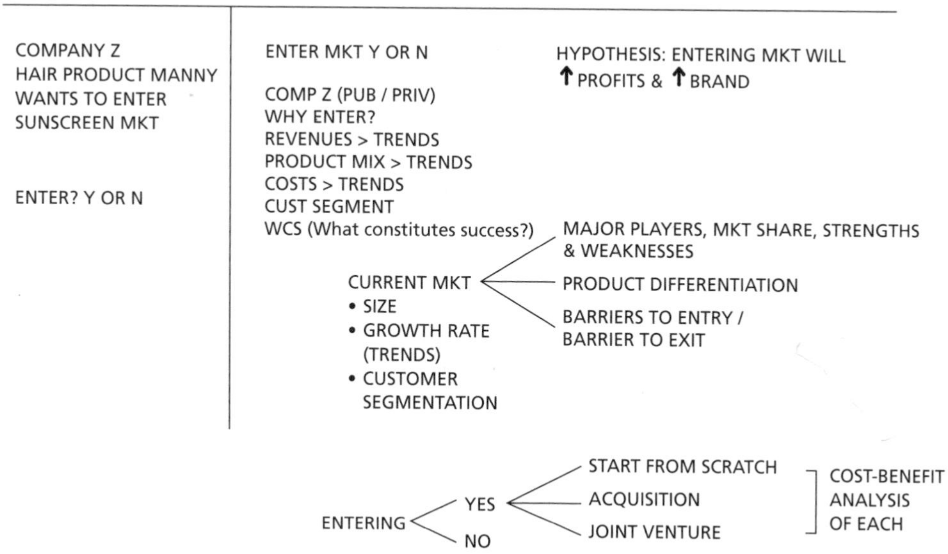

M&A

Many questions about entering a new market are also merger and acquisition questions. The two most important factors about a merger are whether it increases shareholder value and whether the two cultures will mesh well. Cultural mismatch is the biggest reason why mergers either fail or don't live up to their potential.

Here are some key points about an M&A question.

- If the buyer is a private equity firm, ask not only "Why do they want to buy the company? but, "What else do they own?" Many students forget to ask this and they miss out on the countless synergies among portfolio companies.
- If the M&A involves one company acquiring another, ask not only "Why? but also, "What other products do they sell?" The acquisition needs to make good business sense.
- Other reasons to purchase.
  - Increase market access, boost the brand and increase market share.
  - Diversify the company's holdings.
  - Pre-empt the competition from acquiring the company.
  - Inherit management talent
  - Obtain patents or licenses
  - Gain from synergies, cost savings, cultural integration, and the expansion of distribution channels.
  - Gain tax advantages.
  - Increase shareholder value.
- Due diligence. Research the company and industry.
  - What kind of shape is the company you're looking at in?
  - How secure are its markets, customers and suppliers?
  - How is the industry doing overall? And how is the company doing compared to the industry? Is it a leader in the field?
  - What are the margins like? Are they high volume, low margin, or low-volume-high margins?
  - How will competitors respond?
  - Are there any legal reasons why we can't or shouldn't acquire the target company?
  - Are there technology risks?

[3. Pricing Strategies]

Question: Company S is coming out with a new tablet. How should they price it?

Pricing questions can sometimes be a stand-alone question, but just as often part of a larger case. They are one of the easiest categories of questions you'll get. Investigate the company and its objective; learn about the product or service, and the competition; and then pick a pricing strategy.

COMPANY S DEVELOPED A NEW TABLET HOW SHOULD THEY PRICE IT?	DETERMINE PRICE COMP S (PUB / PRIV) MKT LEADER REVENUES > TRENDS PRODUCT MIX > TRENDS COSTS > TRENDS CUST SEGMENT WCS PRICING STRATEGIES COMPANY OBJECTIVES COMPETITIVE ANALYSIS / SUBSTITUTIONS / COMPETITIVE RESPONSE COST-BASED PRICING PRICE-BASED COSTING	HYPOTHESIS: CAN'T FORM YET, LIMITED INFORMATION (need to know company objective)

Step 1: Investigate the company. How big is it? What products does it have, and is it a market leader in this field? **More importantly, what is their objective; profits, market share or brand positioning?** Is it in charge of their own pricing strategies, or is it reacting to suppliers, the market and competitors?

Step 2: Investigate the product. How does it compare to that of the competition? Are there substitutions or alternatives? Where is the product in its growth cycle? Is there a supply-and-demand issue at work?

Step 3: Determine a pricing strategy. There are three main pricing strategies to think about: competitive analysis, cost-based pricing and price–based costing.

Once you have determined the company's objective, you need to run through the three main pricing strategies.

Competitive Analysis: Are there similar products out there? How does our product compare to the competition? Do we know the competitor's costs? How are they priced? Are there substitutions available? Is there a supply-and-demand issue? What will the competitive response be? We need to take that into account.

Cost-based Pricing: Take all our costs, add them up and add a profit to it. This way you'll know your break-even point.

Price-based Costing: What are people willing to pay for this product? If they're not willing to pay more than what it costs you to make the product, then it might not be worth making. On the other hand, consumers may be willing to pay much more than you could get just by adding a profit margin. Profit margins vary greatly by industry. Grocery stores have a very thin profit margin, while drug companies traditionally have a large one. Also consider what your product will be worth to the buyer. Compare it to other products or services in their lives. What did they pay in those cases?

As a special note.
I don't want you to be constrained by percentages. There is nothing wrong with a 1,800% margin if that what the market is willing to pay. That being said, if the product is a life-saving

> **COST-DRIVEN PRICING**
> **(The Deadly Business Sin)**
>
> Before there was Michael Porter and all the other modern-day business gurus, there was Peter Drucker (1909–2005). The following is from Peter Drucker's ***Wall Street Journal*** article "The Five Deadly Business Sins."
>
> The third deadly sin is cost-driven pricing. The only thing that works is price-driven costing. Most American and practically all European companies arrive at their prices by adding up costs and then putting a profit margin on top. And then as soon as they have introduced the product, they have to start cutting the price, have to redesign the product at enormous expense, have to take losses — and often, have to drop a perfectly good product because it is priced incorrectly. Their argument? "We have to recover our costs and make a profit."
>
> This is true but irrelevant: Customers do not see it as their job to ensure manufacturers a profit. The only sound way to price is to start out with what the market is willing to pay — and thus, it must be assumed, what the competition will charge — and design to that price specification.
>
> Cost-driven pricing is the reason there is no American consumer-electronics industry anymore. It had the technology and the products. But it operated on cost-led pricing — and the Japanese practiced price-led costing.*

heart medication for babies think of the public relations issues you might face if word leaked out that children were dying because they couldn't afford your drug. Use common business sense.

In short, when solving a pricing problem, you need to look at all these strategies and see where, or if, they intersect.

NB: Pricing questions become more difficult/interesting when you get a case about partition pricing – meaning that you charge separately for things like delivery, shipping, installation and warranties, versus bundling everything into one price. If you run an airline, do you advertise lower ticket prices and charge for baggage or do you advertise that bags fly for free and charge a higher ticket price? If you're a large electronics store, do you include free delivery and installation on the 70-inch HDTV at a higher price? Or do you charge a lower price for the television (knowing that consumers comparison shop on the Internet even while they're standing in your store) and charge separately for delivery and installation knowing that most consumers can't get a 70-inch television into their car never mind set it up at home. One solution might be to look at industry norms; "Do my competitors offer free shipping?" If you don't consider industry norms: you might very well be at a disadvantage when people comparison shop.

I teach at 50 schools a year. Any price I quote includes my speaking fee and my travel expenses, combined. My competitor charges a fee and charges travel expenses separately. My thought is that my pricing strategy makes it easier for both the school and myself because I don't have to collect, copy and submit a travel report with receipts to the school's accounts payable department. It's just one flat fee. That way I get paid sooner and don't need to wait for my credit card bill to submit my plane ticket cost. I already have an idea what my expenses will be, and that allows the school to budget in advance, which is what *they* like. With my way there are no surprises. So whose way is right? Well, the norm in consulting is to charge a fee plus expenses. That might work well when you have Apple as a client, but not when a client is a cash-strapped university.

[4. Growth and Increasing Sales]

Question: BBB Electronics wants to increase its sales so it can claim that it is the largest distributor of the K6 double-prong lightning rod. How can BBB reach its goal?

Your notes might look like this...

BBB ELECTRONICS
↑ SALES TO BECOME
LARGEST DISTRIBUTOR
OF K6 LIGHTNING ROD

BECOME LGST DISTRIBUTOR
OF K6 RODS

HYPOTHESIS: LOWERING PRICES
WILL INCREASE VOL TO CLAIM
LGST DISTRIBUTOR TITLE

BBB ELECTRONICS

WHY?
- EGO
- PREPARING TO SELL COMPANY
- HIGH MARGIN ITEM, BRINGS IN ANCILLARY SALES

CURRENT VOLUME & TRENDS
TARGET VOLUME
COMPETITORS AND VOLUME

WAYS TO INCREASE VOLUME
↓ PRICES
↑ GROWTH RATE
MARKETING CAMPAIGNS
ACQUIRE COMPETITOR

Hypothesis: By lowering its prices, BBB can increase its sales to become the largest distributor.

Increasing sales or growing the company is not the same as increasing profits. In the former case, you are less interested in costs. Still you want to have an understanding of the company and its objective, its products and the industry. Increasing sales can mean increasing volume, increasing revenues, or both.

Step 1. Learn about the company and its size, resources, and products.

Step 2. Investigate the industry: Is it growing and how is the client growing compared to the industry? Are the clients' prices in line with its competitors?

Increase volume:

- Expand the number of distribution channels.
- Increase product line through diversification of products or services (particularly with products that won't cannibalize sales from existing products).
- Analyze the segments of the business that have the highest future potential.
- Invest in a marketing campaign.
- Acquire a competitor (particularly if the question is about increasing market share).
- Adjust prices (lower them to increase volume and raise them to decrease demand or increase profits).
- Create a seasonal balance. (Increase sales in every quarter – if you own a nursery, sell flowers in the spring, herbs in the summer, pumpkins in the fall and Christmas trees and garlands in the winter).

Another way for a company to grow is to find niches in developing industries with high barriers to entry. There will be less competition and more notice if someone is trying to enter.

+ Key Questions for Additional Scenarios

Following is a quick review of key questions to ask and points to consider after labeling the case.

Industry Analysis: Investigate the industry overall

- Where is it in its life cycle? (Emerging? Mature? Declining?)
- How has the industry been performing (growing or declining) over the last one, two, five and ten years?
- How have we been doing compared to the industry?
- Who are the major players and what market share does each have? Who has the rest?
- Has the industry seen any major changes lately? These might include new players, new technology and increased regulation.
- What drives the industry? Brand, products, size, economics or technology?
- Profitability. What are the margins?

Suppliers

- How many are there?
- What is their product availability?
- What's going on in their market?
- How is the supply chain? Are the companies that supply you getting what the need from their suppliers?

The Future

- Are players entering or leaving the market?
- Are any mergers or acquisitions going on?
- Are there any barriers to entry or exit?
- Substitutions, what alternatives are there?

Developing a new product

- Think about the product.
  - What's special or proprietary about it?
  - Is the product patented? For how long?
  - Are there similar products out there? Are there substitutions?
  - What are the advantages and disadvantages of this new product?
  - How does this new product fit in with the rest of our product line?
  - Can our sales force sell it?

- Think about market strategy
  - How does this strategy affect our existing product line?
  - Are we cannibalizing our own sales from an existing product?

- Are we replacing an existing product?
- How will this strategy expand our customer base and increase our sales?
- What will the competitive response be?
- If we are entering a new market, what are the barriers to entry?
- Who are the major players and what are their respective market shares?

- Think about customers
  - Who are our customers and what is important to them?
  - How are they segmented?
  - How can we best reach them?
  - How can we ensure that we retain them?

- Funding
  - How is this product being funded? Does our company have the cash or are they taking on debt? And can we support the debt under various economic conditions?
  - What is the best allocation of funds?

Consumer Adoption Rates

How many units can we expect to sell? Sometimes you will get a case involving a new product, particularly in the high tech field. The interviewer may ask you "What is the market size for this product and how many units can we expect to sell the first year?" There are two things to keep in mind. First, it is very rare for a new product; no matter good it is, to get more than 10 percent of the market the first year. It is more likely to be between three and five percent. It depends on the market, the strength of the competition and how much better this new product is than its competitors. Second, you should take into consideration the Rogers Adoption / Innovation Curve. Draw the curve, then turn your notes toward the interviewer and walk them through your thought process.

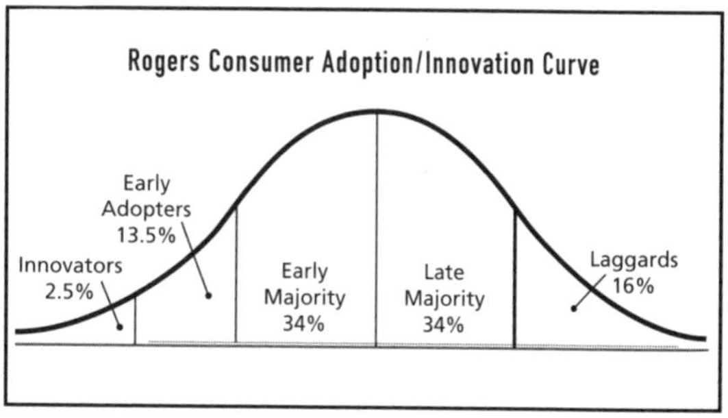

Starting a new business

Starting a new business encompasses entering a new market, as well – the first step is the same. Investigate the market to determine whether entering it makes good business sense.

- Who is our competition?
- What market share does each competitor have?
- How do competitors' products or services differ from ours?
- Are there any barriers to entry or exit?

Once we determine that there are no significant barriers to entry, we should then look at the company from a venture capitalist point of view. Would you, an outsider, invest in this start-up? Would you risk your own money? Venture capitalists don't simply buy into an idea or product they invest in:

- Management
  - How experienced is the management team?
  - What are its core competencies?
  - Have they worked together before?
  - Is there an advisory board?
- Market and Strategic Plans
  - What are the barriers to entering this market?
  - Who are the major players and what are their respective market shares?
  - What will the competitive response be?
- Distribution Channels
  - What, and how many distribution channels can we rely on?
- Products and services
  - What is the product, service or technology?
  - What is the competitive edge?
  - What are the disadvantages?
  - Is the technology proprietary?
- Customers
  - Who are the customers?
  - How can we best reach them?
  - How can we ensure that we retain them?
- Finance
  - How is the project being funded?
  - What is the best allocation of funds?
  - Can we support the debt under various economic conditions?

Competitive Response

There are two-sides to the competitive response coin. What will you do if a competitor comes out with a new product or service and starts to steal your market share? Or, what will your competitor do if you come out with a new product aimed at steal their market share?

- Again, you'll want to understand the situation by asking multiple probing questions, repeat the situation adding in your analysis, devise a plan and implement it.
- If a competitor introduces a new product or picks up market share, we want first to ask such questions as:
- What is the competitor's new product and how does it differ from what we offer?

- What has the competitor done differently? What changed?
- Have any other competitors picked up market share?
- Have the consumer's needs changed?
- Did they increase or expand into new channels?

Responses might include:

- Analyze our current product and redesign, repackage or move upmarket.
- Introduce a new product.
- Increase our profile with a marketing and public relations campaign.
- Build customer loyalty.
- Cut prices.
- Lock up raw materials and talent.
- Acquire the competitor or another player in the same market.
- Merge with a competitor to create a strategic advantage and become more powerful.
- Copy the competitor.

When planning a product launch, or making a price change, you should take into account competitive response. Too many firms seem to have a wait and see attitude which may erase much of the advantage it had hoped to gain with its new strategy.

Turnarounds

If you get a case where the company is in trouble and you've been brought in to save it and turn it around, you might want to consider:

Gather information

- Analyze the company and industry
  - Why is it failing? Bad products or services? Bad management? Bad economy?
  - Are our competitors facing the same problem?
  - Do we have access to capital?
  - Is the company publicly-traded or privately-held?
- Possible actions
  - Learn as much as possible about the company and its operations.
  - Analyze services, products and finances.
  - Secure sufficient financing, so your plan has a chance.
  - Review the talent and temperament of all employees, and get rid of the "deadwood."
  - Determine short-term and long-term goals.
  - Devise a business plan.
  - Visit clients, suppliers and distributors, and reassure them.
  - Prioritize goals and get some small successes under your belt ASAP to build confidence.

✢ Ivy Case System at a Glance

Type	Approach	Elements
Entering a New Market	Market	Competition Market share Comparative products and services Barriers to entry
	Entry	Start from scratch Acquire an existing player Form a joint venture/strategic alliance with existing player
Industry Analysis	Current Industry Structure	Life cycle (growth, transition, maturity) Performance, margins Major players and market share Industry changes (new players, new technology) Drivers (brand, size, technology)
	Suppliers	How many? Product availability? What's going on in their market?
	Future	Expanding or shrinking? Mergers and acquisitions? Barriers to entry or exit?
Mergers & Acquisitions	Objectives	Increase market access Diversify holdings Pre-empt the competition Enjoy tax advantages Incorporate synergies Increase shareholder value
	Price	Fair? Affordable? How to pay? If the economy sours...?
	Due Diligence	What shape is the company in? The industry? How secure are its markets and customers? What are the margins? What is the best competitive response to acquisition? What are the legal issues
	Exit Strategies	How long to keep it? Divest parts of the organization?
New Product	Product	Special or proprietary? Financing? Patented? Substitutions? Advantages and disadvantages? Place in product line? Cannibalizing our own products? Replacing existing product?

Ivy Case System, continued

Type	Approach	Elements
	Market Strategy	Expansion of customer base Prompts to competitive response Barriers to entry Major players and market share
	Customers	Who? How to reach them? Retention — how to hold them?
	Financing	How funded? Best allocation of funds? Debt viable?
Pricing Strategies	Pricing	Company objective Competitive pricing Cost-based pricing Price-based costing
Growth Strategies	Assessment	Is the industry growing? How are we growing compared to the industry? Are our prices relative to competitors'? What are our competitors marketing and development strategies? Which segments have the most potential? Funding for higher growth
	Strategies	Increase distribution channels Increase product line Invest in major marketing campaign Diversify products or services offered
New Business	Market	Who is the competition? What is their market share? Products comparison Barriers to entry
	Cost Benefit Analysis	Management Marketing and strategic plan Distribution channels Product Customers Finance
Competitive Response	Why?	New product? Competitor's strategy changed? Other competitors' increased market share
	Strategy	Acquire a competitor Merge with competition Copy competitor Hire the competitor's management Increase profile with marketing campaign

Ivy Case System, continued

Type	Approach	Elements
Increasing Sales	Assessment (increasing sales doesn't necessarily mean increasing profits)	Growth relative to market share Changes in market share Customer polls Prices competitive? Competitor's strategies (marketing and product development)
	How?	Increase volume Increase amount of each sale Increase prices Create seasonal balance
Reducing Costs	Assessment	Get cost breakdown Investigate for irregularities Benchmark competitors Consider labor-saving technologies
	Cost analysis — Internal	Union wages, suppliers, materials, economies of scale, increased support system
	Cost analysis — External	Economy, interest rates, government regulations, transportation/shipping strikes
Increasing Profits	Revenue E (P = R – C) M Always look at external factors first.	Identification of revenue streams? Percentage of total revenue of each? Unusual balance? Have percentages changed?
	Costs	ID fixed costs ID variable costs Shifts in costs Unusual costs Benchmark competitors Reduce costs without damaging revenue streams
	Volume	Expand into new areas Increase sales (volume and force) Increase marketing Reduce prices Improve customer service
Turnaround	Strategy	Learn about company Review services, products, finances Secure funding Review talent and culture Determine short term / long term goals Write a business plan Reassure clients, suppliers, distributors Prioritize goals and develop some small successes for momentum

In this section, we will explore some supplements to the Ivy Case System. These include both other frameworks and additional tools so that you have an understanding of what else is out there. I've purposely limited the number of alternatives, because I've learned from experience that too many options can become a burden. Keep in mind that none of these frameworks or tools was specifically designed to answer case questions. It is far better to understand the underlying problems of the case and logically address those problems than to try to apply a "fix-all" framework. That being said. . .

+ Five C's and Four P's

These are two elementary frameworks that can do the job. You're not going to blow anyone away with these, but you won't drown either. They will allow you to touch on all the main points and appear fairly well organized.

There are two secrets to using these frameworks. First, since every case is different, the C's or the P's have to be rearranged to fit the case. If you treat these frameworks like a laundry list, your answer will seem nonlinear and possibly disorganized. Second, you need to kick up some dust to conceal the fact that you're using these frameworks. If your interviewer discovers you're using the Five C's or Four P's, you might lose some points; neither of these frameworks is particularly impressive.

[Five C's]

- **Company:** What do you know about the company? How big is it? Is it a public or private company? What kinds of products or services does it offer to its clients?

- **Costs:** What are the major costs? How have its costs changed in the past year? How do its costs compare to those of others in the industry? How can we reduce costs?

- **Competition:** Who are the biggest competitors? What market share does each player hold? Has market share changed in the last year? How do our services or products differ from the competition? Do we hold any strategic advantage over our competitors?

- **Consumers/clients:** Who are they? What do they want? Are we fulfilling their needs? How can we get more? Are we keeping the ones we have?

- **Channels:** Distribution channels. How do we get our product into the hands of the end users? How can we increase our distribution channels? Are there areas of our market that we are not reaching? How do we reach them?

[Four P's]

▶ **Product:** What are our products and services? What is the company's niche?

▶ **Price:** How does our price compare to the competition's? How was our price determined? Are we priced right? If we change our price, what will that do to our sales volume?

▶ **Place:** How do we get our products to the end user? How can we increase our distribution channels? Do our competitors have products in places that we don't? Do they serve markets that we can't reach? If so, why? And how can we reach them?

▶ **Promotions:** How can we best market our products? Are we reaching the right market? What kind of marketing campaigns has the company conducted in the past? Were they effective? Can we afford to increase our marketing campaign?

✛ BCG Matrix

In 1998, Wiley Press published *Perspectives on Strategy*. The book is a collection of articles and essays written by senior members of The Boston Consulting Group. One popular and useful framework is the BCG "Product Portfolio Matrix." This matrix is designed to place a product or group of products into one of four categories while taking into account a company's relative market share. BCG has been kind enough to let us reprint Chapter Three.

The Product Portfolio *(Bruce D. Henderson, 1970)**

To be successful, a company should have a portfolio of products with different growth rates and different market shares. The portfolio composition is a function of the balance among cash flows. High-growth products require cash inputs to grow. Low-growth products should generate excess cash. Both kinds are needed simultaneously.

The Matrix

MARKET SHARE

	HIGH	LOW
HIGH (GROWTH)	★ STAR	? QUESTION MARK
LOW	$ CASH FLOW	X PET

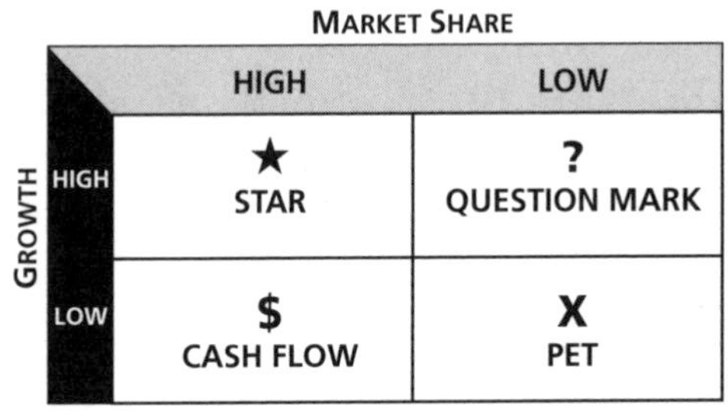

Four rules determine the cash flow of a product.
• Margins and cash generated are a function of market share. High margins and high market share go together. This is a matter of common observation, explained by the experience curve effect.

• Growth requires cash input to finance added assets. The added cash required to hold market share is a function of growth rates.

• High market share must be earned or bought. Buying market share requires an additional increment of investment.

* Used with permission of The Boston Consulting Group. Bruce D. Henderson, "The Product Portfolio," *Perspectives on Strategy*, from The Boston Consulting Group, ed. Carl W. Stern and George Stalk, Jr. (New York: John Wiley & Sons, Inc., 1998), pp. 35–37.

• No product market can grow indefinitely. The payoff from growth must come when the growth slows, or it never will. The payoff is cash that cannot be reinvested in that product.

Products with high market share and slow growth are cash cows. Characteristically, they generate large amounts of cash, in excess of the reinvestment required to maintain share. This excess need not, and should not, be reinvested in those products. In fact, if the rate of return exceeds the growth rate, the cash cannot be reinvested indefinitely, except by depressing returns.

Products with low market share and low growth are pets. They may show an accounting profit, but the profit must be reinvested to maintain share, leaving no cash throw-off. The product is essentially worthless, except in liquidation.

All products eventually become either cash cows or pets. The value of a product is completely dependent upon obtaining a leading share of its market before the growth slows.

Low-market-share, high-growth products are the question marks. They almost always require far more cash than they can generate. If cash is not supplied, they fall behind and die. Even when the cash is supplied, if they only hold their share, they are still pets when the growth stops. The question marks require large added cash investments for market share to be purchased. The low-market-share, high-growth product is a liability unless it becomes a leader. It requires very large cash inputs that it cannot generate itself.

Optimum Cash Flow

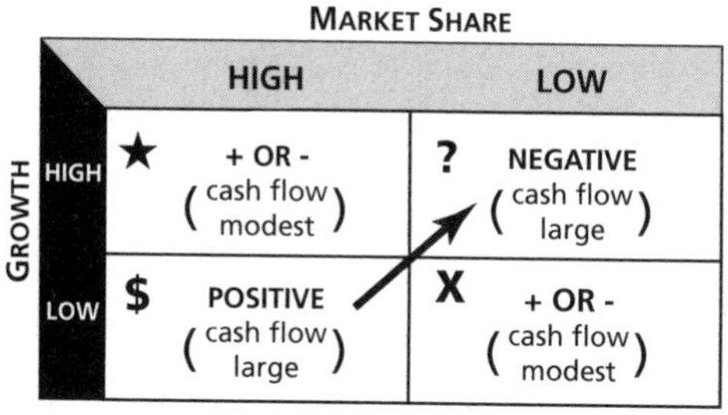

Success Sequence

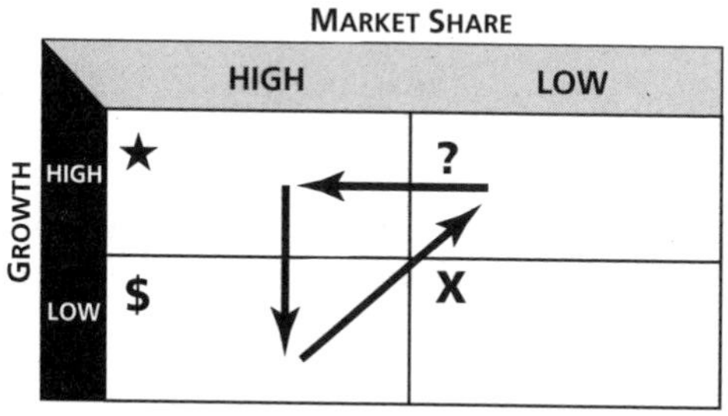

Disaster Sequence

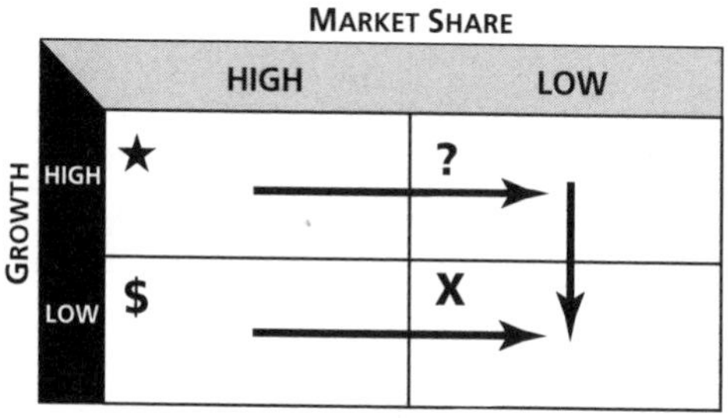

The high-share, high-growth product is the star. It nearly always shows reported profits, but it may or may not generate all of its own cash. If it stays a leader, however, it will become a large cash generator when growth slows and its reinvestment requirements diminish. The star eventually becomes the cash cow, providing high volume, high margin, high stability, security and cash throw-off for reinvestment elsewhere.

The payoff for leadership is very high indeed if it is achieved early and maintained until growth slows. Investment in market share during the growth phase can be very attractive if you have the cash. Growth in market is compounded by growth in share. Increases in share increase the margin. High margin permits higher leverage with equal safety. The resulting profitability permits higher payment of earnings after financing normal growth. The return on investment is enormous.

The need for a portfolio of businesses becomes obvious. Every company needs products in which to invest cash. Every company needs products that generate cash. And every product should eventually be a cash generator; otherwise, it is worthless.

Only a diversified company with a balanced portfolio can use its strengths to truly capitalize on its growth opportunities. The balanced portfolio has:

- stars whose high share and high growth assure the future
- cash cows that supply funds for that high growth
- question marks to be converted into stars with the added funds

Pets are not necessary. They are evidence of failure either to obtain a leadership position during the growth phase or to get out and cut the losses.

+ Michael Porter's "Five Forces" / The Structural Analysis of Industries

Michael Porter didn't develop his "Five Forces" as a case framework. However, when you are given a case dealing with developing a new product, entering a new market or starting a new business, this framework works quite well. (e.g., A regional food manufacturer is thinking of entering the gourmet toothpaste business. Should the company take the plunge?)

Please refer to Michael Porter's bestseller *Competitive Strategy* for a more in-depth explanation of his "Five Forces" model.

Porter writes that the state of competition in an industry depends on five basic competitive forces:

1. The threat of new or potential entrants. This includes new companies or acquisitions of established companies by a new player. If barriers are high or if newcomers can expect entrenchment or retaliatory measures (such as a price war) from existing competitors, then the threat of entry is low. According to Porter, barriers of entry include:

- economies of scale
- capital requirements
- government policy

- switching costs
- access to distribution channels
- product differentiation
- proprietary product technology

2. Intensity of rivalry among existing competitors.

3. Pressure from substitution products, for example, sugar vs. high-fructose corn syrup and artificial sweeteners

4. Bargaining power of buyers. Buyers compete with the industry by forcing down prices, bargaining for higher quality or more services, and playing competitors against each other — all at the expense of industry profitability.

5. Bargaining power of suppliers. Forces 4 and 5 have to do with supply and demand. When there are many suppliers but few buyers, the buyers have the upper hand. When there are many buyers, but few suppliers, the suppliers have the advantage.

Michael Porter's Five Forces:
Forces Driving Industry Competition

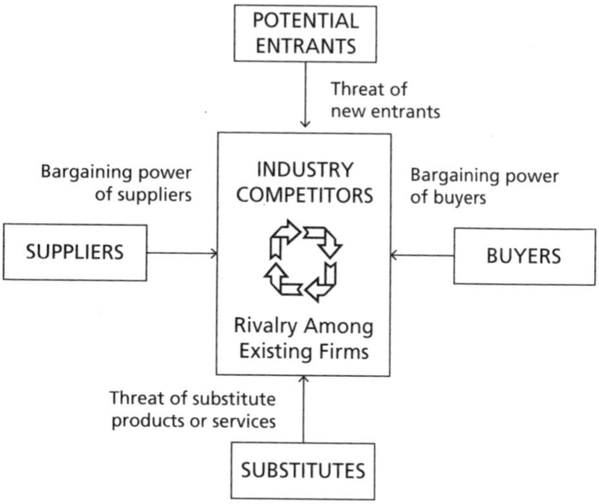

+ The Value Chain

In his 1985 book *Competitive Advantage*, Michael Porter introduced the value chain. It's a framework that follows the company's internal product processes starting with raw materials and ending with customer purchase and service. Questioning the effectiveness and efficiencies of these steps during a case question not only shows an understanding of product flow, but can lead to relevant information to help you solve the case.

Raw Materials >>> **Operations** >>> **Delivery** >>> **Marketing & Sales** >>> **Service**

Raw materials and inbound logistics: receiving materials into the warehouse, relationships with suppliers, "just in time" (JIT) delivery, etc.

Operations: processing raw materials into product through the use of capital equipment and labor

Delivery: warehousing and distribution channels

Marketing and Sales: marketing strategy, identification of customer base and the cost of customer acquisition, sales force issues (e.g., commission, company car, etc.)

Service: customers support, customer retention (It's cheaper to retain a customer than to go out and bring in a new one.)

+ Income Statement

While you may never have to draw up an income statement, you may be handed one in an interview and asked to analyze it. Understanding the basics of an income statement is essential for answering product and company profitability questions. How do the costs stack up? Do any numbers seem out of line or a bit high? For example, if Joe's Shoe Company's labor costs were $50,000 instead of $15,000, that should send off warning bells that something is wrong. Why are labor costs $50,000, or 50% of gross revenues?

Joe's Shoe Company
Income Statement

	Gross Revenues (units x price)		**100,000**
(–)	Returns and discounts	(5,000)	
	Net Sales		**95,000**
(–)	Cost of goods sold		
	Direct labor	(15,000)	
	Direct material costs	(10,000)	
	Overhead	(5,000)	
	Delivery costs	(5,000)	
		(35,000)	
	Gross Margin		**60,000**
(–)	Selling, general and admin.	(20,000)	
(–)	Depreciation	(5,000)	
		(25,000)	
	Operating Profits		**35,000**
(–)	Interest expense	(3,000)	
	Profit before Taxes		**32,000**

✛ An Aristotelian Framework

Aristotle's book *The Rhetoric and the Poetics of Aristotle* was really the first case question interview prep book. His book is about persuasion and, after all, that's what we're trying to do — persuade the interviewer that we have what it takes. Aristotle lays out a tripod (a framework) and argues that persuasion relies on the relationship between logos, ethos and pathos. As you probably remember from Philosophy 101, logos is a logical, well-reasoned argument based on facts and figures, charts and graphs. Ethos deals with the speaker's (that's you) personal voice and character. How likable and believable are you? In other words, fit. How would I feel if we were snowed in for nine hours at the Macedonian Chariot Station? Would you be an interesting companion? Finally there is pathos, your audience's frame of mind. This is often tough to determine or control, but it can be massaged by incorporating logos and ethos into your answer. The point is that you need the tripod: the combination of logos, ethos and pathos to do well in a case interview. Too much logic and not enough personality results in a tipped tripod. As you prepare for your interviews, remember to concentrate on all three. It is as much about the presentation as it is about the logic.

✛ 21 Ways to Cut Costs

Many case questions will ask you to come up with ways to cut costs, and it has been my experience that students tend to struggle with this request. Below are numerous ways to cut costs in the areas of labor, production and finance. Memorize them and when they ask you, rattle off two or three in each area.

Before you answer, the *McKinsey Quarterly** reminds us to consider the company's strategic needs and to think about the long-term consequences under a range of various economic scenarios. Do these areas "drive value" and do they help make the company "competitively distinctive"? Don't just cut equally across the board.

▶ Labor

1. Cross-train workers.
2. Cut overtime.
3. Reduce employer 401(k) or 403(b) match.
4. Raise employee contribution to health-care premium.
5. Institute four 10-hour days instead of five eight-hour days.
6. Convert workers into owners (if they have a stake in the company they will work longer, and harder and constantly think of ways to cut costs in a way that they might not have done before).
7. Contemplate layoffs.
8. Institute across-the-board pay decreases.

* Heywood, Layton and Penttinen. "A better way to cut costs," *McKinsey Quarterly* (2010). No. 1.

Production

1. Invest in technology.
2. Consolidate production space to gain scale and create accountability.
3. Create flexible production lines.
4. Reduce inventories (JIT).
5. Outsource.
6. Renegotiate with suppliers.
7. Consolidate suppliers.
8. Import parts.

Finance

1. Have customers pay sooner.
2. Refinance your debt.
3. Sell nonessential assets.
4. Hedge currency rates.
5. Redesign health insurance.

+ "If" Scenarios to Remember

Sales Scenarios

- If sales are flat and profits are taking a header, you need to examine both revenues and costs. Always start with the revenue side first. Until you identify and understand the revenue streams, you can't make educated decisions on the cost side.
- If sales are flat but market share remains relatively constant, that scenario could indicate that industry sales are flat and that your competitors are experiencing similar problems.
- If your case includes a decline-in-sales problem, analyze these three things:
  - overall declining market demand (e.g., soda sales have dropped as bottled water becomes the drink of choice)
  - the possibility that the current marketplace is mature or your product obsolete (e.g., vinyl records give way to CDs, which give way to digital)
  - loss of market share due to substitutions (e.g., video rentals have declined because there are numerous substitutions vying for the leisure dollar, such as dining out, movie attendance, pay-per-view, Direct TV and the Internet)
- If sales and market share are increasing but profits are declining, then you need to investigate whether prices are dropping and/or costs are climbing. However, if costs aren't the issue, then investigate product mix and check to see if the margins have changed.

Profit Scenarios

- If profits are declining because of a drop in revenues, concentrate on marketing and distribution issues.

- If profits are declining because of rising expenses, concentrate on operational and financial issues — i.e., COGS (cost of goods sold), labor, rent and marketing costs.
- If profits are declining, yet revenues have gone up, review:
  - changes in costs
  - any additional expenses
  - changes in prices
  - the product mix
  - changes in customers' needs

Product Scenarios

- If a product is in its emerging growth stage, concentrate on R&D, competition and pricing.
- If a product is in its growth stage, emphasize marketing and competition.
- If a product is in its mature stage, focus on manufacturing, costs and competition.
- If a product is in its declining stage, define niche market, analyze the competition's play or think exit strategy.

Pricing Scenarios

If you lower prices and volume rises, and then you are pushed beyond full capacity, your costs will shoot up as your employees work overtime, and consequently your profits will suffer.

Prices are stable only when three conditions are met:*

- The growth rate for all competitors is approximately the same.
- The prices are paralleling costs.
- The prices of all competitors are roughly of equal value.

The volume (the amount that you produce) and the costs are easier to change than the industry price levels, unless all parties change their prices together (e.g., airline tickets or gas prices).

The perfect strategy for the high-cost producer is one that convinces competitors that market shares cannot be shifted, except over long periods of time. Therefore, the highest practical industry prices are to everyone's advantage** — meaning that price wars are detrimental and everyone will profit more by keeping prices high.

General tips

- How the Internet affects the company should be in the back of your mind in every case.
- How the economy affects the company should be in the back of your mind in every case.
- How the competition — both internal to the industry and external (substitutions) — affects the company should be in the back of your mind in every case.

---

* Henderson, Bruce D. "The Product Portfolio," *Perspectives on Strategy from the Boston Consulting Group*, eds. Carl W. Stern and George Stalk, Jr. (New York: John Wiley & Sons, Inc., 1998), 21.

** Ibid., p.27.

+ Business Case Tips

- If you ever get a case that you have already heard, as tempting as it might be to answer it, your best strategy is to tell the interviewer. Interviewers usually know when someone has heard a case. You tend to do things too quickly and your thought process is different. It is hard to reenact discovery.
- Take graph paper into the interview. It helps you organize your thoughts, keeps the numbers lined up when you multiply and add and reminds you to try to graph part of your answer.
- Ask for numbers. If the numbers aren't an important part of the case, the interviewer will more than likely tell you not to focus on them.
- Practice your math, particularly multiplication and percentages. Almost all recruiters **will not** let you take a calculator into the interview. Most students make math mistakes. They are usually off by a zero or two (see p. 31).
- Interact with the interviewer as much as possible. Remember, it should be a conversation.

A final word before you tackle the cases.

Peer Advice. Here's advice from some students who had just gone through the process. They all received offers from BCG, McKinsey or both.

"As you go through the math portion of the case, think out loud. Let the interviewer know what is going through your mind. If you are unsure of what to say, pretend the interviewer is on the telephone and you are explaining it to her over the phone."

"For me, one of the unexpected challenges of final round interviews was their sheer length. After five hours of intense interviews, I felt like a slouching, mumbling mess with any spark of creativity long since extinguished, and I was far more likely to make simple mistakes. Before the last couple of interviews on any given day, take a few minutes, and pause to reenergize. Splash water on your face, grab another cup of coffee, take a brisk walk up and down the hallway. Do anything that keeps your brain awake and your personality alive during that final stretch."

"Motivation. Students in non-business disciplines who are looking to land a job in consulting must be able to justify their motivation for the transition. The interview process is expensive and time-consuming for firms, and interviewers are looking for clear, logical answers that will convince them of a candidate's seriousness. Additionally, candidates must be prepared to discuss how consulting fits into their long-term professional goals. Because firms recruiting outside business schools could easily fill their incoming classes entirely with business school students, the burden is greater for non-MBAs."

"Preparation. Preparing for interviews in consulting should not be limited to practicing cases. Interviews also include discussions of experiences in various environments, such as ambiguity and rancor, as well as questions related to leadership and teamwork. The candidate must be prepared not only to discuss these subjects, but also to answer subsequent questions which interviewers will ask to uncover various layers of the topic in addition to the candidate's personality. For preparation, one should practice with a group of friends. This setting, along with the resulting constructive feedback, will help one anticipate the string of questions that will inevitably be asked and improve one's communication skills. Sound preparation will give one the confidence needed during the actual interview — confidence that will create a positive impression with the interviewer. After all, while the interviewer is there to assess whether the candidate is able to structure a problem well, he or she is also judging whether or not the candidate can be put before a client."

"In preparing stories for various settings, candidates must identify and select the most appropriate anecdotes. It is unnecessary for every story to portray the candidate as a hero. A failure through which one learned about one's weaknesses can be just as effective, if not more. Conversely, an experience through which one strengthened a skill or developed a new skill through perseverance will score well. Fabricating an event, however, will result in certain doom, as interviewers are adept at digging deeper into an issue and determining gaps or untruths. Therefore, a successful candidate must select and prepare honest stories that provide insight into one's personality."

"The Ivy Case System was like a roadmap. As soon as I got a question, I was immediately able to identify what type of question it was and what types of questions to ask to tease further information out of the interviewer. This is the advantage the Ivy Case System gives you. Then, having Porter's Five Forces and the Five Cs is also useful in your toolkit."

With regards to interviewing abroad: "Make sure you know what types of projects the country office is involved in. For example, offices in China are doing many 'market entry' projects. So it is important to understand the varieties and complexities surrounding 'entering a new market' and to practice those types of cases."

"Go through the interview process without second guessing how you're doing. It only handicaps your performance. Prepare and then let the cards fall. Be confident. It's impossible to know what the interviewer is thinking. They may do things intentionally to throw you off. Don't let the little things, like screwing up a math problem, upset you."

Practice, practice, practice!

Practice online interactive cases at:

www.apd.mckinsey.com: click on "Interview Prep."
www.bcg.com/careers/careers_splash.jsp: click on "Interview Prep."
www.bain.com/bainweb/join_bain/join_bain_overview.asp: click on "Case Interview."

This chapter is broken down into four sections. The first section is the "Anatomy" section. In this section we have a breakdown of the two most popular types of cases, profit and loss (Harley-Davidson), and entering a new market (Coors Brewery). Motorcycles and beer: Some might say this is a recipe for disaster, but not us. As you go through these two cases, not only will you read the dialogue between the interviewer and the student, you'll read my analysis of how the interviewee is doing.

The second section is made up of ten "case starts". Read the problem statement, then take a minute to lay out your structure and make a list of questions and concerns that you would have wanted to ask the interviewer in a real interview. Then compare your structure to mine. Remember, there are no right answers so it's okay if our structures don't match up. Do one or two at first, then save the rest for when you are more confident.

In the third section you'll find twenty dialogue cases, similar to the ones in the first section, but without my analysis. Read the problem statement and then jot down your structure and key issues. The cases are categorized by difficulty. See the case index for this section on page 92.

Finally, starting on page 160, you'll find the index for the "Partner Cases". These are the cases you and a partner can give each other. They are written so anyone, business savvy or not, can ask you these questions and give you solid feedback. Again, they are divided by difficulty.

As with all case questions, we assume facts not in evidence, as well as generous assumptions. Familiar companies are used for examples because of the power of their brand and their familiarity to the general public. The information concerning these companies may not be accurate and should not be used as reliable up-to-date data.

✛ Harley-Davidson®

Interviewer: Our client is Harley-Davidson Motor Company. Its stock fell from $54 a share to $49 a share on news of declining profits. What's going on and how can we turn this around?

Student: Our client is Harley-Davidson. Its stock fell from $54 to $49 a share on news of declining profits. We need to figure out what's going on and how to fix it. Are there any other objectives I should be aware of?

Interviewer: Yes, maintaining market share.

Analysis: The student was right to summarize the case; however, she would have made a better impression if she had tried to quantify the case. Instead of saying the stock price dropped from $54 to $49 a share, she should have said that the stock dropped about 10 percent. Remember, so much of this is how you think — what goes through your mind when you hear some numbers.

She was also right to verify the objective and to ask if there were any other objectives she should be concerned with. Without asking, she never would have known that maintaining market share was an issue.

Student: I just want to take a moment to jot down some notes.

Interviewer: That's fine.

The student writes on her paper E(P=R–C)M.

Analysis: This is the framework you want to use for a P&L case. Inside the parentheses is the classic "profits equal revenues minus costs." That tells us what's going on inside the company. But you want to look at external factors first. Is this a Harley problem or an industrywide problem? She starts with the E.

Student: I'd like to start with external factors first. Can you tell me what's going on with the economy?

Analysis: The student would have made a much greater impression if she had told the interviewer about the economy. If you are applying for a job in business, you should know what's going on outside the classroom, particularly with the economy. The other reason to tell the interviewer what's happening with the economy is that it gives you more control over the interview. It allows you to frame the economic environment in which this case takes place. So many of these cases take place in a vacuum and you don't know what the economy is like. When you frame it yourself, there are fewer surprises. When you talk about the economy, pick out the main factors that will affect Harley's business. Let's try it again...

Student: I'd like to start with some external factors first. I'd like to start with the economy. I know that the US is at the tail-end of a recession; it is in the middle of a mortgage crisis and unemployment remains high, so people have less disposable income. Gas prices have topped $4 a gallon. I know that the US dollar has been gaining strength against the euro and pound, but is still fairly weak against Asian currencies, particularly the yen. And I know that interest rates have fallen dramatically and are now close to a 30-year low. (*Note: US economy in 2013*)

Analysis: Much better. Do you need to go into this much detail? Yes. You'll see how everything she brought up will tie into her answer later on. Make sure that you write everything down; it will give you some place to go if you get stuck.

Interviewer: Good. What's next?

Student: I'd like to know about the motorcycle industry. Can you tell me what's been going on?

Analysis: No one expects you to know what is going on in the motorcycle industry. The interviewer has a lot of information that he wants to give the student. Sometimes it takes a series of questions from the student to extract the information. Sometimes it only takes one, and the interviewer does a data dump. It is then up to the student to sort through what's relevant now, what's smoke and what might become relevant later.

In this case the interviewer is going to do a data dump.

Interviewer: I have some industry information. Last year the industry grew by 5 percent; Harley grew by 2 percent; the small, less expensive motorcycles and scooters grew by 8 percent. Female riders were up 12 percent and now make up 10 percent of all motorcycle riders, but they only make up 2 percent of Harley riders.

I have some market share for you, but I want you to assume that each of these companies only makes one model. For Harley it is the big Harley Hog.

Student: Okay.

Interviewer: The market leader is Honda, with 27 percent; Harley, with 24 percent; Yamaha, 17 percent; Suzuki, 10 percent; Kawasaki, 8 percent; BMW, 6 percent. The remaining 9 percent is made up of two scooter companies, Vespa and Scooter Do. What else do you want to know about the industry?

Student: It looks as though Harley is not growing as fast as the industry overall. That might be because it has few female riders. The trend seems to be headed towards smaller, lighter, more gas efficient bikes. If Harley—

Interviewer: I know where you are headed. We'll talk about strategies in a minute. Do you have any industry questions?

Student: No.

Interviewer: Do think that this is a Harley problem or an industry problem?

Student: At this point I think it is a Harley problem.

Analysis: Whenever they give you a number, like the fact that the industry grew by 5 percent, don't be happy with it. It doesn't tell you nearly enough. You always want to ask for trends. If the industry grew by 10 percent the year before, and 5 percent this year, then the 5 percent looks very different to me than if the industry had gone from 2 percent to 5 percent. Very few students ever ask for trends. Ask for them and you'll stand out from your peers. Again, they are trying to learn how you think, and if you don't ask for trends, you're not thinking like a consultant.

Interviewer: What's next?

Student: I'd like to look inside the parentheses to see what's going on inside the company. I'd like to start with the revenues first. What are the major revenue streams and how have they changed over time?

Interviewer: Okay. I'm going to give the four major revenue streams for Y1 and Y2. The four major revenue streams are domestic motorcycles sales, international motorcycle sales, replacement parts and garb.

Student: "Garb" being merchandise?

Analysis: If you ever get a phrase, industry jargon or a string of initials that you don't understand, ask for clarification. You don't lose any points for clarification questions up front.

Interviewer: Yes, garb is merchandise. For Year 1, domestic motorcycles made up 45 percent, international 40 percent, replacement parts 10 percent and garb, 5 percent. For Year 2, domestic motorcycles made up 35 percent, international 40 percent, replacement parts 15 percent and garb 10 percent. I'd like you to look at those numbers and how they changed over the last year, and in four sentences or less tell me what's going on with Harley customers.

While the interviewer was stating those numbers, the student was making a chart. The student wrote down the following chart.

Revenue Streams	**Y1**	**Y2**
Domestic	45%	35%
International	40%	40%
Replacement parts	10%	15%
Garb	5%	10%

Student: It looks as if Harley customers are buying fewer new bikes, fixing up their old bikes and buying some garb to make themselves feel good and look bad.

Interviewer: (smiles)

Analysis: She did a great job. She kept it to one sentence and added a little humor to the interview as well.

Interviewer: Okay, good. Let's talk about costs.

Student: Before we do, can I ask about volume? Do we have any numbers on volume of bikes sold?

Interviewer: I do. In Year 1 Harley sold 350,000 bikes and in Year 2 it sold 330,000 bikes.

Students: Thanks.

Analysis: Good move on the student's part. Volume is part of revenue so asking for that number was appropriate and she scored some points.

Student: What are the major costs, both fixed and variable, and how have they changed over time?

Interviewer: The only cost you need to worry about is the cost of steel. We are in the middle of a steel contract that expires in 24 months. We currently have a good deal, but we are concerned about getting slammed with high steel costs in 24 months, as the economy improves. I just want you to keep that in the back of your mind.

What I'd like you to do now is to come up with some short-term strategies that will help turn Harley around. By "short term," I mean 18 months or less.

Student: Okay. The first thing they should do is market to women.

Interviewer: What would they market?

Student: They could design a new bike...

Interviewer: It is going to take more than 18 months to design, manufacture and distribute a new bike. Leave that for the long-term.

Student: They could market the Hog to women.

Interviewer: They'd have to be pretty big women. The Hog is a hard bike to handle. That's why only 2 percent of Harley owners are women.

Student: Then they could market the garb. Women like to look—

Interviewer: What else?

Student: They could raise the price of garb and the price of replacement parts. We know that people are going to continue to buy those items.

Interviewer: What else?

Student: I'm not sure. They could lay people off?

Interviewer: Are you asking me or telling me?

Analysis: Whenever you are answering a P&L case and they ask you for strategies, you want to do two things: (1) write revenue-based strategies and cost-based strategies on your paper, and (2) ask for a moment to jot down some ideas.

By writing revenue-based strategies on your paper, you are showing the interviewer that you are well-organized and thinking two steps ahead. It is easier to think of some ideas if you are looking at a heading on a piece of paper instead of a blank page. It also keeps you from ping-ponging back and forth between revenue-based and cost-based ideas. You want to present all the revenue-based ideas first, then the cost-based ideas.

The reason to ask for a moment to jot down some ideas is that it allows you to think of ideas in any order, but present them in the right order. It also gives you some place to go. Keep in mind that the interviewer has probably given this case ten times. He knows every answer that you can think of and he's heard them all before. There is a good chance that he will cut you off as soon as he knows where your answer is headed. It is very difficult for people to drop their secondary thought and then come up with a new thought right away. When cut off in mid-thought, people tend to panic, scramble and then shut down. They can't think of another idea to save their lives.

If you take the time to jot down some ideas and he cuts you off, then you can just look at your notes and give him another idea. It takes a lot of stress out of the process and makes you look more professional.

Also, if you hit a wall and can't think of anything, try looking at your first page of notes.

Remember, the student told us a couple of great things about the economy: Interest rates are way down and the dollar is still down against the yen.

Let's take it from the top.

Interviewer: Come up with some short-term strategies.

Student: Can I take a moment to jot down some ideas?

Interviewer: Absolutely.

The student writes revenue-based and cost-based strategies on her paper, then jots down some ideas.

Student: Okay. I'd like to break them down by revenue-based and cost-based. I'll start with revenue-based. Harley can raise the prices of its garb and replacement parts because we know people will buy them anyway. We can increase international distribution channels.

Interviewer: Where?

Student: In Asia, where the dollar is still weak.

Interviewer: Okay, what else?

Student: Because interest rates are so low, we can offer low financing packages and give high trade-in values to encourage customers to buy a new bike.

Interviewer: What else?

Student: On the cost side, because interest rates are so low, we can refinance our corporate debt.

Interviewer: Okay, good.

Student: And we can look at laying people off. You said the volume dropped from 350,000 bikes to 330,000. That's a about a 5 percent drop.

Interviewer: We are thinking about changing the price. I have some data. I want you to run the numbers and then tell me what you want to do, and, more important, why you want to do it.

If we leave the price the same, Harley will sell 330,000 motorcycles and make a net profit of $10,000 each. If we discount the price, Harley will sell 440,000 motorcycles and net $7,000 each. And if they raise the price, they will sell only 275,000 motorcycles and net $12,000 each.

Analysis: The student should take some time to run the numbers. You are better off taking a little extra time and getting the right answer than rushing through and getting the wrong answer. Before you give your answer, ask yourself if the number makes sense. If it doesn't, go back and figure it out. You can't un-ring the bell. I'd hate to see you lose a great opportunity over a silly math mistake.

Remember, silence is okay as long as you are doing calculations, writing notes or drawing a chart.

Student: If we keep the price the same, then our net profit will be $3.3 billion. If we lower the price, our net profits will be $3.08 billion, and if we raise the price, our net profit will also be $3.3 billion.

Interviewer: So if we raise the price or leave it alone, we'll make the same net profit. What do you want to do, and why?

Student: I'd like to keep the price the same. You said market share was a key objective, and if we raise the price, we are going to sell 55,000 fewer bikes. That's about a 5 percent drop, which will probably lower our market share. If we sell more bikes, we'll sell more garb and evidentially more replacement parts. And even if we cut production, we will still probably have a lot of Year 2 inventory left over. What do we do with it when the Year 3 models come out? If we sell it at a discount, we'll probably cannibalize our Year 3 sales.

Interviewer: That's all very interesting, but let me tell you why you're wrong. If we raise the price, we'll have lower labor costs because we'll be able to lay more people off. In addition, the higher price will enhance the brand. As far as your other concerns go, you told me that you plan to increase international distribution channels where the dollar is still weak. If we do that, any extra inventory can be shipped overseas and sold at the new higher price. Garb sales tend to be higher when you enter a new territory. So market share shouldn't be an issue. Besides, how do you measure market share? Is it number of units sold or total revenues?

Analysis: Ouch. The interviewer got right in her face even though she gave a well-thought-out answer. Luckily she knows that this "let me tell you why you're wrong" business is just a test. She keeps her emotions in check and does what the interviewer wants her to do: stick with and defend her answer.

Student: You make an interesting argument; however, I don't find it compelling enough. I can't believe that you can do all that within an 18-month period. Therefore, I think the best option in these economic conditions would be to keep the price the same.

Interviewer: Okay, good. Give me two long-term, revenue-based ideas and two long-term, cost-based ideas.

Student: Can I take a moment to jot some ideas down?

Interviewer: Certainly.

Student: Okay. On the revenue-based side, the first thing I'd do is come up with a new bike that is geared not only toward women but to younger men as well. This will give us something to market to women besides garb. I'd also look to see if we can acquire a scooter company. We couldn't put the Harley name on it, but we can take advantage of the fastest growing segments of the market, women and scooters. Besides, there will be a number of synergies we would be able to take advantage of. On the cost side, we were concerned about the price of steel. We can buy some steel futures to hedge against a steel increase. We could stockpile some steel at the current price, and because we are developing a new bike, we can make more parts out of composites instead of steel. We could modernize the plant with new technologies and maybe have some parts made overseas.

Interviewer: Good. Why don't you take a moment and summarize the case for me.

Student: Our client is Harley-Davidson. Its stock dropped around 10 percent on news of declining profits. We looked at external factors first and determined that it was more of a Harley problem than an industry problem. They are out of step with the two fast-growing segments of the industry, women and scooters. So we came up with some short-term and long-term strategies both on the revenue and cost side. An example of a short-term, revenue-based strategy is offering low financing to customers. On the cost side, we could refinance our debt. In the long term we would produce a new bike geared toward women and younger men and acquire a scooter maker. On the cost side, we could hedge steel prices and have certain new parts made out of composite instead of steel. If Harley follows these strategies as well as some of the others we talked about, it should be on its way to higher profits in 24 to 36 months.

Analysis: She came on very strong at the end. The turning point was when she defended her decision to keep the price the same. That gave her additional confidence, and it showed through the rest of the interview.

+ Coors Brewing Company©

Interviewer: Our client is Coors Brewing Company and for the last 50 years it's been advertising the fact that a key ingredient in Coors beer is Rocky Mountain spring water. The CEO calls you into his office and says that Coors is considering entering the bottled water market. I want you to analyze the market, identify any key issues and make a recommendation.

Student: So our client is Coors and it's thinking of entering the bottled water industry. Besides conducting an industry analysis and identifying any major issues, are there any other objectives I should be concerned with?

Interviewer: Yes. The CEO told the board of directors that he would increase revenues by 50 percent in five years or he would resign.

Analysis: It was important that he asked about other objective; otherwise he would have never found out about the needed 50 percent increase in revenues. If he hadn't asked the interviewer would have had to feed him that information during the case and he would have lost points.

Student: I'm assuming that's overall company revenues. So my hypothesis is that by entering the bottled water industry, Coors will increase overall company revenues by 50 percent. I just want to take a moment to draw out my notes.

Analysis: Because this is an interviewee-driven case he stated a hypothesis within the first five minutes of the case. He also took time to lay out his structure.

(Once he's done, he turns his notes toward the interviewer and walks her through them.)

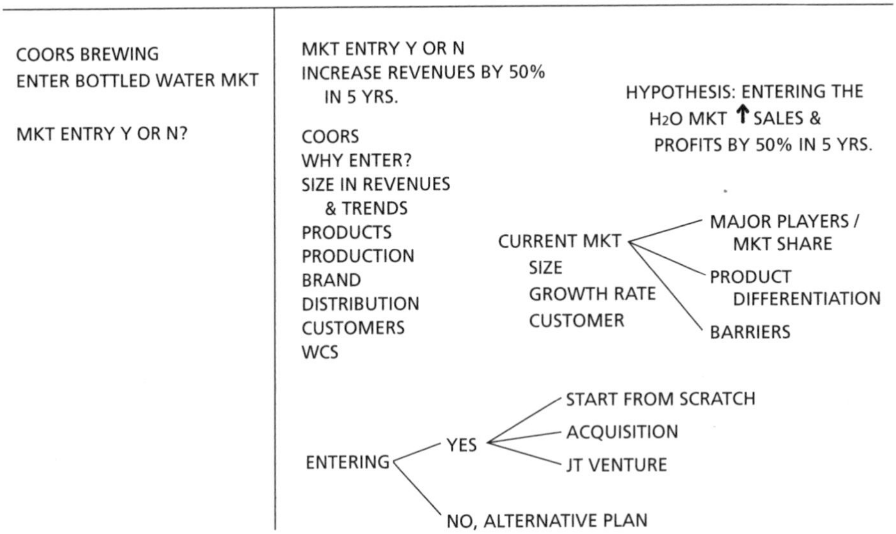

Student: First I'd like to look at Coors. Why does it want to enter this market? If it needs to increase revenues by 50 percent, I need to know what its revenues are today. I'd like to know what its product line looks like and get an understanding of its production process. Is bottling beer similar to bottling water? Branding is also important. Will it call this Coors water or will they use another name? Next is distribution. I'll assume that it currently has beer distributors all around the United States; will it use those same distributors to distribute their water? Will the customer segmentation be similar? I'm betting a lot more people drink water than beer. And finally what constitutes success in the mind of the client? What percentage of the bottled water market does Coors expect to capture in five years?

Next, I'd like to look at the bottled water industry. What were its revenues last year and how has it been trending over the last three years? Do we have any forecasts? I'd like to know who the major players are and what market share they have? How do their products differ from Coors'? Are their any other companies that sell Rocky Mountain spring water? Then the last thing I'd like to know about the industry is whether there are any barriers to entry or barriers to exit.

Finally, I'd like to think about how best to enter the market. Coors can start from scratch and grow organically; it can buy its way in or it can do a joint venture. I'd like to look at the advantages and disadvantages of each.

Analysis: He did a great job. By turning his notes toward the interviewer he brought her into the case and made her feel more like a client and less like an interviewer.

The student started off analyzing the client company. Many students make the mistake of starting off with the water industry. It's important to understand why Coors wants to enter. He also made a pretty exhaustive list of company issues that he wanted to investigate, particularly what constitutes success in the eyes of the client. It's critical to know this, so you have a goal and can reality-test the client's response.

Next he asked for all the important industry information. And finally he laid out options on how to best enter the market.

Interviewer: Sounds good. Where do you want to start?

Student: Why enter the water market?

Interviewer: The CEO has a goal of increasing company sales by 50 percent in five years. He will never make it with beer alone. Assuming the beer market to be a zero-sum market, beer sales have been flat and are forecasted to remain that way for the next five years. Any new product would only cannibalize sales from an existing product.

Student: What were its revenues last year?

Interviewer: $5.2 billion.

Student: So it would have to increase its revenues by [quick calculation] $2.6 billion for a total of $7.8 billion.

Interviewer: That's right.

Student: I know it produces Coors and Coors Light; what other products does it have?

Interviewer: Besides those two, it has Keystone and Keystone Light. That's the beer you buy when you only have $1.50 left to your name. It also produces Killian's Irish Red and Blue Moon.

Student: No non-beer products?

Interviewer: Assume no. You asked about brand and distribution channels and we'll talk about them in a little bit. Who do you think drinks Coors?

Student: Blue-collar beer drinkers, construction workers, college students and sports fans, mostly male.

Interviewer: Okay. In your notes you also asked what percentage of the water market did Coors expect to get in five years. It expects 10 percent. What else do you want to know?

Student: I want to know about the bottled water industry, growth trends, major players, market share, product differentiation and barriers.

Interviewer: Last year, the bottled water industry did $11 billion in revenues. It's forecasted to grow 5 percent a year, every year for the next five years. Flat water makes up 96 percent of the market compared to sparkling's 4 percent. The three major players are Coke, Pepsi and Nestlé. Assume that together they share 60 percent of the overall water market. There are about a dozen other players, some international and some regional. Some of the regional players produce private-label water as well as produce under their own name. They make up 36 percent of the market. The final 4 percent is the sparkling water. The major players there are San Pellegrino, Pierre, Voss and Poland Springs Sparkling.

Also, assume that there are three levels of water. The premium level consists of brands like Fiji, Evian and San Pellegrino, to name a few. The big three, Coke, Pepsi and Nestle, dominate the national mid-level water market. This is where Coors wants to enter, mid-level. The lower tier is made up of regional waters, which are usually priced lower. What's next?

Student: I just want to take a minute and figure something out. Coors needs $2.6 billion in five years. It thinks it can take 10 percent of the market in five years. Is 10 percent of the bottled water market greater than or equal to $2.6 billion? If the market was $11 billion last year and it is growing 5 percent a year for the next five years, we need to figure out what the water revenues are five years from now. (The student writes down A = 11b (1+.05)5, then thinks better of it.)

If the industry is growing at a rate of 5 percent a year for the next five years, that's 25 percent. However, we need to take compounding into consideration. So I know that's it's going to be more than 25 percent but less than 30 percent. So my best guess is around 28 percent. So $11 billion times 1.28 equals... [Writes out the calculation] around $14 billion. Ten percent of that is $1.4 billion, so he's going to be short by $1.2 billion.

Analysis: He almost made the math much more complicated than it needed to be. Interviewers make you do math without a calculator for two main reasons: to see how you think and to see if you think before you speak. No interviewer would want to sit there and watch him struggle with the exponents or do the same calculation over and over again if he had decided to take 5 percent of 11 billion, than 5 percent of that number, and so on.

The other concern would be if he had trouble with the zeros and came up with $140 billion instead of $14 billion. $140 billion doesn't make any sense and even if he caught his mistake right after he had said it, you can't un-ring the bell. You're not thinking before you speak and if you do that in an interview, what are you going to do in front of a client? I can't trust you. And if I can't trust you, I'm not going to hire you.

Interviewer: What percentage of the bottled water market would he need to get in order to reach his goal of $2.6 billion?

Student: Well, 10 percent is 1.4, and 20 percent is 2.8, so a little less than 20 percent. Around 18 percent.

Interviewer: Good. There is no way he's getting 18 percent of the bottle water market in five years. He'll be lucky to get 10 percent. What's the quickest way to increase market share?

Student: Lower prices.

Interviewer: What's the quickest way to increase market share?

Student: A marketing campaign?

Interviewer: What's the quickest way to increase market share?

Student: An acquisition?

Analysis: He lost his confidence. The interviewer asked him a question, didn't like the answer and asked him the same question two more times. While he was confident about his first answer, he stumbled when he was asked again and again. If you take this whole case interviewing process and boil it down, the two most important things are structure and confidence. Usually one follows the other.

Interviewer: Good. Say that Coors is going to buy a regional player with 4 percent national market share called Bulldog water, out of Athens, Georgia. Now, Bulldog's water source is Athens tap water and Coors's water is Rocky Mountain spring water. Two very different water sources about 2,000 miles apart. So Coors will run two separate companies, which is fine. Coors will be in the middle tier and Bulldog in the lower tier. Besides the increase in market share, what are two other advantages to buying Bulldog?

Student: Expertise. Coors is new to the water ...

Interviewer: Good. What else?

Student: Production facilities...

Interviewer: Coors isn't going to ship water by tanker 2,000 miles to save on production costs. What else?

Student: Distribution channels. They...

Interviewer: Good. Coors can piggyback on Bulldog's distribution channels.

Analysis: The student handled that well. He was cut off in the middle of an answer and was able to come up with additional answers.

Interviewer: Before, you asked me about branding. Should Coors call its water Coors Water or something else?

Student: What will be the market acceptance of a beer company selling water? That's the question. Is the Coors name too closely associated with beer? I'm betting that it is. Water is seen as pure and healthy, beer is not. I don't think mothers would like to see their kids drinking Coors. Besides Coke, which is one of the best-known brands in the world, didn't call its product Coke Water; they called it Dasani.

Interviewer: Coors ships beer to independent beer distributors all over the US. Should they use their beer distributors to distribute water?

Student: Yes. It will save on shipping and the cost of building a new network.

Interviewer: Let me tell you why you're wrong. Water is sold in three times as many places as beer. You can't buy beer in a vending machine; you can't buy it at McDonalds' and you can't buy it at school. If Coors wants 10 percent of the water market, it has to have its product in every possible venue. Besides, I don't want a beer truck pulling up in front of an elementary school and unloading water. It sends a bad message. And my last point is that if Coors is interested in increasing revenues, why are you focusing on costs?

Student: Those are all valid points. I think that you're right. They should build a new network of distributors.

Analysis: Interviewers will often take the other side of a question to see if you can defend your answer without getting defensive and come back with a persuasive argument. In this case the student was wrong and he knew it. There is no shame in admitting that you are wrong. It is better to admit it than to come back with a weak case just because you don't want to admit that you are wrong.

Interviewer: Okay, so say Coors calls its water Rocky Mountain Spring Water; it builds a new network of distributors, it comes out with a national marketing campaign, maybe even gets a celebrity spokesperson and offers an introductory low price. How will Coke respond, or will it?

Student: To quote Churchill, I think Coke will try to strangle the baby in the cradle. Coors is too much of a...

Interviewer: Wait a minute. You're comparing Coors to fascism?

Student: The quote was about Bolshevism: Strangle Bolshevism in its cradle.

Interviewer: Are you sure? I was a history major at Williams.

Student: Positive. Coke will respond, and quickly. It won't want Coors to get a foothold in the market and start stealing market share.

Analysis: The case almost went off track, but the student kept the focus. It would have been easy to go off on a tangent about Churchill or World War II, but he took control and steered it back.

Interviewer: Say Coors does all that. We are still $1.2 billion short. How are we going to close the gap? And keep in mind that we already spent our allowance and can't buy another company, and the margins aren't there for exporting.

Student: [Thinks for a minute] Coors spent a lot of time, effort and money building a new brand. They spent a lot of time, effort and money building new distribution channels. And they did it all for one bottle of water. They've done all the hard part. So now they increase their product mix. They could add flavor waters, but also Rocky Mountain Spring lemonade, ice tea, green tea and maybe sports drinks. Not only under the Rocky Mountain label, but under the Bulldog label as well.

Interviewer: Excellent. Let's say we did all that and we figure that we will be $50 million dollars short of our goal. You have a meeting with the CEO. What are you going to tell him?

Student: I'd like to take a moment. Because if I go in now, I'm going to have to tell him that we'll be short of his $2.6 billion revenue increase. I'd like to think about how I can go in and tell him yes to everything. First, the economy will be in better shape five years from now. So most of that $50 million will come from increased beer sales. Second, we can look at other alcoholic products, such as vodka, tequila or alcapops — like Mike's Hard Lemonade. I'd also like to point out that the original assignment was to analyze the bottled water industry and determine if it was a good idea for Coors to enter. The water takes us 95 percent of the way there. Do we throw the baby out with the bathwater even if we are $50 million short?

Interviewer: So what's your recommendation?

Student: Yes, we enter the water market. We do it under a new brand, Rocky Mountain Spring; we do it by acquiring Bulldog Water for its market share, expertise and distribution channels. We build a new network of distributors and then introduce additional products to the mix, like lemonade and ice tea.

Interviewer: Good.

Analysis: He came on strong in the end. The interview was starting to get away from him and he was just answering questions instead driving the question. He was creative in coming up with additional products for both of the water companies. But the thing that clinched it was the fact that he was determined to go into the meeting with a "yes" and a way to get there. Most students would have left it at, "It looks promising but we're going to be $50 million short."

In additional he stated his recommendation first, then backed it up with a plan. He got beat up along the way but kept his cool and regained the control of the interview.

+ Case Starts

Many people struggle with getting started: thinking about the key issues, asking the right questions and crafting their structure. This section was designed to help you with your case starts.

Some cases are very vague and broad: "Here's my problem. What do I do?" With cases like these (more common to BCG and Bain & Company); you need to take great care in drawing your structure. Also, with BCG your structure should be "hypothesis driven." A hypothesis is the assumed answer. "Hypothesis driven" means you need to consider the case from the answer.

Other cases are: "Here's my problem. I want to you to determine market size, price, breakeven and profits." These are less structured cases because the interviewer has given you a laundry list of information to determine (more common to McKinsey). Keep in mind that you don't necessarily have to answer the questions in the order in which they are given. One mistake candidates often make is to quickly jump into calculating the market-size. Determining the market-size first is probably the right thing to do 80 percent of the time; however, you need to make sure that you have enough information to figure it out. If it is a new product, make sure you know the price. If you don't know the price, you can't accurately determine market size. You'll probably also want to know about product differentiations as well. When the interviewer gives you a list of issues, oftentimes you can take the opportunity to quickly draw up a final slide. It will act as your structure, a scorecard for the interviewer to follow, and your summary. You'll see an example in the pages that follow. Also, read more about final slides on page 33.

Keep in mind that some frameworks are as simple as short-term and long-term; and internal and external. Take a step back and look at the big picture. Don't try to force it and don't use the same structure all the time. I've seen many students use P = R – C as their structure for every case. To me that is the same as using one of the cookie-cutter frameworks like the 5Cs or 4Ps. They have, in fact, turned the profit formula into a checklist. By doing so, they'll lose points for lack of creativity, imagination and intellectual curiosity.

With all cases you should summarize the case, verify the objective, ask clarifying questions and then lay out your structure. (See the "The First Five Steps" section in the Ivy Case System chapter on page 35.) There is one exception, the profit and loss case. With a P&L case you lay out your structure before you ask the questions. The structure for a P&L case is E(P=R-C)M. This is the only structure that is set in stone; all others should be handcrafted (see "Profit and Loss" in the Ivy Case System chapter page 37).

To get the most out of this chapter, read the case out loud, pretending it is a real interview. Make an audio recording of yourself as you work through the first few steps, summarize the case, verify the objectives and **ask key questions**. Write or draw out your notes as you would in a real interview and then compare your notes to those found on the following pages. It's okay if they don't match up. Remember, there are no right answers; the interviewer is looking to see how you think, how you structure your thoughts and how you communicate. Play the case start back and listen to the speed, tone and confidence level of your voice. At first you're not going to be happy, probably downright embarrassed, but the more you practice the stronger you become.

+ Case Starts

Cases

CS1: Power plants, chemical, paper and textile factories have polluted about 70 percent of China's lakes and rivers. Water quality is a major concern for Chinese consumers. They are turning toward bottled water as a safer alternative. The cities continue to grow, as does the bottled water market. Nestlé wants to know how best to grow its market share.

CS2: Hacker Guard is the industry leader in the US identity-theft monitoring market. It wants to do an IPO but has seen inconsistent profits and losses six out of the last ten quarters. How can it stabilize the turmoil and increase its profits? (The interviewer hands you a chart.)

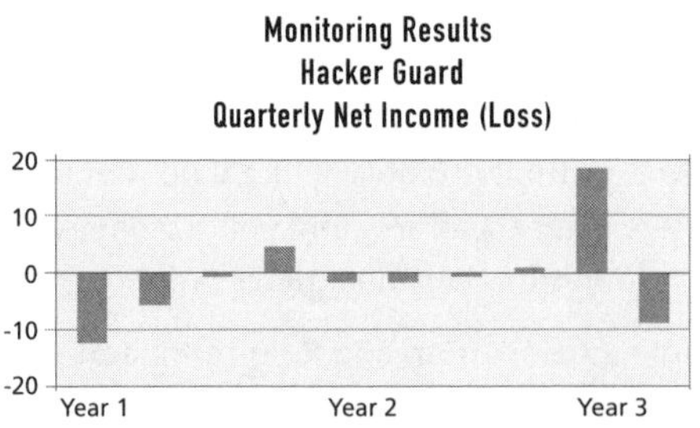

Source: the company

CS3: A Hong Kong company is acquiring a US video game maker. What considerations should be made?

CS4: Flintstone, Potter and Coke is a midsized ad agency. It was established as a regional player but soon picked up some national accounts, including FedEx, Kellogg's and Johnny Walker Scotch. However, last year it lost two of its national accounts and hasn't been able to replace them. The CEO wants to buy a running shoe company that was big during the 1950s – 1980s until it was pushed out of the spotlight by Nike and Reebok. Is this a good idea? At first blush, what are the pros and cons of this idea? (I want you to list the pros and cons before you draw your structure.)

CS5: The CEO of a large Italian electronics firm has come out with a new computer tablet, which is much like the iPad. How should it price its product?

CS6: A major foods company acquired a diet-drink company (similar to Slim-Fast) for $2.2 billion four years ago and had ambitions to increase the diet-drink revenues five-fold in three years. That didn't happen. In fact over the last three years its revenues have fallen 40 percent in the US, to $196 million, and profits have fallen 33 percent. What's going on and how can we turn this around?

CS7: Our client is a global automaker headquartered in Detroit. Its motor parts division, with 20 percent industry market share, carries almost 500,000 parts, options and accessories for vehicle customization. The client has not been profitable for several years and the CEO suspects that the company's high degree of vertical integration is hurting them. The client makes about 80 percent of its own parts, compared to 40 percent at its primary competitors. The CEO has asked for our help. How would you approach this issue?

CS8: You have been brought in as the CEO of Hootie, Inc. The company started making surfboards in the 1960s. Hootie was the market leader, with a 75 percent market share, well into the 1980s. However, competition increased as the sport became more popular, and Hootie missed the trend toward smaller boards. Last year, Hootie had a 10 percent market share. How can we grow the company, regain market share and return the brand to its former glory?

CS9: Palm Tree Plantation Exports grows, sells and leases twenty different varieties of palm trees and other tropical plants throughout the United States. It posted a net income of $95 million, down from $105 million last year. Yet its market share grew by 7 percent. What's going on and how can we turn it around?

CS10: A large Japanese electronics company wants to enter the high-end headphones market. Is this a good idea?

CS1: China Water

Power plants, chemical, paper and textile factories have polluted about 70 percent of China's lakes and rivers. Water quality is a major concern for Chinese consumers. They are turning toward bottled water as a safer alternative. The cities continue to grow, as does the bottled water market. Nestlé wants to know how to grow its market share.

Summarize the case. China's drinking water, particularly in the cities, is horrible. The bottled water market is growing and Nestlé wants to increase its market share. Are there any other objectives I should be concerned with?

Assume no.

Lay out your structure. First, you should ask about Nestlé and its position in the Chinese bottled water market; current market share; growth rate and WCS (what constitutes success in the mind of the client?) What percentage of the market is the company hoping to get and is that realistic? How many brands does it sell under? What is its pricing strategy? How is it priced compared to the market leaders?

Second, investigate the Chinese water market: growth rate, major players and their market share, changes in the industry (mergers? new players? new technology?) and barriers to expansion. Are there restrictions on foreign companies holding more than a certain percentage of market share? Are the home delivery and retail markets growing faster than the office delivery market?

Third, I'd like to investigate several key growth strategies that will serve as a foundation; increase distribution channels (other-people stores, Nestlé stores, home delivery and street carts); increase and diversify product line (more brands, more types of water i.e. vitamin water, flavored water); invest in a major marketing campaign; acquire competitors and create seasonal balance (vitamin C water in winter).

And fourth, I'd like to know about Nestlé's market share in other key water markets, such as North America and Europe. How are those markets growing and would it be wiser to allocate more resources there or in China?

Your notes should look something like this...

CHINESE DRINKING WATER
IS POLLUTED

BOTTLED WATER MKT ↑

NESTLE WANTS TO ↑
MKT SHARE

GROW MKT SHARE

<u>NESTLE</u>
CURRENT MKT SHARE
GROWTH RATE
WCS
BRANDS
PRICING STRATEGY

<u>GROWTH STRATEGIES</u>
↑ DISTRIBUTION CHANNELS
OTHER STORES
NESTLE STORES
HOME DELIVERY
STREET CARTS
OFFICE DELIVERY
↑ PRODUCT LINE
↑ BRANDS, TYPES OF WATER
↑ MKTG CAMPAIGN
ACQUIRE COMPETITOR
CREATE SEASONAL BALANCE
↑ PRICES?

<u>CHINESE H_2O MKT</u>
SIZE
GROWTH RATE
MAJOR PLAYERS / MKT SHARE
Λ'S IN INDUSTRY
(MERGERS, NEW PLAYERS,
NEW TECH?)
BARRIERS – GOV'T REG
MARKETS
HOME, OFFICE, RETAIL

<u>ALTERNATIVE MKTS:</u>
N AMERICA, S AMERICA,
EUROPE, ASIA

FYI. China's bottled water industry will climb to $16 billion by 2017, up from $9 billion in 2012 and $1 billion in 2000. North America will increase 18 percent by 2017, to $26 billion, and Europe will remain flat. Nestlé's current Chinese market share is 1.7 percent. Its Chinese water revenues climbed 27 percent last year. The market leader is Hangzhou Wahaha Group, with 14 percent market share.

CS2: Hacker Guard

Hacker Guard is the industry leader in the US identity-theft monitoring market. It wants to do an IPO but has seen inconsistent profits and losses six out of the last ten quarters. How can it stabilize the turmoil and increase its profits? (The interviewer hands you a chart.)

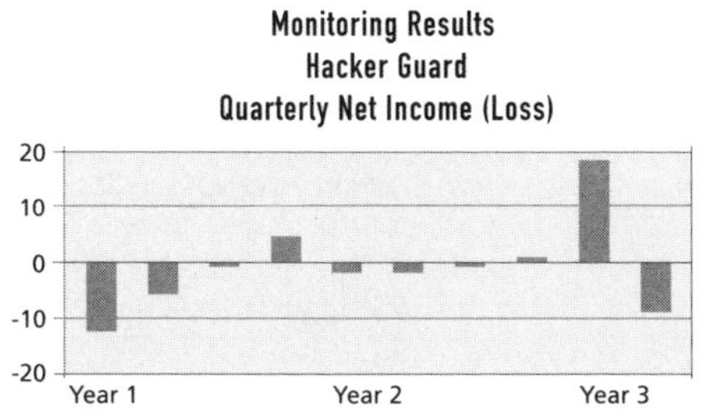

Source: the company

Summarize the case. Hacker Guard wants to do an IPO but needs to stabilize its P&L statement. We need to figure out why this is happening and come up with ways to increase profits. Besides identifying the problems and increasing profits, are there any other issues I should be concerned with?

Assume no.

First, take a minute to study the chart. What does it tell you? There doesn't seem to be any pattern to the swings and some of them are sizable. What would cause Hacker Guard to lose $12 million one quarter and make $18 million in another quarter?

Lay out your structure. Because this is a P&L problem, immediately lay out the P&L framework and then build on it. E(P=R-C)M is the initial framework. To start, look at external factors. Is this just Hacker Guard's problem or are all companies in this space having a similar problem? Touch on a few things in the domestic economy: the unemployment rate, interest rates, the mortgage crisis, and anything else that might affect the disposable income of a US household.

Next, look at the identity-theft industry. What market share does the company have? What are the industry revenues and what have the trends been in the last three to five years? Are other firms' P&Ls all over the place or just Hacker Guard's? Were there profit spikes at the same time with all firms, meaning something happened in the market, such as a large corporate breech like those at Sony or TJ Maxx?

Once you have an understanding of the industry, look inside the company. Start with the revenue streams. What are the major revenue streams and how have they changed over time? Customer segmentation: Who are its clients? Middle-class households? How many clients does it have and how much do they pay a month or a year? How long do customers stay? Is there a contract like that for a cell phone? What is its churn rate? How does that compare to churn rates for others in the industry and for other industries like cell phones?

Next up are its costs. What are its major costs and have they changed over time? Can we benchmark them to the competitors? Were there any large purchases like an acquisition or major upgrades to the company's computer system?

Your notes might look like this...

HACKER GUARD
MKT LEADER IN ID THEFT

TRYING TO DO AN IPO, BUT
INCONSISTENT P&L

WHY & FIX / STABILIZE
REVENUES

WHY & FIX / STABILIZE REVENUES

E(P=R–C)M

HIGH UNEMPLOYMENT	INDUSTRY REV TRENDS (3 YRS)
MORTGAGE CRISIS	COMPETITORS, SAME ISSUE?
LESS DISPOSABLE INCOME	SAME PROFIT SPIKES
	SAME LARGE LOSSES
REVENUES	COSTS
ANY Λ IN REVENUES?	ANY Λ IN COSTS?
CUSTOMER SEGMENTATION	ANY COST SEEM OUT OF LINE?
NO. OF CUSTOMERS	BENCHMARK COSTS
AVG REV PER CUSTOMER	PURCHASES
CONTRACT LENGTH	ACQUISITIONS?
CHURN RATE	IT UPGRADES?

FYI: The real company that this case is based on went public in October at $9. Five months into its trading life, the high has been $11.39 and the low, $6.80.

CS3: Hong Kong Video Games

A Hong Kong company is acquiring a US video game maker. What considerations should be made?

Summarize the case and verify the objective. This is a pretty short case, so instead of repeating the question, just state, "Besides determining the key factors to this acquisition, are there any other objectives I should be concerned with?"

Assume no other objectives.

Lay out your structure. This is a merger and acquisition case. Break it into five main buckets: company; current market analysis; due diligence and risks; costs; and exit strategies.

Your notes might look something like this...

HONG KONG COMPANY

IS BUYING US VIDEO GAME MAKER

WHAT ARE THE KEY ISSUES?

KEY ACQUISITION ISSUES

<u>HONG KONG COMPANY</u>

WHO ARE THEY?
- PE FIRM?
- COMPETITOR?

WHY BUY?
- STRATEGIES
- PATENTED TECH
- ↑ MKT SHARE
- COST SAVINGS SYNERGIES

WHAT ELSE DOES IT OWN?

COSTS
FAIR VALUATION?
CAN THEY AFFORD IT?

CURRENT MKT
SIZE & GROWTH RATE
PLAYERS AND MARKET SHARE
PROD DIFFERENTIATION
CUSTOMER SEGMENTATION
Λ IN INDUSTRY – MERGERS, EXITS, NEW PLAYERS

DUE DILIGENCE & RISKS
- ECONOMY
- MARKET LEADER?
- SECURE
  - CUSTOMERS, SUPPLIERS, DISTRIBUTORS AND TOP MANAGERS
- CULTURAL MIX
- MARGINS
- COMPETITIVE RESPONSE

EXIT STRATEGIES
- SELL
- SPIN OFF AND TAKE PUBLIC
- CLOSE DOWN AND SELL ASSETS

Company. I'd first ask about the Hong Kong Company. Who are they? Is it a private equity firm or a competitor? Why does it want to buy this company? Is it for access to the US market? A special patented technology? To increase its market share? Or to take advantage of cost-saving synergies? What else does it own? Does it own other gaming companies?

Industry. What's the current industry like? Is it growing and what are the trends and forecasts? Who are the major players and what market share do they have? How are their products different than those of the targeted company? What is the industry segmentation and have there been any changes taking place in the industry? Mergers? New players?

Due diligence. I'd want to look at the overall economy. Is the targeted company an industry leader? How secure are its customers, suppliers, distributors and top management? Will the cultures of the two companies mesh well? Are the margins what we anticipated? What will be the competitive response to our buying this video game maker?

Exit strategies. What's the game plan if this fails? Do we sell, spin-off the company and do an IPO, or do we break it up and sell off the pieces?

CS4: Flintstone, Potter and Coke

Flintstone, Potter and Coke is a midsized ad agency. It was established as a regional player but soon picked up some national accounts, including FedEx, Kellogg's and Johnny Walker Scotch. However, last year it lost two of its national accounts and hasn't been able to replace them. The CEO wants to buy a running shoe company that was big during the 1950s – 1980s until it was pushed out of the spotlight by Nike and Reebok. Is this a good idea? At first blush, what are the pros and cons of this idea? (I want you to list the pros and cons before you draw your structure.)

Summarize the case and verify the objective. Summarize the question and verify the objective, to determine if this is a good idea. The interviewer also asked for a pros and cons list.

In a question like this, the interviewer would probably want you to list the pros and cons first, before getting into a deeper discussion. He will usually tell you if he wants the list first.

Pros and cons list. The first thing you want to do is to draw a line down the middle of your paper and label one side "pros" and the other "cons." Then ask for a minute to jot down your thoughts. (You do this for several reasons.) Write them down however they pop into your head, but you'll want to present the pros first and then the cons. Also, if you try to do this off the top of your head, there is a good chance that the interviewer will cut you off in mid-sentence because he knows where you are headed. It is very difficult to come up with another answer when you are cut off in the middle of your original thought. By writing them down first, it will save you a lot of stress and make you look more professional.

PROS	CONS
Diversifies portfolio	They know nothing of operations
National showcase	Draws resources away
Could bring in new retail clients	Expensive
Possible cost synergies	What if they fail
Shows innovative thinking	Company cultures are different
Possible tax advantages	May compete against existing client
Turn it into a reality TV show	

Ask questions. Once the pros and cons are out of the way, you have the opportunity to ask some questions. The big questions are: Why do they want to do this? Can the company afford it? Does it have any experience running a shoe company? What have been the trends in the running shoe industry? Who are the major players and how do their products differ from ours? Is there a better way to enter this market?

CS5: Italian Computer Tablet

The CEO of a large Italian electronics firm has come out with a new computer tablet, which is much like the iPad. How should it price its product?

Summarize the case and verify the objective. Ask if there are any other objectives — such as why the CEO wants to enter this market.

Lay out your structure. Your notes might look something like this...

ITALIAN ELECTRONICS CO
MAKING A TABLET

HOW DOES IT PRICE IT?

DETERMINE PRICE

ITALIAN ELECTRONICS CO
WHY ENTER?
SIZE IN REVENUE & TRENDS
BRAND
PRODUCTS
PRODUCTION
DISTRIBUTE
CUSTOMERS
WCS

INDUSTRY
CURRENT MKT SIZE AND GROWTH RATE
ΛS IN INDUSTRY
NEW PLAYERS, NEW TECHNOLOGY

COMP OBJECTIVE → PROFITS? / MARKET SHARE? / POSITIONING?
COMPETITIVE
ANALYSIS
COST-BASED PRICING
PRICE-BASED COSTING

First, I'd like to know about the company. Why did it want to enter this market? How big is the company revenue-wise and what have the trends been? Does it have a well-known brand? What other products does it have? Where is the production of the product taking place? Does it have established distribution channels? Does this fit in with its current customer segment. And what constitutes success in the mind of the client?

Second, I'd look at the industry: current size, trends and forecasts. Are there any significant changes in the industry, like new players or new technology? Remember how HP came out with a tablet, pulled it three weeks later and came out with another one a year later.

Third, I'd look at four pricing strategies. The first one is **company objective**. This ties in with "what constitutes success" in the mind of the client? Is it looking for profits and wanting to price the tablet at a premium (like Apple)? Is it looking for market share (like Samsung) and thus pricing it a little lower; or is it interested in market positioning (like Amazon), selling at around cost and hoping to make profits on the ancillary products? The second is **competitive analysis**. Who is our competition, how do their tablets differ from ours and how much to they charge? Are there any substitutions? How will the competitors respond to our entering their market? Third is **cost-based pricing**. What does it cost our client to manufacture, distribute and market? Make sure all those costs are baked-in to your number. What sort of margin does the company make on its other products? The fourth is price-based costing. What is the market willing to pay? Is it more than our costs?

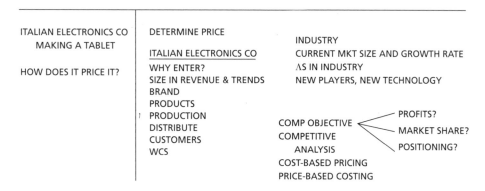

CS6: Diet-drink Loss

A major foods company acquired a diet-drink company (similar to Slim-Fast) for $2.2 billion four years ago and had ambitions to increase the diet-drink revenues five-fold in three years. That didn't happen. In fact over the last three years its revenues have fallen 40 percent in the US to $196 million and profits have fallen 33 percent. What's going on, and how can we turn this around?

Summarize the case. A major foods company purchased a diet-drink company for $2.2 billion four years ago. Its goal was to raise revenues five-fold within three years. Instead, revenues dropped 40 percent to $196 million and profits fell 33 percent. Besides identifying the problems and turning the company around, are there any other objectives I should be concerned with.

Assume no.

Lay out your structure. First, learn about the company. How has the company been doing overall? What percentage of revenues did this product make up three years ago and what percentage does it make up today? What is the company's current market share? Is it giving this product support or letting it die on the vine? How have complementary products been doing? Are they all branded under the same name? What is their customer segmentation? What would constitute success in the mind of the client?

Second, I'd like to know about the diet industry. Is it growing and by how much? What are the trends for the last three years and are there any forecasts? Has there been a sea change in the way people are dieting? Are they moving away from a diet in a can? If we are losing market share, who's taking it? Who are the major players and how do their products differ from ours? Have there been new players to this market?

Your notes might look like this...

MAJOR FOOD COMPANY
ACQUIRED DIET-DRINK
COMPANY FOR $2.28

EXPECTED REV. ↑ FIVE-FOLD
INSTEAD REV. ↓ 40%
TO $196M

PROFITS ↓ 33%

FIX & ↑ REVENUES

FIX & ↑ REVENUES

FOOD COMPANY

OVERALL CO. TRENDS
% OF REV/DIET DRINK
MKT SHARE TRENDS
CO. SUPPORT FOR PRODUCT
ANCILLARY PRODUCT TRENDS
ARE THEY BRANDED THE SAME?
WCS (WHAT CONSTITUTES SUCCESS?)
PRICING STRATEGY

DIET INDUSTRY

GROWTH TRENDS?
SEA-CHANGE?
PLAYERS & MKT SHARE
PROD. DIFFERENTIATION
NEW PLAYERS

GROWTH STRATEGIES

ANALYZE BRAND – REBRAND?
↑ DIVERSIFY & INCREASE PROD. LINE
↑ BRANDS – SEASONAL BALANCE
↑ MKTG CAMPAIGN
(ONLINE, APP, INFOMERCIAL, CELEBRITY)
ACQUIRE COMPETITOR
CREATE SEASONAL BALANCE
↓ PRICES?
↑ DISTRIBUTION CHANNELS

Third, investigate several key growth strategies that will serve as a foundation: Take stock of the brand (does this product need to be rebranded?), increase and diversify product line (taking seasonal balance into consideration), invest in a major marketing campaign (online, smartphone app, infomercials, celebrity spokesperson), increase distribution channels and acquire competitors and build on that brand.

CS7: Global Motor Cars

Our client is a global automaker headquartered in Detroit. Its motor parts division, with 20 percent industry market share, carries almost 500,000 parts, options and accessories for vehicle customization. The client has not been profitable for several years and the CEO suspects that the company's high degree of vertical integration is hurting it. The client makes about 80 percent of its own parts, compared to 40 percent at its primary competitors. The CEO has asked for our help. How would you approach this issue?

Summarize the case and verify the objective. Repeat the question to make sure that you and the interviewer are on the same page. Then verify the objectives. In this case the objectives are to come up with a strategic plan to make the company profitable. While you might think that this is a P&L case, I'd approach it a little differently.

Lay out your structure. Your notes might look something like this...

AUTO MAKER

PARTS DIVISION W / 20%
MKT SHARE
500,000 PARTS

NOT PROFITABLE
HIGH VERTICAL
INTEGRATION

MAKES 80% OF OWN
PARTS COMPARED TO
40% AT ITS COMPETITORS

COME UP WITH A
STRATEGIC PLAN TO
MOVE FORWARD

STRATEGIC PLAN TO MOVE FORWARD

AUTO MAKER REVENUES
PARTS DIV. REVENUES & TRENDS
PARTS DIV. PROFITS & TRENDS
PARTS DIV. MKT SHARE TRENDS
Δ IN COSTS
WCS

AUTO INDUSTRY
CURRENT MKT
SIZE
GROWTH RATE
Δ'S IN INDUSTRY,
NEW TECHNOLOGY

STRATEGY

COSTS
- INTERNAL (UNION WAGES, RAW MATERIALS)
- EXTERNAL (INTEREST RATES, FUEL, TRANS, ECONOMY)

STRATEGIC VALUE
- CHEAPER
- PATENTED TECHNOLOGY

ALTERNATIVES
- REDUCE # OF PARTS
- REDESIGN CARS TO USE SAME PARTS

EXIT STRATEGY
- SELL TO PE OR MANAGEMENT
- SPIN-OFF AND TAKE PUBLIC

Ask questions about the company and the parts division. What are the overall company revenues and what have the trends been? What are the parts division revenues, their trends and what percentage of the overall company revenues do they account for? What have been the trends? Has the parts division been gaining or losing market share over the last three years? Have there been changes in costs? What constitutes success in the mind of the client?

Ask questions about the industry. What have been the overall trends for the auto industry? Have there been any changes in the parts industry, new players or new technology?

Strategies. I'd break this down into three buckets: costs, strategic value and exit strategy.

Costs. I'd look at both external costs (the overall economy, interest rates, fuel costs, transportations costs, etc) and internal costs (union wages, raw materials, etc).

Strategic value. What is the true strategic value of making our own parts? It might have been cost-saving initially, but that might have changed. Is there a patented technology that only our cars have?

Alternatives. This could mean reducing the number of individual parts per car, or having new models using as many common parts as possible. This is tricky; some believe this is what got GM in trouble because all its cars seemed the same. Would it be cheaper to buy our parts from another vendor?

Exit strategy. Does the company sell its parts division to a private equity firm, to management? Does it spin the parts division off from the automaker and make it its own company? What would the company get for it and what would it do with the money?

CS8: Hootie Surfboards

You have been brought in as the CEO of Hootie, Inc. The company started making surfboards in the 1960s. Hootie was the market leader, with a 75 percent market share well into the 1980s. However, competition increased as the sport became more popular, and Hootie missed the trend toward smaller boards. Last year, Hootie had a 10 percent market share. How can we grow the company, regain market share and return the brand to its former glory?

Summarize the case and verify the objective. Repeat the question to make sure everyone is on the same page and then verify the objectives. In this case the objectives are to grow the company, regain market share and rebuild the brand in the eyes of consumers. There are no other objectives.

Lay out your structure. Break it down by company, industry and growth strategies.

Ask company questions. What is Hootie's image in the eyes of the consumer and the industry? What are its revenues and what are the trends for the last three years? What products does it sell? And what is the revenue percentage breakdown by product? Are its prices in line with the rest of the industry's? What kind of distribution channels does it have and has it been shrinking? What is the breakdown of sales by distribution channel, company owned stores, other retailers and online sales? What is its customer segmentation and has that changed? What constitutes success; what market share percentage does it expect? Can the company afford to fund the changes needed?

Your notes might look like this...

HOOTIE SURFBOARDS
FOUNDED IN 1960

HAD 75% MKT SHARE
↓ TO 10% MKT SHARE

STRONG COMPETITION

MISSED TREND TOWARD
SMALLER BOARDS

OBJECTIVES: GROW THE COMPANY, REGAIN MKT SHARE AND RESTORE BRAND

GROW REV. & MKT SHARE
RESTORE BRAND

<u>HOOTIE SURFBOARDS</u>
CURRENT IMAGE / BRAND
SIZE IN REVENUES & TRENDS
PRODUCTS
PRICES
DISTRIBUTION
CUSTOMERS
WCS
$$ FOR FUNDING Λ

CURRENT MKT
- SIZE & GROWTH RATE
- PLAYERS AND MKT SHARE
- PROD DIFFERENTIATION
- CUSTOMER SEGMENTATION
- Λ IN INDUSTRY — MERGERS, EXITS, NEW PLAYERS

GROWTH STRATEGIES
PRODUCTS
- RE-EVALUATE PROD MIX & PRICING
- DESIGN NEW PRODUCTS

DISTRIBUTION CHANNELS
- ↑ OWN STORIES
- ↑ OTHER RETAILERS
- HOOTIE'S ONLINE

BUILD BRAND
- NEW PRODUCTS, MKTING CAMPAIGN
- ENDORSEMENTS, SPONSORSHIPS

ACQUISITION OF SMALLER PLAYER
- KEEP THEIR NAME, BUT USE OUR CHANNELS

Ask industry questions. What have the industry growth trends been over the last three years? Who are the major players, what market share do they have and how do their products differ from Hootie's? Have there been any changes in the industry; mergers, new entrants, or exits?

Growth strategies: I'd break this down into four buckets: products, distribution channels, brand and acquisitions.

Products: Re-evaluate current product mix and pricing structure. Design new products.

Distribution channels: Increase through a combination of company-owned stores, Hootie's online store and other retailers, both domestically and internationally.

Build brand: Consider new products, marketing campaign, endorsements and sponsorships.

Acquisition: Look to see if there are some up–and-coming companies to acquire, keep their brand but use our distributions channels.

CS9: Palm Tree Plantation Exports Notes

Palm Tree Plantation Exports grows, sells and leases twenty different varieties of palm trees and other tropical plants throughout the United States. It posted a net income of $95 million, down from $105 million last year. Yet its market share grew by 7 percent. What's going on and how can we turn it around?

Summarize the case. Whenever you get a question with numbers and the numbers are related, as in this case (net income fell from $105 million to $95 million), you should quantify the numbers. So instead of saying that net income fell from $105 million to $95 million, or that it fell $10 million, you should say the net income fell about 10 percent.

Verify the objective. Determine what's going on and how you can turn it around. There are no other objectives we need to be concerned with.

Lay out your structure. Because this is a P&L case, you should use E(P=R-C)M. Look at external factors first because we want to find out if this is a company problem or an industry problem. Economic factors in this case should include unemployment, the mortgage crisis, housing starts, state and city budgets, interest rates and water and gas prices. All those things are important not only to the company, but to the industry as a whole.

Ask industry questions. Interviewers have a lot of information they want to give you, but you need to ask for it. Did you ask about industry growth trends? Competition? Changing landscape? Environmental factors like drought and disease? Who are the main customers and what is their industry like (states' and cities' budgets are down, housing starts are down and shopping mall and office building development is also down)?

Ask company questions. Once you have a feel for the industry, go inside the parentheses to get a feel for the company. Always start with the revenues. Ask what are the major revenue streams and how have they changed over time? What are the major costs, both fixed and variable and how have they changed over time?

PALM TREE
PLANTATION EXPORTS

SELLS & LEASES PALM TREES
NET INCOME FROM $105
TO $95M
MKT SHARE 7%

WHY & FIX

FIX & ↑ NET INCOME

E(P=R–C)M

HIGH UNEMPLOYMENT MORTGAGE CRISIS LESS DISPOSABLE INCOME CITY & STATE BUDGETS ↓ ↑ WATER & GAS PRICES	INDUSTRY REV TRENDS (3 YRS) COMPETITORS, SAME ISSUES? Δ IN INDUSTRY MERGERS OR EXITS? ENVIRONMENTAL ISSUES DRAUGHT OR DISEASE?
REVENUE STREAMS ANY Δ IN REVENUES? CUSTOMER SEGMENTATION NO. OF CUSTOMERS	COSTS ANY Δ IN COSTS? ANY COST SEEM OUT OF LINE?

CS10: Japanese High-end Headphones

A large Japanese electronics company wants to enter the high-end headphones market. Is this a good idea?

Summarize the case and verify the objective. Ask, besides entering the high-end headphone market, are there any other objectives you should be concerned with?

Your notes should look something like this...

JAPANESE ELECTRONICS

ENTER HIGH-END
HEADPHONES
MARKET

MKT ENTRY Y OR N?

ENTER MKT Y OR N

JAPANESE ELECTRONICS
WHY ENTER?
PRODUCTS
PRODUCTION
BRAND
DISTRIBUTION
CUSTOMERS
WCS

CURRENT MKT
SIZE
GROWTH RATE
CUSTOMERS

MAJOR PLAYERS / MARKET SHARE
PRODUCT DIFFERENTIATION
BARRIERS

ENTERING
YES
START FROM SCRATCH
ACQUISITION
JT VENTURE
NO, ALTERNATIVE PLAN

Start with the company: Why does it want to enter? How big is the company? What are the revenues and trends? What other products does it manufacture? Does it sell other headphones; will this product cannibalize sales from existing products? Does it have the manufacturing capacity to make the headphones or will it outsource production? Does it have a well-known brand to consumers? How will the headphones be distributed? Has the company served this customer segment before? And what constitutes success for the client; how much market share does it expect to get the first year?

Analyze the new market: What is the current size and growth rate? What is the customer segmentation for this market? Who are the major players, what market share do they have and how do their products differ from ours? And are there any market barriers to entry or exit?

Determine how best to enter the market: There are three ways to enter the market. The company can produce this product on its own and grow it organically. It can buy its way in through an acquisition of an existing player. Or it can do a joint venture or strategic alliance with another company. Look at the advantages and disadvantages of all three.

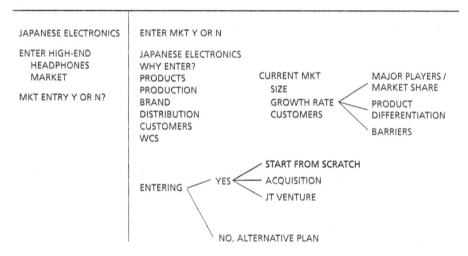

+ Case Practice

While nothing beats live practice, the next best thing is reading as many cases as possible. This builds up an archive in the back of your mind and allows you to draw from one case to help you answer another. The best way to utilize this section is to read the case, then write out your structure. Your answer and my answer will probably not match up. There is no way for you to predict the added variables and twists and turns in the case. So once you draw your structure, sit back and read the cases, making notes in your journal of anything you might not have thought about. Then reread it. You'll pick up more the second time through.

+ Case Index

✣ Mexican Bank

Case 1: Our client is a major commercial bank in Mexico. Despite the fact that the bank has experienced increased revenue growth, for the past two years its profits have declined and even become negative. You have a meeting with the CEO of the bank in a week and you have to come up with answers to two questions: What is the main cause of this decline in profits, and what can we do to restore the bank's profitability?

Besides finding out why our client is experiencing declining profits and determining a strategy to get itself out of trouble, are there any other objectives I should be concerned about?

– No.

I would like to approach this case in two parts. First, I will try to diagnose the cause of the decline in profits, despite the growth in revenues. Then, based on the findings in the first part, I will try to come up with solutions to our problems and put the bank on a path to profitability.

Let's start with the first issue: the diagnosis of the problem. Here, I would like to look at three main aspects: the overall banking industry in Mexico, our bank's revenues and, finally, the costs.

– Sounds like a good plan. What would you like to know?

The student writes down E(P=R–C)M? (see page 38).

First, I would like to look at the banking industry in Mexico. Is this an industrywide problem or does it primarily affect our client? Also, can you tell me more about our client's competitive positioning within this industry?

– It's actually just our client that's experiencing the severe decline in profits. While the other banks have also experienced declines, they have been more moderate. Our client is a major player in the industry, owning 20 percent of the market share. There are three other major national competitors with similar market shares and many smaller, regional competitors. Anything else?

It looks like it is mainly an internal problem rather than an industrywide problem. Before analyzing the bank's costs, both fixed and variable, I'd first like to look at the bank's revenues in more detail. I'm assuming that banks make their money from interest income and from fees. Also, on the cost side, I would like to analyze both the fixed costs and the variable costs.

– That's right. The bank makes money in two main ways: interest income and fee income. Our client has about 70 percent of its revenues coming from interest and the remaining 30 percent coming from fees. However, I would like you to look at the following graph and analyze it for me. Our client currently has 8 million customers.

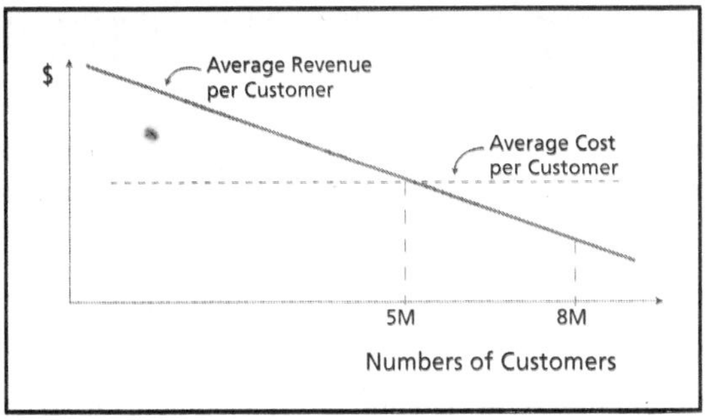

That's a very interesting graph. If our client has 8 million customers, the average cost per customer is higher than the average revenue per customer, thus resulting in a loss. Let's take them one by one.

Our client is experiencing declining average revenues per customer. There are several hypotheses why this might be happening. As the bank was growing, it was acquiring new customers that are not as profitable as the initial customers. For example, instead of signing up more doctors, lawyers or consultants, it is now signing up students or blue collar workers that don't produce as much revenue, thus resulting in the observed decline in average revenues per customer.

On the cost side, the average cost per customer is staying constant, instead of declining. We can see that there are little or no economies of scale. Potential reasons behind this would imply that as the bank was adding new customers, the costs were also increasing proportionally.

– That's great — and accurate. Due to the incentive structure, which rewarded new customer acquisition, branch managers have added customers that were not as profitable as the initial ones. In addition, the bank has aggressively expanded its branch structure and has increased the number of tellers to accommodate the increased number of customers. What should the bank do?

Well, now that we have diagnosed the main reason for the decline in profits as a combination of newer, less profitable customers and the proportional increase in costs, we can propose a solution. A simple but not ideal solution would be to eliminate the additional, less profitable customers while simultaneously reducing the number of branches and tellers to bring us to the initial profitability.

A second, better solution would include two concurrent approaches. First, we should try to increase average revenues per customer, and second, we should decrease average costs per customer. In increasing the revenues, we would come up with new products that would result in increased interest income. We can also increase the fees we charge our customers. In decreasing costs, we could attempt to close off our least profitable branches and reduce our teller personnel.

My proposed solution, however, will produce even better results. I propose segmenting our current customers into several customer tiers and adjusting the service level, and implicitly, the costs according to the customer tier. For example, high net worth individuals would have unrestricted access to personal bankers and new services would be tailored to their specific needs.

At the other end of the spectrum, our client should educate the students about the benefits of using cheaper delivery systems like ATMs or online services. They would still have access to the tellers; however, we would limit their free access to two free teller visits per month. After those visits, we could start charging 30 pesos per visit or around $3US. In effect, we would adjust our service delivery model based on the customer's value to the bank. This would achieve both our goals; of increasing revenues, by better addressing the needs of each customer segment, and reducing costs by redirecting the lower value customers to the cheaper servicing channels.

– Okay, good.

- **Type of case: Profit and loss, marketing, customer segmentation**
- **Comments: What started out as a profit and loss case quickly changed into a marketing / customer segmentation case. The student did a good job analyzing the chart and came up with a number of good possible solutions for the client.**

✛ Yellow Stuff Chemical Company

Case 2: Our client is a manufacturer that makes industrial cleaning solvents and pesticides. Recently, sales have been declining, mostly due to new EPA guidelines. The company has been "dumping" its old products overseas into countries that have less stringent environmental laws as well as re-engineering its products to fit the new EPA guidelines. Further evaluation of sales, both past and future, indicates that the chemical industry has, and will, continue to grow slowly over the next five to seven years, with 3 percent annual growth.

Management has decided to diversify. While Yellow Stuff wants to keep its chemical business intact, it also wants to enter an industry that has long-term, high-growth potential. Yellow Stuff has hired us to help determine what industry or industries it should enter.

While I don't want you to come up with a list of industries, I do want you to tell me what sort of things you should be researching to determine what industry our client should diversify into.

So, as I understand it, our client is a chemical manufacturer who wants to diversify outside the chemical industry into a high-growth industry.

– That's right.

And you want me to come up with a strategy on how to find the best possible match.

– Yes.

Besides diversification and profit, are there any other objectives that I should know about?

– No.

What does the company define as high growth?

– 10 percent a year.

Well, the first thing I'd do is obtain a list of all the industries and eliminate the ones that are growing less than 15 percent or have a potential in the next year of growing less than 15 percent. How much risk is Yellow Stuff willing to take?

– Medium.

Then, I'd also eliminate any high-risk or volatile industries. Next, I'd study the list to see if there are any synergies that we can share.

– Such as?

One example might be to look to see if there is a sister industry where our customer list is the same. If we sell cleaning solvents to Pepsi and then we get into manufacturing aluminum, maybe we can sell Pepsi soda cans. We also have a history of marketing and selling business-to-business, so we might want to stay away from consumer products. We could look at other commonalities, such as distribution channels and sales force.

Once we narrow the list, we need to analyze the market to find out who the major players are and what, if any, the barriers to entering the market are.

– Okay, what else?

There are three ways to enter a new market: Start from scratch, acquire an existing player or do a joint venture. Depending on the industry and the barriers...

– What sort of barriers are you talking about?

Could be government regulations. If you try to start a business and your products have to get approved by the FDA or the EPA, then that could take years. In a case like that, you might want to acquire an existing player. A barrier might be a stranglehold on the market — if, for example, two companies hold an extraordinarily large market share and have a habit of destroying new entries. If raw materials or supplies proved hard to come by, that would be another barrier.

– Okay.

Did I mention substitutions as a barrier?

– What's next?

I'd look very carefully at the future of the industry. It currently may be growing over 10 percent, but is that going to last; and for how long? Is the market growing or shrinking? Is the number of players growing or shrinking? Have there been many mergers or acquisitions lately? And I'd take some time to think about exit strategies as well.

– Summarize for me.

I'd identify all the relevant industries, analyze their markets and determine the best way to enter that market. I'd also conduct an analysis to see if the company might not be better off just investing the money into the stock market. It may make a better return and its investment would be a lot more liquid.

- **Type of case: Entering a new market**

- **Comments: Ninety percent of this question is irrelevant fluff. It's not about the chemical industry, it's about entering a new market. The candidate took the time to ask for the company's definition of high growth. From there, it was straight logic. Now, some of you might argue that this was really a growth-strategies question, but the question tells us that the client really wants to diversify, which narrows the growth strategies to one: diversification. The question then becomes one of identifying the new industry.**

+ Eastern Training Network

Case 3: Our client is a midsize training company that serves New England and the Atlantic Seaboard regions. It offers a variety of computer training and consulting services. Eastern just found out that IBM is going to enter its segment of the market. What does it do?

Eastern Training Network just found out that IBM is entering its segment of the market and wants to know what to do. I'm assuming that the objectives are either to keep IBM out of our market or to maintain as much market share as we can. Is that a fair set of assumptions?

– Yes.

Are there any other objectives that I should be aware of?

– No.

Are there other firms in our area that we currently compete with?

– Yes. Including us, there are three major players that do what we do and maybe three smaller firms that serve one or two clients exclusively.

Do we know what Eastern's market share is?

– Eastern's market share within the region is 24 percent.

Do we know what our two other competitors are doing to keep IBM out?

– No. Good question, but not relevant.

Since one of my major objectives is to maintain market share, I'd break my strategy down into three prongs. First, I'd try to keep IBM out. Second, I'd try to protect what's mine. And third, I'd go after new customers.

– Explain.

I would try to figure out what I could do to raise the barriers of entry and keep IBM out. Since IBM has almost unlimited resources and because this is an unregulated industry, I think the chances of that are pretty nil.

Second, I'd try to protect what's mine. It is much cheaper to keep your current customers than it is to go out and get new ones. So I'd do three things. I'd raise switching costs, make it so that it wouldn't make sense to leave us for IBM.

– Give me an example.

Since I don't know the industry that well, I'd like to give another example. AOL makes it hard for customers to leave because they have what are called "sticky" features. Customers have their e-mail address with AOL; they have their address book with AOL; and their customers have access to certain web information and additional benefits. So to switch over to another Internet provider becomes a hassle.

– Point taken. What's next?

I'd protect what's mine. I'd visit with my customers and find out what is important to them. Maybe increase my promotional efforts. Maybe come up with customer loyalty programs. Make them feel wanted and special. Everyone likes to feel appreciated. And second, I would do everything I could to establish long-term contracts to lock customers in. To go along with that, I'd build in incentives or give commissions to our sales staff to re-sign a client.

– Third?

Bring in new customers. I'd increase my marketing efforts, place ads, go to conventions, lobby for state contracts. I'd try to steal sales staff and customers away from my competition. And finally, I would grow through acquisition. You mentioned that there were a number of smaller players that had one or two big accounts. I'd see if they would like to sell their businesses.

– Don't you think that's risky? To lay out capital to buy up small firms when IBM is coming to town? What's to guarantee that the small firm's clients won't jump to IBM?

There are no guarantees. However, being IBM is a double-edged sword. On the one hand, IBM is big, has an incredible amount of resources and the potential to do great things. On the other hand, it is because it is so big that things might very well fall through the cracks. Am I wrong in thinking that the training we offer is similar to what IBM offers? I think the things that will differentiate us are our people and our customer service. We're going to fight and do everything we can to hold on to our customer base while we prospect for new business. Being the biggest isn't always an advantage.

– What if IBM comes in and offers the same services you do, but offers a steep discount for clients to sign up? Do you lower your prices?

No. I wouldn't engage in a price war with IBM. There is no way to win. I believe that Eastern offers great products at competitive prices. If customers like us, they're not going to go to IBM to save a little money. This is not like shopping around for the best deal on a new refrigerator. We're in the services business; it's all about the service. That doesn't mean I wouldn't be flexible in cutting existing customers a favorable deal to sign a long-term contract.

– I think I almost believe you. Summarize for me.

My strategy would be three-pronged. One, keep IBM out by raising the barriers to entry. Two, do whatever it takes to keep our current customers. We talked about raising switching costs, increasing promotional efforts — things like customer loyalty programs and establishing long-term contracts. And, finally, grow through acquisition and a major marketing effort.

– That was good.

Type of Case: Competitive response

Comments: The three-pronged approach served the student well. He was able to lay out his strategy in a clear and logical manner that was simple and easy to follow. The student stood his ground when pushed about a price war. Whether you agree with him or not, he articulated his point and stuck with it.

+ Coke®

Case 4: Coca-Cola® is trying to boost profitability domestically by raising its prices. It's focusing on the grocery store market, where the volume is high but the margin is low. What are the economics of raising the prices, and is this a good idea?

So, Coke plans to increase profitability by raising prices. It wants to know if that's a good idea.

– That's right.

I know that raising profitability is its main objective. Are there other objectives that I should be aware of?

– It doesn't want to lose market share.

Are we just focusing on Coke and not any of its other brands?

– You can think of all Coke products as one product, Coke.

What's Coke's current market share?

– Not relevant to the question.

How much does it cost to make a can of Coke?

– Not relevant to the question.

How many cans does Coke sell to US grocery stores and at what price?

– Coke sold 100 million cans at 23 cents each to grocery stores last year. If prices remain stable, it expects volume growth of 6 percent. It wants to raise the price to 27 cents per can and forecasts volume growth of only 1 percent.

Let's see. First I can multiply and then find the difference:

100,000,000 cans x .27 x 1.01 = $27,270,000
100,000,000 cans x .23 x 1.06 = $24,380,000
$ 2,890,000

So even though Coke would be selling 5 million fewer cans, it'd be making more of a profit, about $3 million more.

– Profitability would be boosted by what percent?

I can take 27 minus 24 equals 3 divided by 24 equals approximately 12 percent.
By raising prices and selling less, Coke can boost its sales by approximately 12 percent.

– To maintain market share, Coke needs to stir up consumer demand with a major marketing campaign to raise brand awareness and focus on lifestyle issues. Knowing that, if you were Pepsi, what would you do?

Pepsi has three choices. It can follow Coke's lead and raise its prices to match Coke's; it can leave prices the way they are; or it can take advantage of the price change and lower its price.

If Coke spends a fortune marketing its product and does its job and gets people into the stores, Pepsi can snatch sales away at the last minute with a lower price. We are talking grocery stores here. Women do most of the buying in grocery stores and are often price conscious. If they saw two brand-name colas, Pepsi and Coke, and Coke sold for $2.99 a 12-pack compared to $2.59 for a 12-pack of Pepsi, then most shoppers would choose the one on sale or the one with the lower price.

Pepsi might even want to lower its price so it could increase its market share.

In sailing, if you are behind, you're not going to catch up with or beat the opponent by sailing the same course. You have to take a different tack. If Pepsi lowers its prices and cuts marketing costs, it can steal customers away from Coke, through in-store promotions and point-of-contact displays.

– So, if you were Pepsi, what would you do?

Let's run some numbers. How many cans does Pepsi sell to grocery stores?

– Pepsi sells 80 million cans at 23 cents a piece.
If Pepsi follows Coke and raises its prices, its volume will drop from 6 percent to 3 percent.
If Pepsi keeps its price the same, its volume will increase from 6 percent to 12 percent.
If Pepsi lowers its prices to 21 cents, Pepsi's volume will increase from 6 percent to 20 percent.

80,000,000 x 1.03 = 82,400,000 x .27 = 22,248,000
80,000,000 x 1.12 = 89,600,000 x .23 = 20,608,000
80,000,000 x 1.20 = 96,000,000 x .21 = 20,160,000

I'd follow Coke's lead.

– Even if you knew that Coke's volume would rise from 1 percent to 3 percent?

Yes.

– Interesting. Thanks.

- **Type of case: Strategy based on numbers**
- **Comments: It's a straightforward case once you have the numbers.**

✢ Longest-lasting Light Bulb

Case 5: GE® ("We bring good things to life") has invented a new light bulb that never burns out. It could burn for more than 500 years and it would never blink. The director of marketing calls you into her office and asks, "How would you price this?" What do you tell her?

Let me make sure I understand. GE has invented a light bulb that never burns out, and the marketing director wants us to help her decide on a price.

– That's correct.

Is coming up with a price the only objective? Or is there something else I should be concerned about?

– Pricing is the only objective.

Is there any competition for this product, and do we have a patent?

– We have a patent pending, and there is no other competition.

We know that the advantage is that this bulb never burns out. Are there any disadvantages to this product? Does it use the same amount of electricity?

– There are no disadvantages, except maybe price. And that's why you're here.

What did you spend on R&D?

– It cost $20 million to develop this product.

What are the costs associated with a conventional light bulb?

– It costs us five cents to manufacture. We sell it to the distributor for a quarter, the distributor sells it to the store for 50 cents and the store sells it to the consumer for 75 cents.

And what does it cost us to manufacture the new light bulb?

– Five dollars.

So, if we use the conventional bulb-pricing model, that would mean the consumer would have to pay $75 for this light bulb. If we use another simple model and say that a light bulb lasts one year and people will have this new bulb for 50 years, that's an argument for a retail price of $37.50 (50 years x $0.75). Then we need to ask ourselves whether a consumer would pay $37.50 for a light bulb that never wears out. Now we're looking at price-based costing. What are people willing to pay? And is it enough to cover our costs and give us a nice profit?

The other main issue is that the more successful we are, the less successful we'll be in the future. For every eternal light bulb we sell, that's 50 or 75 conventional bulbs we won't sell in the future. In a sense, we're cannibalizing our future markets. So, we have to make sure that there is enough of a margin or profit to cover us way into the future.

– Good point.

I'll tell you, I have reservations about selling to the consumer market. I just don't think the opportunity for pricing is there.

– So, what do we do, scrap the project? We've already spent over $20 million in R&D.

Not at all. We turn to the industrial market. For example, the City of Cambridge probably has two thousand street lamps. Those bulbs cost maybe $20 and have to be changed twice a year. The real expense there isn't the cost of the bulb; it's the labor. It might take two union workers. In addition, you have to send out a truck. It probably costs the city $150 in labor costs just to change the light bulb. Now, if we were to sell them this ever-lasting bulb for $400, they would make that money back in less than two years and we would make a handsome profit.

– Not bad.

- Type of case: Pricing

- Comments: First, the candidate looked at cost-based pricing and realized that the price was too high and that the typical consumer would not shell out $75 for a light bulb. Then he looked at price-based costing and concluded there wasn't enough of a margin built in to make it profitable. Thinking outside the outline given in the pricing case scenario, the student also realized that he would be cannibalizing his future markets. Thus, he decided that neither pricing strategy made sense for the retail market. So, instead of suggesting that GE just cut its losses and walk away from the project, he went looking for alternative markets and concluded that there was great potential in the industrial market.

Because this product has yet to be released, and is without competition, the supply and demand theory doesn't work in this case.

+ Getting into Diapers

Case 6: DuPont® has just invented a lightweight, super-absorbent, biodegradable material that would be perfect for disposable diapers. What should they do with it?

DuPont has developed a new material that would be great for disposable diapers and they want to know how best to take advantage of this product.

– Yes.

One objective is to figure out what to do with this material. Any other objectives?

– Yes, make a handsome profit. But first, I'd like you to figure out the size of the disposable diaper market.

Okay. I'm going to make some assumptions. I'll assume that the population of the US is 320 million and that the life expectancy of an average American is 80 years. I'm also going to assume that there are even numbers of people in each age group. So, that means that there are the exact same number of three-year-olds as 73-year-olds. So you divide 320 million by 80 and get 4 million people per age group. Children wear diapers from age zero to three, so that's 12 million children. I'm going to assume that 80 percent of the children wear disposable diapers, so that's 9.2 million kids times five diapers a day equaling around 50 million diapers a day. Multiply that by 365 days and you get 18.2 billion diapers times, I don't know, say, $1 a diaper. So the market is $18.2 billion a year.

– So, now we know the market size. What's next?

We look at the market and see who the major players are, what kind of market share each has and what the pricing differentials are. I know P&G has a large part of that market and I know that there are a number of generic brands as well. The competition is tough, but I can't think of any barriers that would really stop us.

– So, you think we should get into the diaper business?

Yes, but we need to figure what part of the business. When I asked you if there were any other objectives or goals, you said profit. What you didn't say was to become a major player in the consumer diapers market. That means that there are several ways we could enter. I'd like to list them, then look at the advantages and disadvantages of each.

We could start up our own diaper company, form a joint venture, buy a smaller player and substitute our product for theirs or manufacture the diapers and license them to a number of companies.

First, let's look at starting our own company. We have name recognition, but not in that industry. We would have to set up a manufacturing plant, hire a management team, marketing team and sales force and establish distribution channels. Time-consuming and expensive, but do-able.

Second, we could form a joint venture with an established diaper company. The advantages are that the company already would have everything in place as far as name recognition, management team, sales force and distribution channels. But we might find this limiting. Depending on the deal, we might only be able to manufacture for them.

Third, we could buy a diaper company and substitute our product for theirs. This has merit for all the same reasons the joint venture has. We need to ask ourselves if we really want to manufacture and market diapers or just manufacture them.

The fourth option would be to license our product to a variety of companies. If our technology were superior to the existing product, we could get multiple companies on board and let their marketing experts fight it out.

– Good. So which one would you choose?

With just the information I have so far, I'd venture to say the last option: manufacture and license the rights, become a supplier and do what DuPont does best — manufacture.

We could even go to the different diaper companies and get pre-orders to ensure that the market is there and our pricing is in line.

Type of case: Market-sizing and entering a new market

Comments: At first, some might consider this a developing-a-new-product question, and they could probably make a decent case out of it. But the question really asks, "What should they do with it?" That implies that the product has already been developed and the company is searching for the best way to exploit this new technology; thus, this is an entering-a-new-market case.

What impressed the interviewer here was the fact that he picked up on what the interviewer didn't say and built on that. That's an extraordinary example of great listening — the best skill a consultant can have.

New York Opera

Case 7: Our client is the New York City Opera. It wants to develop a growth strategy for the next five years. What would you advise it to look at, and what are your recommendations for growth?

The New York City Opera wants us to develop a growth strategy for the next five years.

– That's right.

Besides developing this five-year strategy, are there any other objectives?

– No.

So I don't need to look at increasing sales, reducing costs or increasing profits?

– Those are all key ingredients to growth, are they not?

Yes, I guess they are. I was just trying to determine the direction of the question. I'd like to ask a few questions. Is the industry growing?

– No, it's down 7 percent last year.

How are we faring compared to the industry?

– Better, but not by much. Our growth rate last year was 2 percent.

Who are our competitors and how much market share does each one have?

– Who do you think our competition is?

It's anyone or anything that competes for the leisure dollar. It could be as widespread as a restaurant, a hockey game, events at Lincoln Center or a trip to the Hamptons. But it is also other opera companies in New York. I'm not sure how many opera companies there are in New York.

– There are about four. The biggest is the Metropolitan Opera. Can you name any operas?

Sure. There's *Tommy* and *Figaro*. Oh, and *The Barber of Seville*.

– Okay. That helps me put your answer in perspective. So what do you do?

The first thing I would do is a competitive analysis. I would look at not only the four other New York opera companies, but those in other major US cities and maybe London and Paris as well.

– What would you analyze?

Everything. Revenues and revenue streams, ticket distribution outlets, fixed costs, marginal costs, production costs, season schedule, ticket prices, the names and types of operas produced, marquee names in each production, marketing campaigns and other uses for the venue.

– That's quite a list. After you did the analysis, what would you do?

I'd take the best practices and see if it makes sense to incorporate any of those practices at the New York City Opera.

– You mentioned revenue streams. What do you think the revenue streams are; currently?

Ticket sales, sales of programs, drinks during intermission and merchandise like CDs, t-shirts — that sort of thing. And I think fund-raising is an important revenue stream as well.

– How would you increase revenues?

Three ways. We can look at increasing ticket prices; we can increase our marketing campaign to get more people to come to the opera; and once they're there, get them to spend more money.

– Can you think of additional revenue streams?

Maybe holding lectures and panels or possibly giving lessons?

– We're not offering singing lessons. What else?

I'll assume that an opera does not perform 365 days a year and that there are often stretches of time when the venue is open or in preproduction. Every night that the opera house sits empty, we're losing money. So, why not hold other events in the venue, specifically musical events. I mean, the acoustics have to be unbelievable, don't you think?

– I would imagine. Okay, good. You also mentioned ticket distribution.

Yes. I'd check to see if you can buy tickets over the web and at other ticket outlets. See if we can come up with a few additional and maybe untraditional outlets or distribution channels. I'll assume that they have discounts for season ticket holders, large groups, students and senior citizens.

– That's correct.

I think schools are a good place to educate future opera fans. We have to rebuild the audience. Get the next generation interested in opera.

– The next area you mentioned was costs. I don't want to spend too much time on this, but I'll assume that you'll work hard to reduce all our costs.

Yes.

– To be honest with you, your answer isn't going where I want it to go. I feel like we're getting too bogged down in details. The question was about growth strategy. Unless you have more to say about growth strategies, we'll end this interview right now.

Well, we've talked about increasing sales by bringing in a big-name singer, adding new distribution channels for tickets and merchandise sales, as well as possible new revenue streams. We talked about increasing the product line and the diversity of that product line. That could

mean new merchandise or more operas, but I think it means different shows, concerts or maybe stand-up comic revues — anything that fills the opera house on nights when there is no performance. A third strategy — that doesn't apply, but I thought I would mention — is acquiring the competition, maybe buying one of the smaller opera companies. But it doesn't sound like we have a lot of extra cash on hand, and what we do have can be better allocated toward driving more people in our door.

– That was a nice summation, but there was nothing new there.

One last thing. This summer I worked for a mutual fund company and what we discovered is that 95 percent of the business came from 5 percent of the customer base. This company wasn't fully taking advantage of the opportunities to grow through its existing customer base. Up until this summer, it never differentiated between customers who represented real profits and customers that only represented costs.

– This is good. Continue.

They found that over one-third of the money spent on marketing and customer service was wasted on efforts to acquire new customers who cost us more than we made. In some cases, we were marketing toward our established customers when that money could have been better spent.

– So what are you telling me?

We should focus the company on bringing in new and profitable customers. That may mean changing the way we currently and traditionally market. It means developing better relationships with our profitable customers. And finally, it means abandoning those customers that cause us to lose money.

– I think that theory applies to a mutual fund company better than an opera company, but I'll give you points for trying.

Type of Case: Growth strategies

Comments: Her answer was all over the place. Parts of it were very strong; other parts weren't. She went off on a tangent and got herself into trouble. The other thing is that she never really came up with anything extraordinary. Everything she mentioned had been tried before. The last bit about growing through existing customers and weeding out the dogs was interesting if not totally relevant.

Note: **Many firms have a version of this question. They could ask about a music school, a museum or a symphony.**

+ The Discount Brokerage Race

Case 8: Look at this chart. Your client is a discount brokerage. The majority of its revenue comes from online trading. It achieved a 10 percent growth rate last year (Y1) and was ranked number six in the industry. In Y2 it fell to seventh. The company wants to get back its sixth-place ranking. How much will it have to grow to maintain that sixth-place ranking in Y3, given the rate of growth of its competitors?

Company	Industry Ranking	Current Size in Year 1 (Revenue)	Growth Rate	Year 2	Industry Ranking
A	1	$1000m	1%	1010	1
B	2	$900m	2%	918	2
C	3	$800m	0%	800	4
D	4	$800m	5%	840	3
E	5	$700m	5%	735	5
F	**6**	**$600m**	**10%**	**660**	**7**
G	7	$600m	20%	720	6
H	8	$500m	20%	600	8
I	**9**	**$500m**	**10%**	**550**	**9**
J	10	$400m	30%	520	10
K	11	$300m	20%	360	11
L	12	$300m	30%	390	12

Our client is Company F, a discount brokerage. In Y1 we were ranked sixth with a growth rate of 10 percent and sales of 600 million. In Y2 we dropped to seventh place with a growth rate of 10 percent and revenues of $660 million. You want me to figure out how much we will have to grow by in order to get our sixth-place ranking back in Y3.

– Yes, that's right.

Is it fair to assume that the growth rates of all the other firms will remain the same?

– Yes.

Do you mind if I write on the chart you gave me?

– No, go ahead.

I'm going to do part of this through a process of elimination. Everyone below Company F growing at a smaller or equal rate or whose revenues are significantly below ours can be eliminated. So that's easily the bottom four — I through L.

We also know that A and B will remain the top two. So I need to concentrate on C through H, including us — F. So, first, I'm going to do the calculations for each of those and see where they stand.

Company	Industry Ranking	Current Size in Year 1 (Revenue)	Growth Rate	Year 2	Industry Ranking	Year 3	Industry Ranking
A	1	$1000m	1%	1010	1		1
B	2	$900m	2%	918	2		2
C	3	$800m	0%	800	4	800	5
D	4	$800m	5%	840	3	882	3
E	5	$700m	5%	735	5	772	6
F	6	$600m	10%	660	7	726	7
G	7	$600m	20%	720	6	864	4
H	8	$500m	20%	600	8	720	
I	9	$500m	10%	550	9		
J	10	$400m	30%	520	10		
K	11	$300m	20%	360	11		
L	12	$300m	30%	390	12		

If we stayed at a 10 percent growth rate; we'd have revenues of $726 million, which would put us in seventh place. So, how fast do we need to grow? If we round Company E's sales off to $772; then that's our target number. We need to beat 772. So we need an increase of over $46 million (772 – 726). So 660X = 772. Divide each side by 660 and we get X equals...about 1.17 or 17 percent. A minimum 17 percent growth in Y3 would put us in sixth place.

Company	Year 3	Industry Ranking
A		1
B		2
C	800	5
D	882	3
E	771.75	7
F	772	6
G	864	4
H	720	8

– Okay, good. Which company would you invest in and why?

I'd invest in G, provided it can continue its 20 percent growth rate.

- **Type of case: Numbers**
- **Comments: This case was a pure numbers case. The student did well by eliminating what was obvious and using her time efficiently.**

+ Cow Brothers Premium Ice Cream

Case 9: Cow Brothers is a maker of super-premium ice cream, low-fat ice cream, low-fat yogurt and sorbet. Its products are high quality and the company uses only natural ingredients. Cow Brothers products are distributed nationwide through supermarkets, grocery stores, convenience stores, franchises and company-owned ice cream shops and restaurants.

Cow Brothers has 30 flavors and sells its products in one-pint containers. It also has single servings on a stick.

Cow Brothers has strong brand recognition. Its "Have a Cow" marketing campaign met with great success. Last year, sales were $200 million ($177 million came from supermarket and grocery store sales), which put the company third in the industry behind Häagen-Dazs and Ben & Jerry's. These top three competitors hold 62 percent of the market.

The president, Winston Cow, is still not satisfied. He wants to increase company sales to $250 million by next year. How do you do it?

Let me make sure I understand. Cow Brothers, the number three maker of premium ice cream, wants to increase its sales from $200 million to $250 million next year. That would be an increase of around 25 percent. How much did Cow Brothers' sales increase last year?

– 10 percent.

And that was mainly due to the "Have a Cow" marketing campaign?

– Yes.

One objective is to increase company sales. Are there any other objectives or goals that I should be aware of?

– No.

Is the company privately held?

– Yes.

What was the overall industry growth last year?

– 12 percent.

So Häagen-Dazs and Ben & Jerry's only grew by 12 percent last year?

– No. Ben & Jerry's grew by 20 percent Häagen-Dazs by less.

First, we should analyze what Ben & Jerry's did to increase its sales and compare it to not only what we did but to what Häagen-Dazs did as well.

– Fine. What else?

Student draws the decision tree as she speaks.

We need to not only increase sales but also to grow the company. The three major ways to increase sales are to raise prices, to get customers to buy more when they purchase Cow Brothers and to expand our market base. Are we priced competitively?

– Our prices exactly match our competitors'.

So that's a no for raising prices. You mentioned that Cow Brothers only produces ice cream in the one-pint containers. Have they thought about a two-pint container? That way customers would buy more per transaction.

– That's a possibility.

The third way is to expand our market base. I'd like to talk growth strategies. I know of five main growth strategies: increase distribution channels, increase product line, launch a major marketing campaign, diversify and acquire a competitor. I'd like to look at the advantages and disadvantages of each of these and see which makes sense.

It seems as if we are tied into all the major distribution channels for our products. But there must be areas of the country where distribution is weak. I'd analyze those markets and see if we can't increase the number of outlets that carry our products.

Next, we need to increase our product line: You said we have 30 flavors. How many flavors do the supermarkets and ice cream shops carry?

– The supermarkets carry five at a time; the ice cream shops carry 15.

We don't want to increase the number of flavors because no one can carry them as is. We need to add new sizes, not new flavors. You said that the "Have a Cow" marketing campaign went well. We should look at increasing our marketing budget.

The next idea is somewhat radical, but bear with me. Diversification. Cow Brothers has great brand recognition. It's well known and stands for quality. In marketing class we read Ted Levitt's article "Marketing Myopia," in which he uses an example of the buggy whip company. When the car came along, the demand for buggy whips dropped significantly. Had the buggy whip company seen itself as being in the transportation business instead of the buggy whip industry, it would still be in business today. Likewise, if Cow Brothers pictures itself in the dairy business or gourmet foods business, it can take better advantage of its brand name.

Cow Brothers might want to try a line of gourmet cheeses and cream cheeses. The cream cheeses could be distributed through all the regular distribution channels, but we could also create new distribution channels through various chains of bagel shops, which may also want to sell our single-serve ice cream products.

– That's food for thought.

Now, acquisition might be a possibility if we can get the idea funded without loading ourselves up with debt. We might look to buy one of our lesser regional competitors, particularly in an area of the country where our distribution channels and name recognition are weak.

– Okay, good. So what are your recommendations?

First, I'd continue and probably step up our marketing campaign. Second, I would increase our product line by offering a two-pint container size as well as the original one-pint size. I'd also diversify our product line into other dairy products, like gourmet cream cheeses, to take advantage of our brand name and our established distribution channels. Third, I'd analyze the possible acquisition of a regional competitor, particularly in a region of the country where our sales are weak. That way we can take advantage of its established distribution channels.

- Type of case: Increasing sales and growing the company

- Comments: First, she was quick to realize that this was a two-scenario case: increasing sales and growing the company. She also quickly figured out the client's expectations. Winston Cow wanted to increase company sales to $250 million. What kind of percentage did that represent? And was it feasible? Realizing that ice cream sales alone couldn't reach the client's goal, she looked at the company overall, assessing and changing its strategy. Finally, her ability to look outside the existing business led to a great idea — Cow Brothers Gourmet Cream Cheese.

✦ Hair-raising

Case 10: Our client is a large pharmaceutical company that has developed a cure for baldness. It's a pill that will rapidly (within three months) re-grow your hair to the thickness it was when you were fifteen years old. The pill, called IPP2, needs to be taken every day to maintain that thickness. Please estimate the size of the US market and tell me how you would price the drug.

So, our client is a large drug company that has developed a pill that will re-grow your hair to the thickness it was when you were a teenager. The pill is called IPP2 and needs to be taken daily. You want me to estimate the size of the domestic market and develop a pricing strategy.

– Yes, that's right.

Besides estimating the market size and coming up with a pricing strategy, are there any other objectives I should be concerned about?

– Profits. We want to make sizable profits.

How about market share?

– We're more concerned about profits than market share. You price it right, the market share will come.

Before I tackle the market size, I'd like to ask a few questions.

– Shoot.

Can this be used by both men and women?

– Yes.

Is it covered by health insurance?

– No.

Is it a prescription drug or sold over-the-counter?

– Prescription.

Is this for thinning hair or just for male pattern baldness?

– Can be used for thinning hair as well.

Are there any side effects?

– Yes. It causes sexual dysfunction in 2 percent of men, and women thinking of having children shouldn't take it because it could cause birth defects.

I don't think that's enough to deter men. However, we need to eliminate all women 40 years old and younger, although I realize that there is a small population of women who give birth after 40. So, let's figure this out.

I'm going to assume that there are 320 million Americans and that their life expectancy is 80 years. And I'm going to assume that there are even numbers of people in each age group, and that there is a 50/50 split between men and women. I'll break it down by generation and by sex. So 320 divided by four generations equals 80 million per generation, and each generation has 40 million men and 40 million women. I'll also assume that as men get older, actually as people get older, there will be a greater percentage of them losing their hair.

Age	Men	% w/thin hair		Women	% w/thin hair		Totals
1-20	40m	0%	0	40m	0%	0	0m
21-40	40m	20%	8m	40m	0%	0	8m
41-60	40m	40%	16m	40m	1%	.4	16.4m
61-80+	40m	60%	24m	40m	10%	4	28m
							52.4m

With men ages 1–20, I'll assume that no one or no significant number falls into that category. Same with women. For those 21–40, I'll estimate that 20 percent of men and again 0 percent of women fall into that category. The 41–60 group has a higher percentage — I'd say 40 percent of men and 1 percent of women. And, finally, in the age range of 60–80, I'd guess 60 percent of men and 10 percent of women.

That totals around 52 million. From that number, I'm going to subtract 7 million. The reasons are that some men shave their heads, some don't care about going bald and others can't afford it, although we don't know what the price tag is yet.

So I'll estimate the market size of 45 million American customers.

– Okay, what's next?

We need to price our product. I'd like to look at it three different ways. First, who is our competition and what do they charge? Second, we'll look at cost-based pricing. And third, we'll consider price-based costing. I just want to a take a moment to draw a diagram...

PRICING STRATEGIES

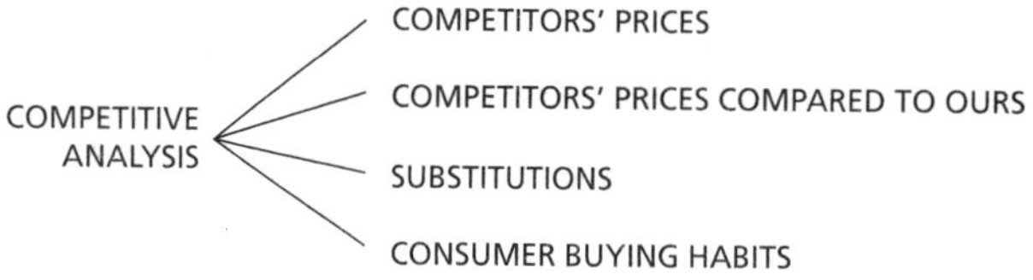

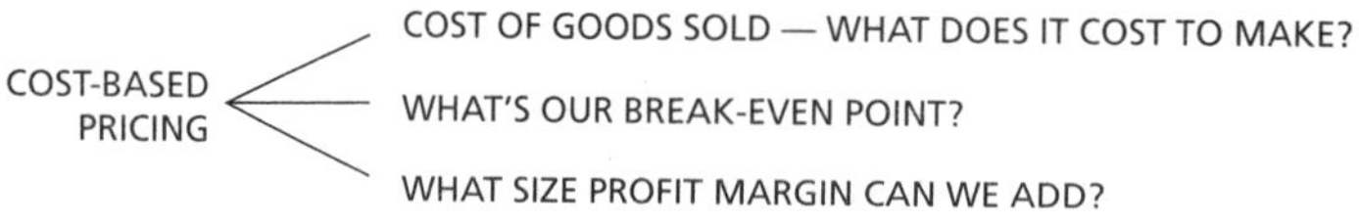

PRICE-BASED COSTING
- WHAT ARE CUSTOMERS WILLING TO PAY FOR THE PRODUCT?
- WHAT'S IT WORTH TO THEM COMPARED TO OTHER THINGS?
- SUPPLY AND DEMAND

Who is our competition and what do they charge?

– There are two major competitors. One is a topical solution that sells for $60 for a month's supply. The second is a pill that sells for $50 for a month's supply.

How does our product compare to the competition?

– We are three times more effective. Thicker hair, faster.

Are there any credible substitutions?

– Assume no.

What about customer loyalty?

– Assume that both the competitors produce the same results and it comes down to application preference.

Let's talk about cost-based pricing. What does it cost us to make, package and market a one-month supply? Were there heavy R&D costs?

– R&D costs were minimal because this was discovered by accident while we were testing a similar drug for a different illness. So the cost of the entire package, everything you need to worry about, is $1 for a month's supply.

One dollar? That's it? That's great. So with production costs of one dollar and no heavy R&D costs, we can dismiss cost-based pricing. If we look at price-based costing, we need to figure out what the market will bear. How much will people be willing to pay for a full head of hair? Currently, they are paying between $50 and $60 a month for products that aren't as good as ours. So that means that they might pay as much as $150 to $180 a month. So now we have parameters of between $2, which represents a 100 percent markup, and $180, which represents 18,000 percent markup.

– An 18,000 percent markup; are you comfortable with that?

I'm comfortable with the markup percentage if that's what people will pay. This isn't a life and death drug, like an AIDS drug. This is purely cosmetic. I'm not convinced that people would pay $180 a month. You're growing a little thin on top, sir. What would you pay?

– Rule number one: Never insult the interviewer.

Sorry, but it looks good on you.

– And you were doing so well. What else do you have regarding pricing?

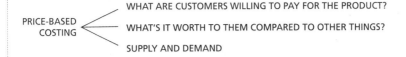

You need to look at what it is worth to them compared to other things in their life. People pay $3 a day for a cup of Starbucks coffee. Is a full head of hair worth a cup of coffee? I'd say yes.

– So, $90 a month?

Student draws this chart.

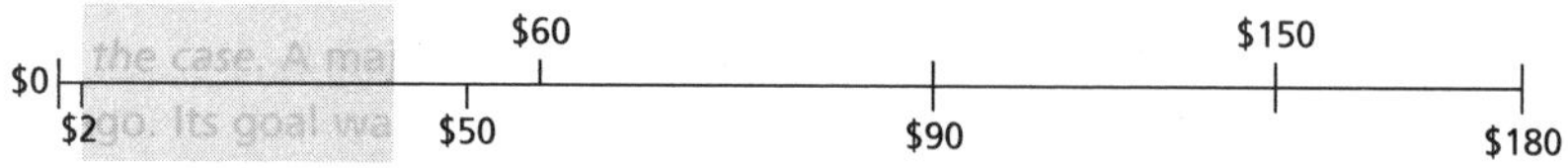

PRICING FOR MARKET SHARE

The objective of this case was profits, not market share. If it were market share, then I'd go in at $40 in order to under-price our competition, gain tremendous market share and then crank the price once we have them as loyal customers — kind of like the pricing strategies of Standard Oil in the 1930s. But I don't think we'll need to do that. If the product is that effective, we'll get heavy press coverage and soon drive the competition out of the market.

One small point as far as market share is concerned: If a large share of the market currently uses a topical solution because they like the application process, then we will have to try harder to get them to switch to a pill, realizing that a percentage of them will never switch.

Type of Case : Market-sizing, pricing

Comments: Our candidate was lucky that the interviewer had more humor than hair. He did a good job breaking down the market-sizing aspect of the case. He used a chart that kept information organized. He also looked at three pricing strategies, quickly dismissing one as irrelevant. I also liked that he took a moment to diagram his pricing strategy. Overall, a nice job.

+ Wireless Worries

Case 11: In Q4, the number-three US wireless carrier slipped further behind its rivals in its number of customers, even as profits rose 35 percent. What do you think is going on?

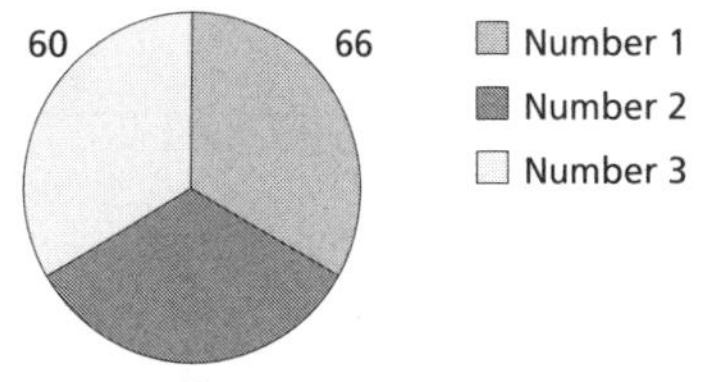

Profits are up, but the number of customers is down. We need to figure out why this is happening.

– That's right.

How many customers did Number 3 lose in Q4?

– As you can see, we closed the year with 60 million customers. That takes into account a loss of 2.5 percent or 1.5 million customers lost in Q4.

Annually, that's 10 percent of our customer base for the year.

– That's right.

Besides figuring out why we're losing so many customers, are there any other objectives I need to be concerned about?

– Not at the moment.

The student writes E(P = R –C)M.

I'd like to start by looking at the industry. Are the other two major wireless companies losing customers as well?

– Yes, but not in such large numbers. Traditionally, wireless companies lose about 1 percent of their customer base each quarter. However, they gain much more than they lose.

Did we gain more than we lost?

– Yes. We gained 2 million new customers that quarter.

Next, I'd like to know why we are losing so many customers?

– Why do you think?

It could be any number of reasons: the other companies might have a better and more reliable network, more effective advertising, better pricing, cooler phones or better customer service.

– Assume all that is true, but it only makes up a small portion of our losses. Why else?

Did we have a satellite problem, causing our network to go down for a while?

– No.

The student struggles to come up with other reasons, so the interviewer tosses her a bone.

– What if we wanted to lose those customers?

I'm not sure I understand.

– One of our major concerns is bad debt. We spend a lot of time, effort and money on bill collection. It's a runaway cost. We spend so much time trying to get new accounts that we don't do a proper job vetting our customers' credit. Here's a chart for you to study. What does it say to you?

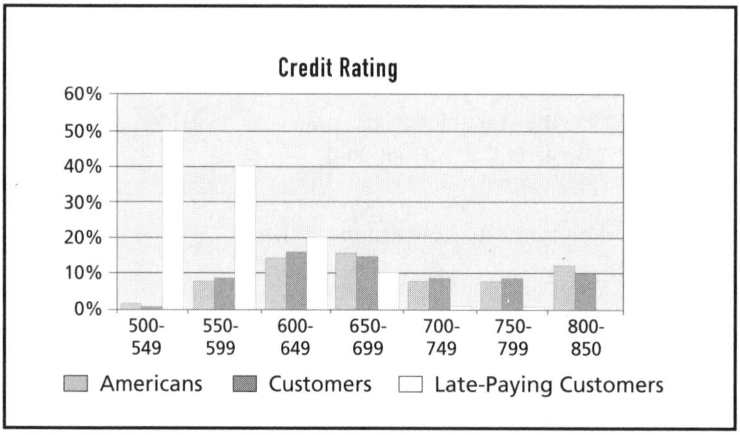

It tells me that people with credit ratings between 500 and 600 are a problem. Is it worth keeping them as customers? Let's figure out how many customers we're talking about. According to the first pie chart, we have 60 million customers. It looks as if 1 percent of our customers fall into the 500 – 549 range. They pay late 50 percent of the time. Is it the same 50 percent who pay late every month?

– Not necessarily. You can assume that everyone in that group has been late paying the bill at some point, some more than others.

If we eliminate them as customers, that's 600,000 customers. The next group isn't much better. We can see that 40 percent of them pay late. This is a bigger pool. We're looking at 9 percent of the customer base, or around 5.4 million customers. If we dropped those two groups from our customer lists, that would set us back 6 million customers and put us at 54 million. In turn we would be 10 million customers behind the number-two wireless company.

– So?

How much does it cost us to collect late payments from each customer?

– $50.

How much is the average bill?

– Overall, it's $40; however, in those categories, it's $75.

So we're paying $50 to collect $75. Are our margins so great that we're still making money off those customers?

– No. Profit margins are 25 percent.

Do we charge a late fee?

– No.

What percentage of those customers abandon their accounts altogether, leaving us holding the bag?

– Good question, but I don't have the figure for that. Run some numbers for me. How much will we be saving if we drop all 6 million customers?

We have 6 million late-paying customers with average bills of $75. That's revenues of...$450 million. Our margins are 25 percent, which brings the number down to a little less than $115 million. We need to add the cost of collection. Some customers pay late 50 percent of the time, others 40 percent of the time. Let's average it and call it 45 percent. So 45 percent of 6 million customers is 2.7. We have 2.7 million customers who pay late. We spend $50 trying to recover the money; that's $135 million. So we're losing $20 million a month going after those customers.

– So what do you suggest?

We can do a couple of things. Shed the high-risk late payers. Vet new customers better. Require them to have a 600 credit rating or better. Start charging a late fee and go after the customer collections every two months instead of every month. If we do that, we're spending $50 to go after $150.

– That's right.

Type of case: Reducing costs

Comments: She just did all right. The student's math was solid. She got stuck and the interviewer came to the rescue, but she didn't pick up on the hint. She came up with a decent list of suggestions, which showed she listened. Also, she did a good job analyzing the second chart. It's a hard chart. It is not well designed and it has a lot of information on it. Oftentimes, the interviewers will give you badly designed charts to test your analytical skills.

+ Blade to Blade

Case 12: Our client is a small privately-held lawn mower manufacturer in lower Alabama. The company makes low-end mowers, the type marketed to low-income households. It has 1 percent of the national market. There are 25 national competitors.

Like the rest of the industry, the company's sales have been flat. But its bigger problem is that the company it has been purchasing its engines from for the last 40 years suddenly called up and said it was filing for bankruptcy and closing its doors.

The client has looked around for another engine manufacturer, but the only one it could find is charging 40 percent more than what our client has been paying. The reason for this is that the engines it uses involve a side-mounted engine; compared to the flat-top engine most other mowers use. They've been using this side-mounted engine for 40 years. It's inexpensive and reliable, a real workhorse. You know the old saying, "They don't make things like they used to." Well, this engine is "like they used to." In addition, the side-mounted engine has become our client's signature over the years.

Here is a chart of the lawn mower industry. As you can see there are 25 competitors. Twenty-three of them make up 98 percent of the market.

Lawn Mower Industry

18%	5	
40%	8	
40%	10	
2%	X	Y
	ENG	

Our client is Company X. Its biggest competitor is Company Y. Together they share the lowest 2 percent of the market. Company Y buys its engines from the same engine maker (ENG), so it is in the same boat. X and Y have been competing against each other in this market for the last 40 years and there is no love lost between them. If both mowers were in the room you couldn't tell them apart, except one has a big X on it. These are basic mowers. You pull the cord to start it, push it and the grass blows out the side. It's one step above Fred Flintstone pushing Dino around the front yard.

If the client raises its price by 12 percent, that increase will push it up into the next level where there are already ten companies fighting over a 40 percent market share. More important; there are big names in that group like Honda, Lawn-Boy® and John Deere. Their mowers have a lot more bells and whistles than ours. We can't compete in that market without drastic redesign and upgrades.

I know I have given you a lot of information, but just one last thing: The client uses "just in time inventory," which is normally a good thing; however, because it didn't see this bankruptcy

coming, it only has enough engines on hand for one month as it heads into its busy season. What does it do?

That was a lot of information. Let me make sure I got it. Our client is a privately-held lawn mower manufacturer in lower Alabama. It has 1 percent of the national market. Its engine supplier suddenly filed for bankruptcy, which left it in a position of low inventory as it heads into its busy season. The only alternative engine is 40 percent higher than what it has been paying. However, if it raises its prices, that action will push it into the next tier where it will have to compete directly with the likes of Honda and John Deere. So its objective, I imagine, is not only to survive this crisis but to maintain or increase sales and market share. Are there any other objectives I should be concerned with?

– No.

Can I ask a few clarifying questions?

– Certainly.

What are its margins?

– Twenty-five percent.

What is the manufacturing cost of the mower and what percentage does the engine account for?

– You can assume that it costs us $100 to manufacture and we sell it to the distributor for $125. The cost of the engine makes up 60 percent of the cost of the mower. The other parts — the wheels, shell and handle — make up 25 percent, and labor accounts for 15 percent.

If the engine makes up 60 percent of the cost of the mower, that's $60. If that component were to jump up 40 percent, that means [student does a quick calculation on his graph paper – 60 x .4 = 24]...that means the engine would jump $24, for a total cost of $84, which would make our new mower cost $124. That takes quite a bite out of our margins if we can't raise our prices.

– You can see their dilemma.

This mower is manufactured in Alabama, so I'll assume our labor costs are reasonable. I don't think we'll gain anything by moving the operation to China or Mexico. Where do we buy the other parts?

– In Alabama. This company supports the surrounding communities. You can assume that buying the wheels from Mexico isn't going to solve this problem.

Do you mind if I take a moment to lay out my structure?

– Certainly.

One last question. How much does the flat-top engine cost compared to the old side-mounted engine?

– The price is the same, although some would argue that the quality isn't as good.

The student draws a line down the middle of his page and starts writing.

I want to divide this into short-term solutions and long-term solutions. In the short term, the company has several options. It can buy the new engine and raise its prices, but that would pin it against Honda, so that's not ideal. It could close its doors and liquidate the company, or even sell its company to a Honda who wants to enter this lower market. Again, not an ideal solution. It could eat its margins for the busy season, and then switch to the flat-top engines when things slow down. Do you know how long it would take to redesign the mower and retool the factory?

– Eight weeks.

Another short-term solution would be to buy the engine company out of bankruptcy. If we can get it up and running again quickly, we'd be able to save our busy season.

– Interesting. What would you want to know before you bought the company?

The first thing I'd like to know is why they went bankrupt.

– They went bankrupt for two reasons. Bad management and they were $2 million in debt. The engine company itself was a cash cow, always has been. It too, has 25 percent margins. However, the owner took out all the cash and signed a big loan to start a new company in another industry, which failed. Now it can't pay back its loan and the bank won't extend it because of the company's bad credit history and the tight credit markets.

Do we have $2 million in cash reserves?

– No, we have $1 million. But the bank is willing to take 40 cents on the dollar based on the value of the company, and it values the company at $2 million. So you get the building and the equipment, which is ten years old and has about two to three years of life left on it. The owners would have been better off investing in new equipment than in racehorses or whatever it threw its money at. With new equipment, he could have built the side-mounted engines for less and built other engines as well.

So the bank will take $800,000. I'm concerned about laying out 80 percent of our cash reserves for an acquisition. How's our bank credit?

– It's good. If we put $500,000 down, we can take out a loan for the rest. What else would you need to know?

I'd need to know if there are any new engine suppliers on the horizon.

– Assume no; what else?

Would we be able to get the workers back, particularly the floor supervisor? And if so, will the cultures of the two companies mesh well?

– This is lower Alabama and they were just laid off, so we could get the workers back. And on one hand you have guys building engines and on the other guys making lawn mowers. They probably play in the same softball league and drink out of the same keg. What else?

Is the side-mounted engine the only product we make? And are the engine company's suppliers in good shape? While there is nothing to indicate that they are in trouble; we need to find out. This is an old design and some of the parts might be tough to find.

– Good. Yes, we only have that one product and the suppliers are in good shape. What else?

We would need to review an exit strategy. What happens if this fails and what happens if we are successful? While an exit strategy might not be that critical; in this case it is something you want to think about.

– Okay, good. Anything else?

One last thing, competitive response. Ninety-eight percent of the industry isn't going to care one way or the other. We need to think about Company Y. How would it react? Would it still buy its engines from us? Do we even want them to buy their engines from us?

– Okay, assume that the engine company and Company Y have been doing business for close to 40 years. There hasn't been a contract between the two of them in 30 years. Thus, we are under no legal obligation to sell to it. We can if we want to, but don't have to. What would you do with Y and why would you do it?

The way I see it, we have three options. First, we can cut Company Y off completely, forcing it to buy its engines from the other guy at a 40 percent premium. That might force it up to the next tier if it raises its prices and we can gobble up its market share, or it might eat its margins for a while and then switch to a top-mounted engine. It would have little choice. It can't live on 1 percent margins.

Second, we can sell to it but increase the price by 30 percent. It would continue to buy our engines but that would still cut deep into its margins, and I think that it would buy from us to get through the busy season, then switch to the flat-top engine. The third option is to sell to it at a 5 percent increase. This would keep it buying from us. This is important because we just laid out $800,000 for this engine company and can ill afford to cut off half our revenue stream. It would also keep Company Y from manufacturing a flat-top mower. This is good because then not only would we still be supplying engines to this entire sector of the market; it would also keep us from having to produce a flat-top mower ourselves. If we did this, I'd probably insist on a two-year contract. But before I did anything, I'd like to run the numbers. We know the engine company's margins are 25 percent. Do we know how many engines they sell a year?

– Good questions. I don't want to get into that. Say we continue to sell to them for the next two years. What additional steps would you take to ensure company X's success?

Do we know how much the new equipment would cost and what the building is worth?

– No.

Well, I'd probably buy the new equipment, if it would allow us to cut our manufacturing costs and to expand our product line. I'd set the new equipment up under the same roof as the lawn mower production. This would allow us to sell the old equipment and the building and put the proceeds toward either buying the new equipment and/or paying down the $300,000 we owe to the bank. There would be some synergies and cost savings we could take advantage of.

– Give me three ways to cut costs in this case, besides moving everything to under one roof.

Now that we have the new equipment, we can produce other engines to sell as well as help our own company expand our product line. We could build weed-whackers and leaf blowers. We could even create some seasonal balance to our production line by building engines for snow blowers.

– Okay, that's one. What else?

We could cross-train the workers to be able to build engines and lawn mowers. Also we could retool the assembly line to be able to quickly switch from one product to the other as demand dictates. The third way is to go back down the supply chain and renegotiate with our suppliers. Maybe sign longer contracts or get bulk discounts if the engines and mowers share parts. In addition, interest rates are at a near 40-year low, so maybe we could refinance our debt.

– Nice. Can you summarize the case for me?

The student starts to summarize almost immediately.

Our client is a small, privately-held lawn mower manufacturer. It has learned that its engine supplier is closing down and is left without a suitable alternative. We investigated several short-term strategies, the best of which was to buy the engine company out of bankruptcy. We've verified that Company Y will remain a customer, while identifying a number of ideas to make our company more productive, including consolidating production space and workers. We also identified several cost-cutting measures, including reducing inventories and refinancing our debt.

– Okay, good.

Type of Case: Merger and acquisition

Comments: The student did very well. He asked some good questions up front, quickly realizing that cost-cutting wasn't going to solve this problem. He broke the problem down into short-term and long-term solutions. Once he did that, he was quick to realize that this was a mergers and acquisitions question. He asked a lot of good questions about the engine company and he analyzed the Y situation, by laying out his three options and not just automatically cutting Company Y off, which would have been an emotional response.

+ World Spacelines

Case 13: World Spacelines has developed a rocket-boosted Spaceplane® that can take off and land like a conventional airplane but can also fly through the atmosphere and orbit Earth. World Spacelines wants to take passengers on a three-hour tour of space. It has built a prototype, which cost it $500 million. Each additional Spaceplane will cost $100 million to manufacture.

- **Estimate the size of the domestic market.**
- **Determine what price it should charge for a ticket.**
- **How many Spaceplanes should it build in the future?**
- **Should it manufacture Spaceplanes for the competition?**

So, let me make sure I understand. World Spacelines has developed a Spaceplane that can take off and land like a conventional plane, and has been designed to take tourists on a three-hour tour of space.

– Yes.

You'd like me to estimate the size of the US market, determine what to charge customers, decide how many of these Spaceplanes to build and whether or not the company should manufacture them for our competitors.

– That's right.

I'll assume one objective is to build a successful business. Are there any other objectives I should be aware of?

– Yes. They want to be the first organization to build a space hotel.

Are there any competitors?

– No.

Do we have a patent on our technology?

– Yes.

How long before someone weasels around the patent and starts to compete with us?

– Three years.

How big is the plane? How many passengers does it hold?

– One hundred.

The trip takes three hours. How many trips per day are you planning?

– Two trips a day, 360 days a year.

Student draws chart (final slide).

Price	
Market-size	
# of Spaceplanes	
Planes for company	

Well, before I can estimate the market size, I need to know the price we are going to charge. Because if it's one dollar, then the market is just about the whole country. But if we charge $1 million, then the market is much, much smaller.

And before I can figure out the price, I need to know what it's going to cost us per passenger. So I'm going to make some assumptions about costs. How long is the life of the plane?

– Twenty years. And, yes, you can allocate the costs over 20 years without interest. What do you think the major costs are?

I figure the major costs are the cost of the plane, labor (both on-board and administrative), maintenance, fuel, airport fees, insurance and marketing.

– Good. I'll give you most of the costs; however, I want you to figure out the fuel costs. The plane burns 10 gallons of fuel for every mile and the fuel costs $10 a gallon.

How far is our trip? How high is the sky?

– The Earth's atmosphere is about 300 miles thick, but most of the atmosphere (about 80 percent) is within 10 miles of the surface of the Earth. There is no exact place where the atmosphere ends; it just gets thinner and thinner, until it merges with outer space. In addition, we use very little fuel when we are orbiting and descending. So we'll estimate our trip goes 500 miles.

So 10 gallons per mile times 500 miles equals 5,000 gallons, times $10 a gallon, is $50,000 per trip. You said two trips per day, 360 days a year. Okay, $100,000 per day times 360 days equals $36 million a year in fuel costs.

Major annual costs are:	
Cost of the plane (prototype)	$25,000,000
Labor (on-board & admin.)	$2,000,000
Maintenance	$4,000,000
Fuel	$36,000,000
Gate & Airport	$1,000,000
Insurance	$2,000,000
Marketing	$2,000,000
TOTAL COSTS	$72,000,000

Our costs are $72 million. We need to divide that by the number of passengers. You said 720 flights per year and 100 passengers per flight, which equals 72,000 passengers a year. Divide 72,000 passengers into $72 million in costs and you get $1,000 per passenger.

– Good. So what are you going to charge per trip?

Well, there are three main pricing strategies: competitive analysis, cost-based pricing and price-based costing. There is no competition, so we have nothing to compare it to, except maybe exotic vacations, but that's a far reach. As far as cost-based pricing goes, our costs are $1,000, so if we double that to $2,000, that's a pretty good margin. However, this is really a special trip. To go where no tourist has gone before, to a place that has been accessible to only a few elite astronauts. To a place that everyone has wondered about, not to mention all the "Trekkies." I think price-based costing is the way to go.

– So, what are you going to charge?

I'd like to figure out what the market is for $10,000 a ticket. Let's start with 250 million Americans. I'll assume that 2 percent of the population makes over $100,000 a year and can afford a $10,000 vacation. So 2 percent of 250 million is 5 million people. Out of that 5 million, maybe 20 percent would want to do it. So that's a base of a million customers.

How long does it take to build another Spaceplane?

– Each Spaceplane takes six months to build.

We have one plane now that we estimate that we can fill for the next fourteen years. So I would build as many planes as I could for at least the next three years, until we see what the competition is like, then reevaluate at that point.

– Really? I think your assumptions are a little too broad. Lay it out for me.

YEARS 1–5

PLANES	Y1	Y2	Y3	Y4	Y5
Plane 1	72K	72K	72K	72K	72K
Plane 2	36K	72K	72K	72K	72K
Plane 3	0	72K	72K	72K	72K
Plane 4	0	36K	72K	72K	72K
Plane 5	0	0	72K	72K	72K
Plane 6	0	0	36K	72K	72K
Passengers	108K	252K	396K	432K	432K
Total	108K	108K	360K	756K	1188K
Running Total		360K	756K	1188K	1620K

By the end of Year 3, we would have six planes up and running and would have carried a total of 756,000 passengers, well below the 1 million market estimate. However, by the end of Year

4, even without any additional planes, our running total would climb to almost 1.2 million passengers. That's 1.6 million passengers the following year. Two things can happen. First, we can lower the ticket price to $5,000 a ticket, which would spike demand. Second, our other objective is to build a space hotel, so we will need Spaceplanes to shuttle people back and forth, provided the space hotel has been built by then. Even if it hasn't been built, the new demand will continue to fill our planes. Third, even though we haven't spoken about this, I think that there will be a large international demand as well.

You also said that competition might show up around this time.

– That's right. The last question I asked was whether you'd sell Spaceplanes to the competition.

Our revenues off the prototype would be $10,000 times 72,000 customers, which equals $720 million, minus our costs of $72 million, which equals $648 million for the first year. If each additional plane costs $100 million, that's going to drop our costs by at least $20 million, if not more, depending on shared costs. But let's reduce our costs by $20 million. So now we have revenues of $720 million minus costs of $52 million; which equals $668 million. For us to sell our Spaceplanes to the competition wouldn't be practical. If we're making $668 million a year off each plane, we'd have to sell them for, like, $2 billion. I doubt that the competition would pay that kind of money.

To answer your questions, the market size is 1 million passengers at $10,000 a ticket. If we drop it to $5,000, we'll see a huge spike in potential customers. I'd build as many planes as I could for the next three years and then reevaluate our situation once we see what the competition is doing and how far along the construction is on our space hotel. And I wouldn't manufacture Spaceplanes for anyone but us.

- **Type of Case: Market-sizing, entering a new market and pricing**

- **Comments: Big points for realizing that she couldn't estimate the market size without first knowing the price of the ticket, and she couldn't estimate the price without first knowing the costs.**

+ Snow Job

Case 14: Snow Shovels Inc. (SSI) imports and distributes snow shovels. The snow shovel market is relatively stable. As expected, sales depend on demand, and demand depends on weather. SSI has to order its shovels four months in advance. How many shovels should they order?

SSI imports and distributes snow shovels. They have to order their product four months in advance. They want to know how many shovels they should order.

– Yes.

Besides deciding how many shovels to order, are there any other objectives I should be concerned about?

– Yes. The goal is to maximize profits with the lowest amount of risk and the least amount of inventory on hand.

What areas of the country does the company cover?

– Just Wellesley, Massachusetts.

I'd look at expanding into other areas.

– No. They just want to focus on their little corner of the world.

Then maybe we can increase their distribution channels. How many distribution channels do they have?

– Good question, but not relevant to what I'm looking for in this question.

How many did the company order last year?

– Two thousand.

What was the weather like last year?

– Cold; with lots of snow.

Did they have any inventory leftover from the year before?

– Yes, 500 shovels.

Is it fair to assume that they sold all 2,500 shovels this past year?

– Yes.

So there is no leftover inventory?

– That's right. SSI hates to carry over inventory.

Could we have sold more? Were there orders left unfilled?

– Yes. It's fair to say that if it's a cold winter, SSI will sell 3,000 shovels. If it's a mild winter, they will sell only 1,000.

Do we know what the forecast is for the coming winter?

– There is a 40 percent chance that it will be a cold winter, and a 60 percent chance that the winter will be mild.

Okay, let me get this straight. There is a 40 percent **chance of a cold winter, in which we could sell 3,000 shovels. There's a 60** percent **chance of a mild winter, in which we would sell 1,000 shovels. And SSI hates to carry over inventory. How much do we pay for the shovels and what do we charge?**

– We buy them for $10 and sell them for $20.

So we make $10 a shovel. Let's figure that 40 percent of 3,000 equals 1,200 and 60 percent of 1,000 equals 600. If you add them together, that equals 1,800 shovels.

– That's it? That's your answer? Why does everyone come up with 1,800 shovels? I've given this case five times today, and everyone has come up with 1,800 shovels. Think about the information I gave you. Think about the objective.

I'd like to look at the estimated value. If we order 1,000 shovels and assume that no matter what kind of winter we had, we would still sell 1,000 shovels; then the estimated value would be:

# Ordered	# Sold	Income	Costs	Net	Times %	Expected Profit
1,000	1,000	1,000 x 20	1,000 x 10	10,000	100%	$10,000
						$10,000

If we order 2,000 shovels and there is a 60 percent chance of a mild winter in which we would only sell 1,000 shovels, and a 40 percent chance of a cold winter in which we would sell all 2,000, the value would be:

# Ordered	# Sold	Income	Costs	Net	Times %	Expected Profit
2,000	1,000	1,000 x 20	2,000 x 10	0	60%	0
2,000	2,000	2,000 x 20	2,000 x 10	20,000	40%	$8,000
						$8,000

If we order 3,000 shovels and there is a 60 percent **chance of a mild winter in which we would only sell 1,000 shovels, and a 40** percent **chance of a cold winter in which we would sell all 3,000, the value would be:**

# Ordered	# Sold	Income	Costs	Net	Times %	Expected Profit
3,000	1,000	1,000 x 20	3,000 x 10	(10,000)	60%	$(6,000)
3,000	3,000	3,000 x 20	3,000 x 10	30,000	40%	$12,000
						$6,000

Based on the numbers above, and assuming that you're relatively risk adverse, I would have to suggest that you order 1,000 shovels. You are pretty much guaranteed a $10,000 profit. If you order 3,000 shovels, you have only a 40 percent **chance of making $12,000 and a 60** percent **chance of losing $6,000.**

– Can you graph it?

Sure. It would look like this.

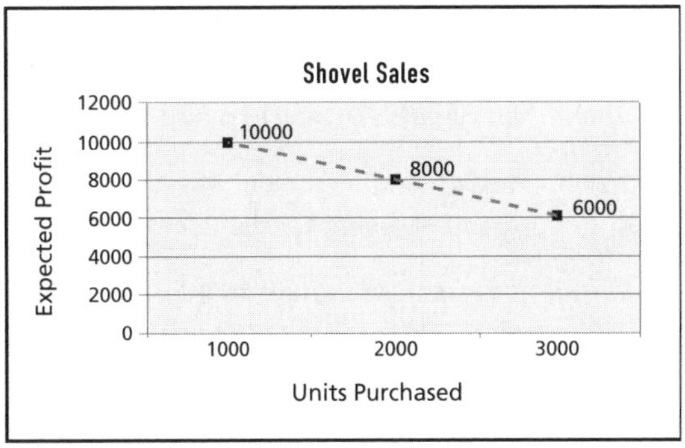

– Good recovery.

One last question. In this case, we assumed that the leftover inventory is a loss in the current period. It's really an asset unless they plan to throw it away.

– Good point. You're right, but in this case we don't want to deal with it.

Type of Case: Strategy

Comments: This case is all about risk. The student tried to come to a fast answer, then pulled back and quickly rethought this strategy based on the interviewer's reaction. Estimated value may not be common knowledge to a lot of non-MBAs, so go back and reread the answer.

Note: I've given this case 40 times to Harvard students, and only two got the correct answer. On a scale of 1 to 10, this is probably a 9.

+ Jamaican Battery Enterprise

Case 15: Our client is the Jamaican Battery Enterprise. Currently, they sell car batteries throughout the Caribbean, Africa and Central and South America. Over the past two decades they have been eyeing the Cuban battery market. However, Cuban Battery Enterprise, a state-owned battery company, currently has 100 percent of the secondary market. The reason they have 100 percent of the secondary market is because the Cuban government imposes a 50 percent tariff on the manufacturing costs and shipping costs on all imported batteries.

The Cuban government has just announced it will be lowering the tariff on batteries by 5 percent a year for the next 10 years until the tariff reaches zero.

The Jamaican Battery Board of Directors wants to know the size of the Cuban market and if, when and how they should enter it.

The Board of directors of the Jamaican Battery Company wants to know the size of the Cuban market and if, when and how they should enter it. We know that currently the Cuban battery market is dominated by the Cuban Battery Enterprise because of a 50 percent tariff on the manufacturing and shipping costs on all imported batteries. But we also know that the government is lowering the tariff by 5 percent a year for the next 10 years until the tariff reaches zero.

– Yes, that's right.

I'll assume that the objective is to gain market share and be profitable. Are there any other objectives that I should know about?

– No.

What is the market share that they would like?

– One hundred percent.

Let me rephrase. What is the market share that they can reasonably expect to gain and under what time table?

– Twenty-five percent within five years of entering.

Let's start by estimating the size of the Cuban secondary car battery market. I'll assume that there are 10 million people in Cuba.

– That's a little low but a good figure to use.

I'll also assume that disposable income is limited and that only one in ten households have a car. So if we estimate that the average Cuban household is made up of five people —

– Where did you get five from?

I'm assuming that there are two generations living in a number of the homes.

– Okay.

So, if there are 2 million households and if only one in ten have a car, that means that there are 200,000 cars. I would also like to add in another 10,000 vehicles, which include taxis, trucks and government vehicles.

– So, 210,000 vehicles.

Yes. I'll also assume that Cubans keep their cars for a long time and that the average car needs a new battery every three years.

– Three years? What were you thinking when you made that assumption?

I was assuming that this is a monopoly in a communist country; thus the quality of the battery might not be competitive with a Jamaican Battery, which probably lasts five years.

– Go on.

So, 210,000 vehicles will need a new battery every three years. But there are two factors we need to figure in. First, let's say that half of the 10,000 "other" vehicles that we mentioned are government or military vehicles. So we need to subtract 5,000 from the total. Now it is 205,000 divided by every three years, which equals around 68,000 batteries.

Also, the number is going to be reduced over the long run because our batteries will last five years, not three. I'm not sure how to factor that in.

– That's okay. It's just important that you brought it up.

If we want 25 percent of that market, we're talking 17,000 batteries a year.

– Okay, what's next?

I'd like to know some costs and prices. What are our costs and prices compared to theirs?

– Prices are irrelevant, but costs aren't. It costs the Cuban Battery Enterprise $12 to produce a battery. Their raw material costs are 20 percent, their labor costs are 50 percent and their overhead and all other costs are 30 percent.

It costs us $9 to produce a battery. Our raw material costs are 20 percent, our labor costs are 25 percent and all other costs, including overhead and marketing, are 55 percent. It costs us $1 to ship it to Cuba.

Let me just write this out.

Cuban Battery Enterprise		**Jamaican Battery Company**	
Production costs:	**$12**	**Production costs:**	**$9**
Raw material 20%		**Raw material 20%**	
Labor 50%		**Labor 25%**	
All other costs 30%		**All other costs 30%**	
Shipping costs	**$0**	**Shipping costs**	**$1**
Tariff	**$0**	**Tariff**	**$5**
Total cost	**$12**	**Total cost**	**$15**

That means it costs us $9 manufacturing plus $1 shipping, which equals $10. Add in the 50 percent tariff and we're talking $15 a battery.

We now need to figure out when we will be competitive. In five years the tariff will drop from 50 percent to 25 percent, which is half. So, it will still cost us $10 to manufacture and ship the battery; however, the tariff will only be $2.50. That makes our total cost $12.50. So I would say, based on sheer numbers, we can enter and compete during Year 6. But if we can market and explain that, for a little bit more, our battery will last five years instead of three years, we might be able to charge a premium, and that could justify entering the market in Year 5.

– Let's switch hats for a second. You now are advising the Cuban Battery Enterprise. What do you advise them?

My first step is to approach the government and try to get them to reconsider lowering the tariff.

– Castro's mind is made up. The tariff will be reduced.

Next, I would want to find out why our labor costs are so high.

– Why do you think?

The two things that jump to mind are technology and medical costs. Maybe our technology is old and our manufacturing process is very labor intensive.

– Yes, that's part of it. What else?

We are in a communist country where health care is free. That's the hidden cost in everything that's done — every service and every manufactured item. Even a country like Canada, with its national health-care program, has higher prices. If the Canadian dollar wasn't so weak compared to the US dollar, the Canadians would price themselves right out of the market in many items.

– We'll save that discussion for another time.

Well, we can't do much about the health-care costs, but we can upgrade our technology. The upgrade would also make our batteries more competitive and able to last five years instead of three years.

– Say we upgrade our technology and are now able to make a world-class battery for $9 a battery. How would that change things?

Well, the tariff becomes moot in the sense that we can be competitive without it. This is good, but we still have a perception problem. I think we need to launch a marketing campaign to show the Cuban public that we have a new battery that is world class. I'd also like to review our customer service and our distribution channels. These are key functions that are often overlooked in a monopoly environment.

– Good point. Our customer service is pitiful and our distribution channels are restricted to two major warehouses, one in Havana and the other in Nuevitas. You said that you would launch a marketing campaign, and I'll assume that there will be a customer service aspect to that. What would you do about the distribution channels?

I'll make two assumptions. First, I'll assume that we have at least two years before the Jamaican Battery Company enters our market. Second, I'll assume that other non-American battery companies will also enter our market, probably about the same time and with a strategy similar to the Jamaican company's.

– Both fair assumptions.

First, I would go to every gas station on the island, both in the cities and in the countryside. I would front each one the cost of the batteries, give them a nice display rack, free t-shirts and maybe some cash. In return, they would have to sign an exclusive agreement to sell only our batteries.

Let me ask you this; Does the government make its own tires? And, if yes, how's the quality?

– Yes, they do, but the quality is poor. However, based on your advice, they will also upgrade their technology and launch a marketing plan because the tire tariff is being eliminated as well.

So, you know what I'm getting at. We can open a service store where residents can get both a new battery and new tires, and maybe an oil change. We can snap up all of the best locations before the foreign competitors come into our market.

– We're switching hats again. You are now back to advising the Jamaican Battery Company. You have seen that the Cuban Battery Enterprise has upgraded its plant, increased its distribution channels, formed a joint venture with the Cuban Tire Enterprise and launched a nationalistic marketing campaign. Do you now enter the Cuban battery market, and if so, how?

Whenever you enter a new market, there are several things you need to examine. Who are the major players? What size market share do they have? How are their products or services different from ours? And are there any barriers to entry? The major player is the Cuban Battery Enterprise. They have 100 percent of the market. Two years ago, their products were inferior, but today they are very similar. The tariff was a barrier to entry, but now it looks as if access to distribution channels could be a threat.

I've learned that there are three main ways to enter a market. Start from scratch, buy your way in or form a joint venture. I'd like to do a quick cost-benefit analysis of each. Starting from scratch would be a fine strategy if we can define our distribution channels. If the Cuban company has all the gas stations tied up and has built tire and battery stores, then our distribution means are limited. Plus, selling 17,000 batteries a year might not justify an investment of building our own battery stores.

The second strategy is to buy our way in. Since this is a communist country, there isn't a lot of buying opportunity. If we were going to buy anyone, it would have been Cuban Battery Enterprise, and we should have bought it when it was a mess and not a formidable competitor.

The third way is to form a joint venture. If I work under the assumption that there are no independent battery distributors, then my first choice is to form a joint venture with one of the tire companies that are entering the market. My guess is that there will be several tire companies and battery companies jumping in, so we need to be part of that coalition.

– So it all boils down to —

So it all boils down to distribution channels.

– Great job.

Type of Case: Strategy / entering a new market / market-sizing

Comments: This was a long case and one that you'd get in the final rounds, where you have about an hour to answer it. It had a market-sizing component to it, but probably the hardest thing was the switching of the hats. It forced the student to come up with counterstrategies to the strategies he had just developed.

Most students would have tried to figure out the reduction in tariff fees year by year, but this student saved time and impressed the interviewer by picking a point in the middle and working from there. He made the math simple and was able to do the calculations in his head.

The student was very well-organized — he even wrote out the costs and percentages in a little chart. This impressed the interviewer and made everything easy for the student to find when flipping back through his notes.

North American Airlines*

Case 16: In an effort to increase in-flight sales, North American Airlines (NAA) is contemplating partnering with JavaMoose, the world's leading coffeehouse chain, to sell several varieties of special-blend coffee. From the perspective of NAA, would such a partnership prove to be profitable?

Okay. So, let me rephrase the scenario. NAA wants to sell several varieties of JavaMoose coffee on its flights; to increase coffee sales. We want to evaluate whether or not this is a good idea for NAA. Did I understand that correctly?

– That's right.

Besides making a profit, are there any other objectives I should be aware of?

– There is the possibility of a joint marketing campaign, but focus on the profits.

I'm going to need some additional information regarding the airline's routes, the products it currently sells, its clientele, and its financial targets with this venture, as well as information about the JavaMoose products it intends to sell.

– All right. What would you like to know?

Let's start with the routes. What routes does the airline serve? What is the duration of each of these routes?

– Okay. Eighty percent of NAA's routes are under two hours. These flights serve New York, Boston, Washington, D.C., and Philadelphia. Recently, NAA has added two routes to its portfolio: one connecting New York to Los Angeles; the other linking New York with San Francisco. These routes comprise the other 20 percent. Each of these flights is direct and lasts about six hours.

I see. Could you tell me how many flights are under two hours and how many over two hours in a given day?

– Sure. NAA makes 50 flights daily.

Okay. So 40 of its flights are short and 10 of them are long.

– That's right.

Let's move on to the products it offers on its flights. Could you tell me what is complimentary, what is sold and what the markup is on the items that are sold?

– NAA offers complimentary soft drinks, bottled water, regular tea and regular decaf and caffeinated coffee on all its flights, regardless of duration or the time during which the flight takes place. On the early flights, NAA charges for specialty juices, bagels and breakfast rolls. Peanuts, chips and fruits are offered only on the two cross-country routes. Beer, wine and champagne are sold on every flight. There is a 50 percent markup on these items.

---

* Special thanks to Mukund Jain.

Now I would like to know something about NAA's fleet, clientele, occupancy rate and the average sales per flight. More specifically, are all planes the same size? What types of passengers are on these flights? What percentage of each flight is full? What type of passenger makes in-flight purchases? Are purchases more prevalent during particular flights and/or particular times?

– Okay. All good questions. All of NAA's planes are the same size — with a capacity of 200 passengers. Its clientele consists of business travelers usually looking to make a day trip. The average occupancy rate per flight is 95 percent. Because they are mostly business travelers on these flights, these are the passengers making in-flight purchases. The average number of sales per flight depends on the flight's time of day and the length of the flight. Sales on morning and early afternoon short flights average $50 per flight. Sales on the long and early flights average $100 per flight. On the other hand, sales on the shorter evening and night flights average $150 per flight, while the later, longer flights average sales of $200.

That helps. Could you tell me how much the average passenger spends?

– Of those who purchase an item, it's $5.

Of the 50 daily flights, how many are early flights and how many are late flights? How many of the early flights are long, and how many are short?

– That's an even split — 25 early and 25 late. In terms of long and short, 80 percent of the early flights are short, and 80 percent of the late flights are short.

All right. I'm going to summarize this information in a table.

	Early			Late			Totals	
	# of Sales	Sales/ Flight	# of Flights	# of Sales	Sales/ Flight	# of Flights	# of Flights	Sales
Short	10	$50	20	30	$150	20	40	$4,000
Long	20	$100	5	40	$200	5	10	$1,500
Totals	30		25	70		25	50	
Total Sales		$1,500			$4,000			$5,500

So, on a given day, NAA's in-flight sales total $5,500; and with a mark-up of 50 percent, that's a cost of $3,666 and $1,833 in profits.

– You're telling me something I already know. We're low on time. Could you move along?

Absolutely. What percentage of NAA's clientele are drinkers of special-blend coffee?

– We don't know.

Okay. With 95 percent occupancy, that makes 190 potential customers per flight. We'll look at the short, early flight first. Ten drinks are sold on each of these 20 flights. I'm going to assume that each of the drinks is purchased by a different passenger. Since these are early flights taken mostly by business travelers who are usually not too price sensitive, I'll suppose that only 10

percent of the remaining 180 passengers will purchase a JavaMoose product. I'm basing that assumption on a couple of facts. First, many passengers taking an early flight may want to take a nap on the flight rather than inject additional caffeine into their system. Second, for an appreciable number of customers, the complimentary coffee presently offered by the airline will satisfy their desire for caffeine. Third, several passengers might have already purchased a JavaMoose product at the terminal while waiting to board the aircraft. Thus, we can assume that 10 percent or 18 passengers, are potential customers on the short, early flights.

– Really? Let's move on.

The late, short flights will probably have an even lesser number of in-flight JavaMoose customers. I'm going to estimate this number at 5 percent of the passenger population not ordering a drink. Justifying this number are two similar facts. First, the sale of coffee generally declines as the day moves ahead. Substitute drinks such as sodas and bottled water contribute to this decline, as does a diminishing need to stay awake with less of a day remaining. Second, coffee is a drink that accompanies breakfast better than it accompanies lunch, an afternoon snack or dinner. Thus, 5 percent of 170 makes 8.5 potential passengers. To be conservative, let us say eight sales.

– Fascinating. Please continue.

In long, early flights, there are currently 30 sales of drinks per flight. That leaves 160 passengers, assuming that those purchasing specialty juices will not purchase coffee. Even though these flights are usually three times longer in duration, I am going to assume that still only 10 percent — rather than 30 percent — of the remaining passengers will purchase a JavaMoose coffee. The same reasons justify this number as the ones I mentioned for the short, early flight. First, a longer flight affords a longer opportunity to sleep. Also, the complimentary coffee provided on the plane is a satisfactory substitute for many. Additionally, the opportunity to drink multiple cups for free on a longer flight is attractive to avid coffee drinkers. So, 10 percent of 160 is 16 passengers.

– We're running out of time.

Sure. That leaves us with the late, long flights. With 40 drinks sold, that leaves 150 passengers who might purchase coffee. Once again, I'm going to estimate that 5 percent of the passenger population not ordering a drink will purchase coffee. Premium coffee is not a drink that one drinks later in the day, especially with the availability of substitute drinks that go better with an afternoon snack or dinner. Thus, the total number of passengers who might purchase some JavaMoose coffee is 5 percent of 150; that is 7.5 or seven to be conservative.

The table below presents a summary of what we've discussed.

	Early			Late		
	# Sales/ Flight	# of Flights	Total # of Sales	# Sales/ Flight	# of Flights	Total # of Sales
Short	18	20	360	8	20	160
Long	16	5	80	7	5	35
Total	34	25	440	15	25	195
Total Sales			635			

Thus, the total number of cups of JavaMoose coffee that might be sold on a given day is 635.

– So, what do you think?

Well, there are a few concerns to selling JavaMoose coffee. First, JavaMoose might object, as this could cannibalize its sales at the terminal. This is a particularly serious concern to JavaMoose since customers who purchase coffee might also purchase something to eat. Second, serving JavaMoose coffee might require special preparation that could raise costs for both parties, particularly if we serve several varieties. Third, storing an additional beverage in an already space-constrained aircraft would be very difficult. Fourth, there is the risk of damaging the JavaMoose brand, a serious risk given JavaMoose's position as the market leader.

– You seem to be looking at this from the JavaMoose point of view, not our client's. So should NAA approach JavaMoose with this opportunity?

I think NAA can pilot this coffee on some of the earlier flights — long and short. To push adoption, they can halt serving the complimentary coffee and offer JavaMoose. Or, they can simply halt the complimentary coffee and charge for the JavaMoose, but that might upset the coffee drinkers looking forward to a free cup of joe. As far as preparation of JavaMoose is concerned, JavaMoose could help out by providing — pre-made — one or two varieties of their more popular flavors that would require minimal work on the part of the flight attendants. Looking at the table, if NAA were to charge $3 for a cup of coffee, they would raise revenues of $3 times 635 or $1,905 on a given day. I assume JavaMoose would also get an appreciable piece of this pie, which would further reduce NAA's intake.

Thus, my recommendation is for NAA not to pursue this opportunity.

– Are you at all concerned about what the competition does? Whether other airlines sell JavaMoose or Starbucks coffee on their flights?

I was going to get to that, but we ran out of time.

– What about the fact that for every cup of JavaMoose we sell, not only do we make a profit on the cup of coffee, but we save some money on the complimentary drink we were going to give them for free. Did that positive cannibalism ever cross your mind?

No, but it's a good point.

– Did you think about whether customers would switch to NAA because we now serve JavaMoose on all flights? It could raise our occupancy rate up a percentage point. That's worth much more than the profit we'd make.

No.

– Did you consider the option of serving JavaMoose for free on all flights?

Given time...

– Did you think about how our competition would respond to our serving or not serving JavaMoose on board our flights?

That would be an interesting analysis.

– It's clear to me that you are unfamiliar with the business traveler market. And I have my doubts whether you'll be familiar with it after graduation. Business traveler purchases are notoriously price inelastic because, for one, these are ends-oriented busy people who cannot be bothered with a price differential under $5. And, two, they are generally not paying for the coffee out of their own pockets — their companies are. As such, I can't imagine anyone who would hesitate before selecting the JavaMoose coffee over airline coffee.

And what about the "wake-up" coffee — for people who rack out on the red eye? Don't you think the percentage that would purchase a "wake-up" coffee is relatively high? In addition, when I travel cross country, I just work or sleep; as does everyone around me. I can't remember more than 10 percent of my flights being 95 percent full. And, finally, you paid zero attention to time zones and jet lag. Caffeine balance is extremely familiar to business travelers.

How do you expect me to move you on to the next round when you missed so many key points?

You told me to focus on profits and, given the time constraints, I think I did a good job at looking at the economics of the situation. I asked a lot of good and relevant questions — did I not?

– Yes, you did.

My quant skills were strong. I did most of the math in my head. I made easy-to-read charts and walked you through my thinking. I'm proud of my answer. Sure, I could have looked at those other things, but I needed to prioritize, given the time constraints. Now, I'll be happy to work out a model to determine whether it makes more sense to give the JavaMoose coffee away if it will boost our occupancy by 1 or 2 percent. I can also look at the effects of a joint marketing program as well as investigate other options such as Starbucks. And I'll be happy to do a competitive analysis within our region as well as other regions of the country.

– No, that won't be necessary. You did do a decent job. I wanted to see if you could handle criticism. And you did a good job of that as well.

Type of case: New product and increasing sales – not a very good fit for either one

Comments: The student did do a good job with the economics of the case. And she defended herself without being defensive. This is an important point to remember. Sometimes the interviewer will bust your chops just to see if you can defend yourself without getting bent out of shape. Roll with the punches and don't take it personally. They're doing their job to see if you do yours.

Texas Star Markets

Case 17: Our client is a large grocery chain throughout Texas. Their stores are concentrated in suburbs outside all the major cities in Texas: Dallas, Arlington, Fort Worth, Houston, Austin, Galveston, San Antonio, Amarillo, Corpus Christi, El Paso and Padre Island. They are looking to grow the company — but only in Texas. They feel that they have saturated the grocery market in the suburbs and have dismissed the idea of opening up stores downtown.

They already have an online grocery ordering and delivery service, so they are thinking of entering into the convenience store business. Is this a good idea? If so, how best to enter the market?

Basically, a large Texas-based grocery chain wants to explore the possibility of entering the convenience market. We need to determine if this is a good idea and, if it is, how best to enter this new market.

– That's right.

Besides the ones stated above, are there any other objectives I should be aware of?

– No.

Talking in broad strokes, I'd like to figure out why the company wants to expand, and what the current convenience store market is like and then discuss ways to enter that market. Does that sound like a good idea?

– Possibly. I wouldn't have done it like that, but let's see how you make out.

I assume the reason or reasons Texas Star is entertaining this notion are: A) They have excess cash on hand and want to see if this is a better return on investment than a money market or other investments they've looked at; B) They want to increase their market share of the Texas in-store food business; C) There has been a decline in their existing business, maybe because of shrinking sales or higher costs; and/or or D) They see this as a growing market.

– Assumptions A, B and D are correct.

May I take a moment to jot a few ideas down?

– Sure.

The student takes a moment to draw a decision tree.

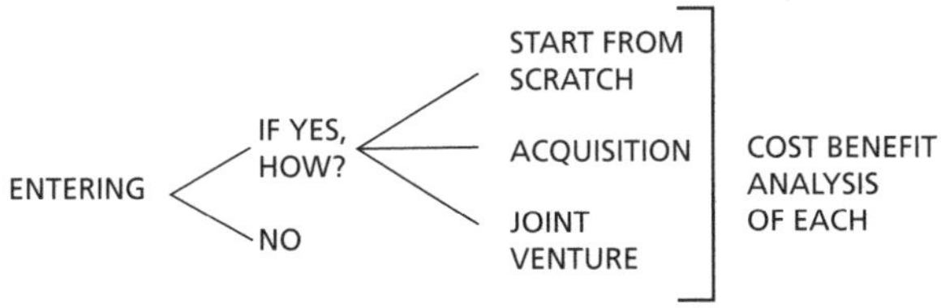

I know that there's plenty of competition with 7-Eleven, Christy's FoodMart, Dairy Mart, White Hen Pantry, Red Apple, and U-Tote Em, just to name a few. Can you give me any market share information?

– I can tell you that the leader is 7-Eleven and that they did over $3 billion in sales last year. That includes both in-store merchandise and gasoline sales, but I don't know what their market share is.

Do you know how many stores they have?

– Over 58,000 in the US and Canada. But I don't think that's relevant.

You're right. The proper question should have been how many of those stores are in Texas and how many convenience stores are there in Texas?

– That's right, but I don't have that information either.

I can't think of any barriers to entry, so I'll assume that's not a concern.

– What are the concerns?

While our grocery stores have name recognition, we need to figure out a way to capitalize on that and any other competitive advantage we might have. A convenience store is a convenience store. We'll probably be selling the same items as the 7-Eleven around the corner. Why would people come to us? I can think of three reasons: location, price or loyalty to the grocery chain.

– Okay, I like that. Explore it some more.

Well, the first one was location. Which leads me to the next question. How do we plan to enter the market? We can start from scratch, buy our way in or do a strategic alliance.

– Texas Star doesn't want to do a strategic alliance.

I'd like to come back and visit this question in a minute. However, we would need to look at the real estate market and see what kinds of locations are available. We may want to see if there is a small chain of existing stores with good locations but poor management that we could take over.

– What else?

Next on the list is price. This is where I think we make our mark. People pay for convenience. Prices are high because costs are high, because stores tend to buy many items in low volumes.

One of our advantages is that we already buy large amounts of all the products we would sell in the store, so we have economies of scale working for us. We should be able to leverage our current value chain components.

– What does that mean?

To be honest, I'm not sure.

– Let's call a time out for a second. Never use jargon or phrases that you don't understand. If you do it in an interview, then I'll assume that you will do it in front of a client. It's easy for the interviewer to lose trust in a candidate, because I can't trust you in front of a client. Now it just so happens that I like you and that you are doing really well on the question, so I'm going to pretend that I didn't hear that. Continue. Where were we?

We were discussing price. If we can price our items somewhere between what we charge in our grocery stores and what our competitors charge in their convenience stores, we could drive in traffic. For instance, if I buy a gallon of milk at the grocery store, it costs me $2.95. If I buy that same product in a convenience store, it costs me $3.95, a dollar more. If we could price it at $3.49, that's a significant enough difference where it would drive people into the store. In addition, I'm assuming that Texas Star, like most large grocery stores, has store-label items, such as their own brand of peanut butter. Those items sell for significantly less than the traditional name brands, so the price difference would be even greater. We could offer all the traditional convenience store items while adding things like a salad bar and prepared gourmet meals. This could change the genetic code of convenience store retailing.

– Let's not get carried away.

Let's look at the company's resources and capabilities. We buy in large volume; we have the management team, the marketing team, trained workers, name recognition; and we have an untraditional marketing channel through our existing stores. I don't think that there would be any cannibalization of existing grocery store sales, because items would still be less expensive in the grocery store. In fact, we could cross market and offer coupons to try our convenience stores.

The last thing on my list was brand loyalty. Texas Star obviously has a strong following, a commitment to Texas and, I'm guessing, to local communities.

– All right, summarize for me.

Texas Star is looking to expand. Their idea of getting into the convenience store market is a viable one. This market will continue to grow and there are no major barriers to entry. It will allow Texas Star to build on their name recognition and take advantage of the organization's existing resources and capabilities. They can offer lower prices and store-brand items, cross market with their grocery stores and offer new items to traditional convenience store fare.

The best way to enter the market is to look for a small chain that has good locations but bad management. Buy the chain, change the name and bring in your own management. All stores

should be in close proximity to a Texas Star grocery store. If the company can't find a buy-out target, they should start from scratch.

And I just want to restate that it is a combination of name recognition, location and prices that will make this idea a success.

– Okay, that was pretty good. Now you got me thinking. Texas Star, as you can tell, is always looking for new ways to increase their revenue streams. They are also considering opening an in-store bank. No other competitors in their area are currently doing it. What do we need to be thinking about?

Again, they are entering a new market. There are a number of things that they need to figure and decide. First, do they have the space in their stores, or will they have to construct additional space? Also, if they do have the space, we need to think about whether that space can be used more effectively. How much space is needed?

– It's the equivalent of a florist department, and we already have one of those. And yes, we do have the space for this. It would take some remodeling, but nothing significant.

We need to look at who the major players are, what size market share they have, whether our products or services will be any different from our competition's and if there are any barriers to entry.

– What would you guess?

That there's plenty of competition and that our products or services might be basic compared to our competitors'. All we really have to offer them is convenience. Hopefully, there will be increased traffic at the grocery stores due to the bank. But now, with ATMs, debit cards and cash back, the basic services are easily covered. I'm thinking that we need to figure out how best to enter the market and determine if this makes sense.

There are three ways to enter the market: start from scratch, buy our way in and pursue a joint venture. What are the costs in each of theses options? What are the potential revenue streams and how do they differ? And what is the risk associated with each?

– Do a quick cost-benefit analysis for each.

Starting from scratch will be time consuming and somewhat expensive. We'd have to hire new people with experience in banking to run the organization. There might be some barriers due to federal and state banking regulations, which might take some additional time. And if it fails or doesn't live up to expectations, it could damage the overall Texas Star brand. On the other hand, we already have locations and our rent would be minimal. Revenues would come from bank transactions and, possibly, increased grocery sales. However, I'm not convinced that this is the best way.

Buying our way in would mean buying an existing bank and taking over its business. We would already have the people in place, a number of existing locations and some brand recognition. It might be expensive. We would have to do due diligence on the entire bank and the banking industry. We might be able to sell some of the branches to other banks to help reduce any debt we would incur. This would be really jumping in with both feet.

The third way would be a joint venture with an existing bank. I think this is the simplest solution and holds the least risk to profits and our brand. We would just lease space to the bank for a monthly fee. We would have to weigh the rental income against the remodeling costs.

– So, what are you saying?

I would tell Texas Market that if they feel that having a bank branch in their grocery stores would result in increased traffic and maybe higher sales, they should form a joint venture with an existing bank and keep risk to a minimum and lease out the space. Starting from scratch or buying an existing player is expensive and risky. We currently know nothing about the industry and a failure could hurt the Texas Star brand.

- **Type of Case: Entering a new market**

- **Comments: Besides getting into trouble for using business jargon that he did not know, the interviewee did pretty well. He laid out his strategy up front and stuck to it, but also added ways that the client could differentiate itself from the competition. He seemed to roll into the banking part of the case with a little more confidence.**

✢ Red Rocket Sports

Case 18: The Red Rocket Sports Company designs and markets apparel and footwear products under many brand names. All products are generally produced using similar manufacturing processes. Additionally, these products share similar distribution channels and are marketed and sold to a similar type of customer.

Take a look at the numbers below and tell me what's going on with Red Rocket Sports and where they should be concentrating their efforts. I'll be back in 30 minutes for your analysis.

Net Sales	Y3	Y2	Y1
Footwear	$2,430,300	$2,226,700	$2,050,000
Apparel	$1,355,000	$1,258,600	$1,050,000
Total	$3,785,300	$3,485,300	$3,100,000

Net Sales	Y3	Y2	Y1
US	$2,070,060	$2,020,000	$1,807,650
UK	$ 474,700	$ 444,700	$ 415,800
Europe	$ 810,400	$ 695,500	$ 607,400
Other	$ 430,140	$ 325,100	$ 269,150
Total	$3,785,300	$3,485,300	$3,100,000

(TAKE 30 MINUTES TO DO YOUR ANALYSIS; THEN READ ON)

Red Rocket Sports Answer:

After 30 minutes the interviewer comes back into the room and the candidate presents his findings to the interviewer.

– Take me through your analysis.

The first thing we need to look at is the yearly percentage changes by type of product and by area. *Pulls out handmade chart.* These numbers are eyeballed but should be pretty accurate.

		Y2/Y3	Y1/Y2
PRODUCT	Footwear	10%	10%
	Apparel	10%	20%
MARKET	US	2%	12%
	UK	7%	7%
	Europe	15%	15%
	Other	30%	20%

There are a number of things we can infer from this chart:

- Footwear has grown consistently by about 10 percent over the last two years.
- Apparel growth has slowed, from 20 percent in Y1/Y2 to just under 10 percent in Y2/Y3.
- The US market has had dramatic declining growth — from 12 percent to 2 percent, although it is still, by far, our biggest market.
- The UK growth has remained steady, at approximately 7 percent.
- The same is true for the European market, with a consistent growth rate of 15 percent.
- The most promising markets are the "other" markets, which I'll assume are Asia and Latin America. They grew by around 20 percent in Y2 and by just over 30 percent in Y3. At this rate, they will bypass the UK in total sales by next year. I believe that the "other" markets represent the highest area of potential growth.
- The action is in apparel, despite the slowdown in Y2/Y3.

Next, I looked at what part of the business each product line and market represents.

		Y3	Y2	Y1
PRODUCT	Footwear	65%	65%	65%
	Apparel	35%	35%	35%
MARKET	US	55%	60%	60%
	UK	12%	12%	15%
	Europe	20%	20%	20%
	Other	11%	8%	8%

What this chart tells us is:

- Footwear represents two-thirds of our sales and has remained as such over the last few years.
- The US is, by far, our biggest market, making up more than half of our sales, but that number is inching down.
- The UK has inched down as well — going from 15 percent to 12 percent.
- Europe has hung in at 20 percent.
- The "other" markets have inched up, now representing 11 percent of sales.

Our traditional markets in the US and UK are mature, while the "other" markets have the highest growth rate. However, the traditional markets still represent the bulk of our business — over two-thirds of sales. And apparel sales have driven the growth rates over the last two years despite the slowdown in Y3.

– How can you say that? Why do you have so much confidence in apparel?

You need to look past the percentages and concentrate on the numbers themselves. Sales went from $3,100,000 in Y1 to $3,785,300 in Y3. That's an increase of $685,300. Of that number, apparel accounted for almost half, despite representing only 35 percent of sales.

– Okay, so what should Red Rocket do about this?

Action 1: Concentrate efforts on growth areas, particularly in "other" markets:
- **Increase the product line, particularly in apparel.**
- **Increase distribution channels.**
- **Reinforce the sales force.**
- **Launch a major marketing campaign.**

Action 2: Secure our traditional markets to maintain business:
- **Launch marketing campaigns to boost sales in mature markets.**
- **Focus on best-performing distribution points and best-performing stores.**

Action 3: Investigate market trends to anticipate future changes:
- **Talk to industry analysts and get their opinion of the trends.**
- **Elaborate our strategy of product/market effort, based on info from experts.**

It's easy to graph these recommendations in a 2x2 matrix.

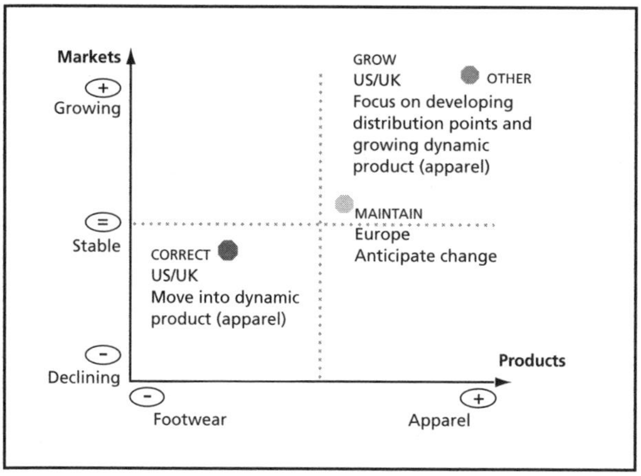

Type of Case: Company analysis

Comments: The student used charts and bullet points to make her presentation. She eyeballed the numbers because of the time constraint and the absence of a calculator. Remember, consultants use charts, graphs and PowerPoint® slides to get their point across with clients — you need to do to the same.

+ The Up-in-Smoke Cigarette Company

Case 19: The Up-in-Smoke Cigarette Company, which manufactures cigarettes, is considering outsourcing its distribution truck fleet to an independent company. To continue providing this service in-house, they would have to significantly upgrade their fleet due to new regulations requiring commercial trucks to provide electronic records of their itineraries — including average and maximum speed, time driven continuously and the length of driver breaks.

The chief operating officer (COO) has hired you to help her decide: Should they outsource, or upgrade the fleet and continue to do distribution in-house?

Our client is a cigarette company that is trying to decide whether to outsource its delivery function. They've asked us to determine whether it is best to outsource the work or keep it in-house. Are there any other objectives we need to focus on?

– No. Do you have a problem with having a cigarette company as your client?

It wouldn't be my first choice, but no.

– We don't always get to pick our clients. If this is going to be a problem, then tell me now.

It's not a problem.

– Okay, then proceed.

To help the COO decide, I will consider two main factors: the economics of such a move and associated risks.

Under the economic factors, I will compare the needed investments in the truck upgrade with the potential costs or savings from outsourcing.

Under the risks, I will look at both the internal and external risks. Internally, I will look at the cultural impact and impacts on labor — like the potential of a strike. Externally, I will look at the bigger macroeconomic risks — cost of gasoline, government regulations and future flexibility vs. competition.

– Okay, good. Where would you want to start?

I would like to start with the economics of the problem. I would like to figure out the costs for both outsourcing and keeping it in-house. Also, I would like to know the estimated investments and the company's required payback period.

– It would cost the company about $1 million to upgrade its fleet, including trade-ins on the old trucks. Essentially, it would have to buy new trucks, as the current trucks are old and the COO figures they are due for replacement soon anyway. The company requires a four-year payback on all its investments.

– For a detailed table on the costs associated with both in-house deliveries and outsourcing, please take a look at the following table.

	In-house	Outsource
# of Deliveries	400	400
Average Cost of Delivery	?	$2,400
Labor Costs	?	N/A
Insurance	$200	$100
Gas	$200	N/A
Maintenance (per Delivery) (Includes oil change, tires, etc.)	$100	N/A
Cost per Delivery	?	?

In order to determine the difference between outsourcing and in-house deliveries, I need to determine the labor cost per delivery. Can you tell me more about labor costs? How many full-time drivers do we have and how much do we pay them on average?

– We have 10 full-time drivers that we employ for $5,000 per month, including benefits.

Great. That means the salary costs are 10 drivers times 12 months times $5,000 per month, which is $600,000 per year. We divide $600,000 by 400 and we now know that the labor cost per delivery is $1,500. When we add the additional costs, we have the total in-house cost per delivery of $2,000. In the case of outsourcing, the total cost is $2,500.

Overall, our client would save $500 per delivery or $500 times 400 deliveries, which equals $200,000 per year; with in-house distribution.

However, when we compare that with the required investment of $1 million dollars, we get a payback of five years, which is longer than the required payback of our client.

– How'd you get five years?

I divided 1 million by 200,000 and got five.

– Okay, good. What's your final recommendation?

Just looking at the economics of the move, I would recommend outsourcing the delivery to the independent company. However, I would like to analyze some of the risks involved.

As I mentioned initially, the internal risks are worth analyzing. For example, I would like to analyze the potential impacts of this move to our internal culture — we'd be firing 10 drivers. Also, I would like to assess the potential for a strike should we decide to outsource this service.

– Those are good points, but our drivers are not unionized and we estimate the culture will not change significantly. Can you think of anything else?

Yes, actually. Looking at external factors, I can see some benefits in outsourcing. By outsourcing — especially if we sign longer-term contracts — we externalize the risk for the increase in the price of gas and the change in government regulations. These are important risks to a company like ours and are significant benefits to our company. Additionally, outsourcing would maintain the flexibility of our distribution in the event our company expands.

– Great answer. Now let's change hats and try to figure out how to make the in-house deliveries work. What would be some of your suggestions?

Well, we have a few variables. For the in-house deliveries to work, we would have to have:

Investment < savings from In-house times payback period.

Therefore, we could do several things.

1. **We could lower the needed investment. We could do this by leasing or renting the trucks instead of buying them.**
2. **We could increase the payback period beyond four years.**
3. **We could increase savings from in-house deliveries. Here, we have several options as well:**
   a. **We could increase the number of deliveries, either for our company or for smaller companies, in order to increase the utilization of our drivers.**
   b. **We could reduce maintenance costs by outsourcing that job alone.**
   c. **We could introduce new software to determine more efficient routing for our trucks, thus saving us gas and maintenance.**

– Excellent. Thank you.

Type of case: Reducing costs, in-sourcing vs. outsourcing

Comments: You're not always going to get the clients you want, and you need to think this through. Many consulting firms will try to reassign you if you have a legitimate reason for not wanting to be on the case, but they can't always control it because it has to do with scheduling. The student did well. He analyzed the simple chart and was able to fill in the blanks. He looked at both external and internal factors and came up with good recommendations on both sides of the issue.

✛ Cabana Feet

Case 20: Cabana Feet, LLC makes gel-flow flip-flops. These are like traditional flip-flops but have the comfort of a gel insole. They come in a variety of sizes and colors. Earlier this year, Brad Pitt wore them in his latest film; and they have become all the rage. Now, Cabana Feet is struggling to keep up with demand. Cabana Feet is the only flip-flop maker producing its footwear entirely in the US. This has been a selling point in their advertisements for the last 10 years. Thus, it can't outsource production to other flip-flop makers. Take a look at the chart below and lay out for me in broad strokes some short-term and long-term strategies that it might review.

Our client is a company called Cabana Feet. They make gel-flow flip-flops. It looks like the company was producing about 6,000 pairs a month. Demand suddenly shot up when Brad Pitt wore their flip-flops in a movie. Cabana can't outsource because they are the only flip-flop maker in the US; and a big part of their advertising rides on the fact that their product is American made.

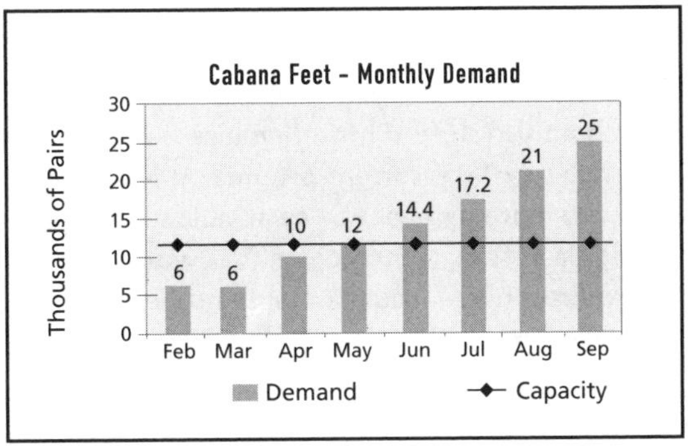

– That's right.

You want me to come up with some short-term and long-term strategies to help the company meet demand. Are there any other objectives I should be aware of?

– No.

Can I ask a few questions?

– Absolutely.

Judging by the chart, our capacity is 12,000 pairs of flip-flops a month.

– Yes.

I'm assuming that the movie came out in April.

– Yes.

What month are we in now?

– Early September.

So the 25,000 number is an estimate?

– That's right.

Have we been able to fill the orders up until now, or are there thousands of pairs back-ordered?

– We've been able to fill the orders because of inventory; however, we'll run out of inventory at the end of the month.

Do we expect the trend to continue? When does the DVD come out?

– The DVD comes out in December. What are your thoughts on the trend?

I would expect the trend to level off after the DVD's release. But our strategy must take into consideration two scenarios. First, what happens if Brad Pitt wears construction boots in his next movie and sales fall back to the 6,000 pairs-a-month number? And what can we do if it levels off at around 25,000 pairs?

– Okay, good. What are you thinking? How can we meet demand?

I have a couple of ideas. First, we put on more shifts if we haven't already. Ask employees if they want to work weekends and a third shift. If not, then hire new employees for those shifts. Second, I'd do a complete analysis of the current production line. See if there are any bottlenecks. See how we can squeeze more pairs out of each shift without compromising quality. Third, look for labor-saving devices or technologies that would boost production without committing to another production line. Fourth, build another production line or even another factory. Fifth, Econ 101 — raise our prices. And, sixth, outsource production.

– There is no one inside the US that can help us. So the only option is to go outside the US.

Then go outside the US.

– And throw away our marketing campaign of the last 10 years? We'd get crucified in the press.

Not if we go to the business press and argue that this is a temporary measure, that for us to meet demand we need to go outside the US. Once we can meet demand with US manufacturing; then we'll bring everything back home. Look, our sales jumped from 6,000 pairs a month to 25,000 pairs a month. Assume that 5,000 out of the original 6,000 customers bought our shoes because they were made in the US. I think that number is high, but let's assume it to be true. That means that we have 20,000 new customers who are more interested in looking like Brad Pitt from the ankles down than whether the flip-flops are made in the US.

We can't miss this opportunity. If we don't get those flip-flops on to the market, someone else will. We have to worry about knock-offs and new competition.

– All right. By what percentage did the company's demand grow from March to April?

It went from 6,000 pairs to 10,000 pairs. That's 10 – 6 = 4 4/6 = .66 or 66 percent.

– I'm going to give you some additional information. At the plant, workers make $15 an hour. Supervisors make $20 an hour. Each shift uses 10 workers and one supervisor. Each shift is eight hours long. Assume 20 work days in a month. Got it?

Got it.

– What would be the labor costs of one shift if benefits equal 30 percent of wages and there is a miscellaneous cost of $232 per shift?

Workers' wages, $15 an hour; times eight hours times 10 workers equals $1,200. The supervisor costs are $160. I got that by multiplying $20 by eight hours. Total wages are $1,360 times 30 percent equals...408. So $1,360 plus $408 equals $1,768, plus the miscellaneous cost of $232, equals $2,000 per shift.

– Good. Now assume that the total costs per shift, fixed and variable, equal $2,000. Cabana makes $8 a pair; up to production capacity. What is the shift break-even point? How many pairs of flip-flops does the company have to make each shift to break even?

That would be $2,000 divided by $8 equals...250 pairs of flip-flops.

– Capacity is 12,000 pairs of flip-flops a month. Capacity equals two shifts a day, five days a week. Given a normal eight-hour shift, what is the maximum production per shift?

For a single shift?

– Yes, a single shift. I want you to think out loud when you do the math.

Okay. I'll take 12,000 pairs and divide that by two shifts. So each shift makes 6,000 pairs per month. Next I'll divide the 6,000 pairs by 20 work days in the month and I'll get 300 pairs of flip-flops per shift.

– How much would a third shift increase our capacity?

It would increase it by 6,000 pairs and push it from 12,000 to 18,000.

– If we started a third shift using our current employees, what would be the cost of the third shift? How much would our profits per pair of flip-flops change? Keep in mind that wages would go to time-and-a-half. And you'll need to add in the miscellaneous cost as well.

Workers' wages at time and a half would jump to...$1,800 ($22.50 x 10 x 8) and the supervisor's costs would be $240 (30 x 8). That totals to $2,040. Multiply 2,040 by 30 percent for bene-

fits and that equals...$612, so that's $2,652 plus the miscellaneous $232. So the total is $2,884. So $2,884 minus $2,000 equals $892 in additional costs. Divide the $892 by 300 pairs and it equals...$2.97. Thus we have $8 minus $2.97 equals $5.03 per pair.

– What are some of the pros and cons of adding a triple shift using our current workers?

Can I take a minute to think this through?

– Sure.

The student draws a line down the center of his page. He writes out the pros and cons and presents them in bulk — all the pros first, then all the cons.

Pros	Cons
Able to meet demand up to 18,000 pairs without major new investment	Possible worker burnout
More total profits	Lowers profit per pair
Helps keep competitors out	Higher wear and tear on the machinery
Saves on hiring and training costs of new employees	Might lower quality of product; may have to throw out some pairs
Easy to get back to normal production levels	Less time for maintenance
Better utilization of equipment	Suppliers might not be able to meet our demand

– By adding a third shift we'll only be able to produce 18,000 pairs a month. You said earlier that you thought demand would level out at 25,000 pairs. If we add a new line that produces 800 pairs a day, this includes two shifts; is this enough?

Well, 800 pairs a day equals 16,000 pairs a month, given 20 workdays in a month. Add to that the current capacity of 12,000 pairs and we total 28,000 pairs a month. If demand is greater than that, we can go as high as 42,000 pairs if we put on triple shifts on the new line and the old line.

– Summarize the case for me.

Our client, Cabana Feet, has seen demand for its flip-flops skyrocket from 6,000 pairs a month to 25,000 pairs within a six-month period. While we'll assume that demand might continue to grow for a few more months, we're thinking that it will settle down at around 25,000 pairs a month. Current capacity is only 12,000 pairs a month. We've been able to meet demand because of inventory on hand; however, the inventory is now down to nothing. We came up with six short-term and long-term strategies to fix the problem. The main ones are putting on more shifts, streamlining our production process and outsourcing production to another manufacturer outside the US.

We learned that our break-even point is 250 flip-flops per shift and that our capacity is 300 pairs per shift. We talked about the pros and cons of putting on a third shift, including watching our profit per pair drop from $8 to about $5 a pair. And finally, we are considering adding a new line, which could increase our overall production to 42,000 pairs a month. That's a 250 percent increase over our current double shift capacity.

– Good. Thanks for coming by.

◗ **Type of case: Production and strategy case**

◗ **Comments: The student did very well. He was quick to come up with some long-term and short-term strategies. He held his own when the interviewer pushed him about the outsourcing question. His math skills were solid and he tried to quantify his answer when he could.**

+ Partner Cases

Partner cases are cases that you can do with your friends, regardless of whether they know how to give a case. There are five easy Level 1 cases, five medium Level 2 cases and five hard Level 3 cases. Your partner first needs to read the Roommate's Guide found on the next page and then read the case all the way through, twice. The case gives your partner plenty of advice and information to make it easy and fun to grill you.

For some of the cases there are charts in the back of the book (see Partner Case Charts, starting on page 221), that need to be photocopied beforehand; if you can't photocopy, then some of the charts can be hand-drawn in a few minutes' time.

There is flexibility built into these answers and, as usual, there is usually no one right answer. Have fun with these. After you have answered the case, turn around and give it to another friend. You learn just as much giving a case as you do answering one. The average student serious about a career in consulting will do at least 30 "live" cases. Nothing beats live case practice.

+ Partner Cases

+ The Roommate's Guide

If you have been begged, bribed or blackmailed into helping your friend(s) prepare for case questions, here are some suggestions.

Your prep

- Read the question and answer all the way through before giving the case.
- Be aware that there are multiple "right" answers.
- It's all right to give them help if they lose their way.
- Don't cop a know-it-all attitude.

Things to watch for at the beginning

- Are they writing down the case information?
- Is there a long silence between the end of the question and the beginning of their answer?
- Are they summarizing the question?
- Are they asking about the client's objective(s)?
- Are they asking clarifying questions about the company, the industry, the competition and the product?
- Are they laying out a logical structure for their answer?

Things to watch and listen for during the course of the question

- Are they enthusiastic and do they project a positive attitude?
- Listen for the logic of their answer. Is it making good business sense?
- Is their answer well organized?
- Are they stating their assumptions clearly?
- Are they being creative?
- Are they engaging, bringing you into the question and turning the case into a conversation?
- Are they asking probing questions?
- Are they quantifying their answer?
- Are they asking for help or guidance?

Review list

- Was their answer well organized? Did they manage their time well?
- Did they get bogged down in details?
- Did they seem to go off on a tangent?
- Did they ask probing questions?
- Did they use business terms and buzzwords correctly?
- Did they have trouble with math, multiplication and percentage calculation?
- Did they try to get you to answer the question for them?
- Were they coachable? Did they pick up on your hints?
- Did they speak without thinking?
- Did they have a positive attitude?
- Did they summarize their answer?

Final analysis

- Did they take your criticism well?
- Did they defend themselves without sounding defensive?

Aftermath

- Go out on the town.

+ Grupo Modelo

Problem Statement

Grupo Modelo® is the leader in Mexican beer production, distribution and marketing, with 64 percent worldwide Mexican beer market share. Currently, it brews and distributes 13 brands, including Corona Extra®, the number one Mexican beer in the world. Grupo Modelo is thinking of taking advantage of its Corona brand by starting a high-end Mexican food company focusing on shelf-stable and frozen food for supermarkets in the US. Is this a good idea?

Guidance for the Interviewer

The student should repeat the question to make sure everyone is on the same page, and she should verify the objective (expanding the brand). The student should also ask if there are any other objectives she needs to be concerned with — in this case the answer is yes, profits.

Data Bank

The student should lay out her structure in these buckets.

- Industry characteristics: major players, market share, product differentiation, barriers to entry
- Industry size and performance: growing, shrinking, size of margins
- Industry future: new players entering, players leaving or merging
- Customers: Hispanics vs. yuppies: What are Corona's demographics?
- Financial state of Grupo Modelo: Does it have the money to invest?

The US market for shelf-stable, frozen and refrigerated Mexican food is $2.4 billion. It's a fragmented market, with specific companies focusing on niche items, such as Amy's Kitchen, Goya Foods , Ortega and Las Campanas. Other threats include local players and private brands.

Ask: Last year, the market grew by 6 percent. What were the industry revenues the prior year? ($2.4/1.06) = $2.26 billion or $2.3 billion.

Ask: Come up with three pros and three cons of this idea. The student might come up with other pros and cons, which is fine; this is just a guideline.

PROS	CONS
Strong brand recognition	Not their core business
Established marketing department	Big investment
Synergies with shipping	Risking brand

Ask: What's the best way to enter this market? What are the advantages and disadvantages? Have the student pick one and elaborate.

License name / joint venture

+ less risk	- less control of product and brand reputation
+ less financial investment	- less percentage of the profits

Buy an existing player

+ management and distribution channels in place
+ instant market share

- big investment
- big risk

Start from scratch by producing it ourselves

+ more control over costs and quality
+ more ownership

- huge investment (plant, workers, trucks)
- longer time to market (need to establish distribution channels, build plant, etc.

Tell the student that the company has decided to start from scratch, but wants to know where to build the factory (US or Mexico?) and how to roll this product out.

A US plant: Advantages are higher perceived quality and easier distribution. Disadvantages are higher costs (wages, construction, energy) and backlash about job loss in Mexico.

A Mexican plant: Advantages are lower wages and construction costs, and good internal PR. Disadvantages include perceived lower quality and major distribution issues; such as border crossings, drug-war violence and empty trucks returning to Mexico.

Product roll-out: Start small and mirror Corona sales and cross market with the beer.

Special note: Instead of a summary, ask the student whether she would recommend moving forward with this project. Whether she thinks the company should choose to move forward or not doesn't matter as long as she can articulate her decision.

Did the interviewee...

A good interview consists of:

Repeating the question, verifying the objective and asking about other objectives

- Making no math mistakes
- Stating fair assumptions
- Keeping well-organized and easy-to-read notes
- Developing well-articulated recommendations

Mark of a good discussion. Because there is little math, this case should be more of a discussion touching on all the key issues. I'm interested in what goes through the student's mind, and in what order, when she receives this problem.

+ Test Prep

Problem Statement

Your client is one of the leading test prep firms in America. It's seen increased revenues but decreased profitability and market share. They're hoping you can figure out why and make recommendations what they should do.

Guidance for the Interviewer

The student should repeat the question to make sure everyone is on the same page, and he should verify the objective (determining why profitability and market share are decreasing). He should also ask if there are any other objectives he needs to be concerned with — in this case the answer is no other objectives.

This is a case where the interviewee needs to get a better understanding of what factors can drive a countercyclical or economically-insulated business model.

Data Bank

A good structure for this case would be to assess behavior in the market (trends and competition), then identify drivers of revenue and costs. E(P=R-C)M is the structure the student should use. E equals the economy; tell him we are in the tail-end of a recession. When he asks about the market (M), hand him Chart 1 and ask him to do a quick analysis.

Number of US students getting tutoring assistance (millions)

	Students	Industry Revenue		
Y1	3	$1,210		
Y2	4	$1,375		
Y3	5.5	$1,595		

The student should first identify that the market has done quite well in the face of the economic downturn, as educational opportunities have become increasingly important and competitive. He should then quantify the growth: the fact that the number of students grew by 83 percent from Y1 to Y3 (5.5 – 3 = 2.5 / 3 = .83) and industry revenues grew by around 32 percent (1,595 – 1,210 = 385 / 1,210 = .318) in that same period. However, revenue per student dropped significantly from $403 to $290, a 28 percent drop: 209 – 403 = -113 / 403 = -28%)

Next, the student should ask about our competitors. By asking about our competitors, he can be provided with the profitability charts shown on the next page. They will paint the picture that while our firm's profitability is increasing, this is happening at a lesser clip than for our leading competitor, and at a far lesser clip than for the start-up entrant, Competitor Two.

Hand the student Chart 2.

Our Company			
	Revenues	Costs	Profits
Y1	500	450	50
Y2	550	495	55
Y3	600	540	60

Competitor One			
	Revenues	Costs	Profits
Y1	500	450	50
Y2	550	475	75
Y3	600	500	100

Competitor Two (start-up–3 yrs. ago)			
	Revenues	Costs	Profits
Y1	100	90	10
Y2	150	100	50
Y3	250	110	140

Guidance for the Interviewer

Give the student a minute to analyze the new data. He should assess revenue and cost drivers. If he doesn't, ask him what he thinks the revenue streams are. In analyzing the revenues, he should note that the revenue streams could be such sources as classes and tutoring, possibly also test-prep book or software sales. The split in that regard is not particularly relevant.

In analyzing costs, the interviewee should propose what potential sources of cost could exist. Major costs could include: development of teaching materials, fixed costs for test prep centers and variable costs to pay teachers. You can say you don't have access to the competition's numbers for cost of development, but there's no reason to believe they do it more cheaply than we do (at $50 million/year). Then he should brainstorm potential factors that could lead to disparate levels of fixed costs for test-prep centers and variable costs.

Once he tells you his thoughts on costs, tell him that in practice, the up-and-coming firm has virtually no costs for real estate. And our leading competitor has not shown an increase in its land holdings line item. **Additionally, the up-and-comer's wages equal 20 percent of its booked revenues. The lead competitor's wages equal 35 percent of booked revenues. Ours are half of booked revenues.**

Ask what are the takeaways: One big takeaway is that this business has not fully embraced outsourcing of tutoring work online, and thus does not generate the same economies of scale that online tutors can generate. In other words, this test prep company keeps opening up conventional brick and mortar stores and pays tutors (thus incurring consistent fixed and variable costs) whereas the other firms have been employing tutors across America and in India to tutor students online using their proprietary teaching materials. These online tutoring operations have a single, upfront fixed investment (web infrastructure and test materials) and smaller variable cost (cheaper tutors), with no costs of maintaining large amounts of real estate. They are achieving far better economies of scale and volume for their investment in test development. Thus, they can charge less for their service while making more profit per student.

Recommendations

A good interviewee should come up with recommendations for what can be done by the firm. Recommendations should include:

Exploring online tutoring by the firm's US tutors
Developing tutoring within India
Undermining the company's competitors' positions by:

- marketing the superiority of its products
- playing to the premium market

They could also consider a non-market strategy of aligning with teachers' unions, etc., who feel that Indian tutors aren't sufficiently equipped to teach to specific state accreditation standards.

Summary

The student needs to jump right into this without any down time to collect his thoughts. A good summary is about a minute, minute-and-a-half long. It is not a rehash of everything you spoke about; it is a short recap of the problem and two or three main points and recommendations that he wants the interviewer to remember.

Our client has seen increased profits but decreased profitability and market share as the market has grown over the last three years. A new start-up has gobbled up market share and has been growing at a faster clip than has our client. The start-up's percentage of costs is less than half of our costs because it has virtual offices and very low fixed costs. Some of our recommendations are to add an online service using lower-paid tutors from India while attacking the start-up as an inferior service.

Did the Interviewee...

- repeat the question, verifying the objective and asking about other objectives?
- analyze the numbers without being asked to, and with no math mistakes?
- keep well-organized and easy-to-read notes?
- develop a good short summary touching on the most critical points?

Mark of a Good Case Discussion: The student had to make a lot of assumptions about costs and a lot of fast calculations. I would look to see how quickly he came up with the fact that the new company has a virtual model and how our company should respond to that growing threat.

✢ Online Movies

Problem Statement

Last year Wal-Mart entered the online digital download-movie store market through the acquisition on of VuDu.com. They paid $100 million for it. So now consumers can download movies to rent or purchase on either Vudu.com or Walmart.com. I need you to find these four things.

1. Wal-Mart's online movie store revenues
2. The number of years for the acquisition payback
3. Wal-Mart's first year ROI
4. Should Wal-Mart keep the Vudu.com site?

Hand the student this chart.

US Digital Movie-Download Market Share By Downloads

	Market share	Δ in market share
Apple	65.8%	↑ 1%
Microsoft	16.2%	↓ 2%
Wal-Mart	5.3%	↑ 4.3%
Sony	4.47%	↓ 4%
Amazon	4.2%	↑ 2%

Data Bank

Movies rent for $5; movies sell for $15.

Wal-Mart's profit margins are 30 percent.

Sales are split between rentals and sales are 4 to 1.

Movies can be viewed on Playstation, Blu-Ray, HDTV, computers, tablets and smartphones and downloaded through Walmart.com and Vudu.com.

Movies can be viewed the same day they are released as DVDs.

Market-Sizing

There are a couple of ways to do this; the best is as a household problem. The key is to be able to follow the student's logic. Have him walked you through his thoughts. Watch out for broad assumptions and don't be afraid to ask him to justify an assumption if you feel it is too broad or that he skipped a step.

320 million Americans > 3.2 people per HH > 100 million US households

US HHs with Internet access > 60 percent.

From that group I'm going to subtract:

- people who don't download movies
- people who don't want to put their credit card on the Internet
- households with dial-up service
- some Netflix customers
- Direct TV or cable-streaming customers

\+ people w/o Internet who can download movies from Starbucks, or in school.

Taking all that into consideration; I'll assume 50 million HHs renting or buying movies through downloads. HHs with teenagers or road warriors might download more; but on average I'll assume they download a little less than 2 movies a month or 20 movies a year.

50 million HH downloading 20 movies a year = 1 billion downloads

Wal-Mart has 5 percent – 1b x .05 = 50 million downloads

4 to 1 spilt:
40 million rentals @ $5 = $200 million and 10 million buys @$15 = $150
Total $350 million in revenues

$350 million in revenues with 30 percent margins = 350 x .3 = 105 million
Cost of acquisition – $100 million
Payback: around 12 months, depending on cash flows

ROI
$105 in profits – $100 million price = $5 million 5/100 = 5 percent ROI

Should WM keep VuDu.com?

If Yes	If No
Added expense, steals ad dollars	Different customer base, if VuDu shuts down; many customers will go to Apple because WM's not hip
Maintains its 1% market share for a while.	VuDu demographics 17 – 35, hip. Early adaptors. They spend five times the money on the web than the average WM customer. WM demographics, families and low-to-middle income shoppers – just the name VuDu indicates that it is not family-friendly
No way to drive them to WM.com	Could lose as much as 1% of your market share

The key to this part of the case is demographics. If the student doesn't mention it, ask him what he thinks the demographics are for both sites. One option is to sell the name and the customer list to someone who has the higher demographics; that way the owner can help pay off the acquisition costs, reduce the payback period and increase their ROI.

Did the student draw up a final slide at the beginning of the case? It should look something like this.

Final Slide	
Revenues	$350m
Breakeven	1 year
ROI	5%
VuDu	sell

Summary

He needs to jump right into this without any down time to collect his thoughts. A good summary is about 30 seconds to a minute, possibly a minute-and-a-half long at the most. It is not a rehash of everything he spoke about; it is a very short recap of the problem and two or three main "take-a-ways" that he wants the interviewer to remember. If he made the final slide; then that will serve as his summary. He should turn it toward you and walk you through it.

Did the interviewee...

A good interview consists of:

- Repeating the question, verifying the objective and asking about other objectives
- Asking solid and poignant questions
- Making no math mistakes
- Keeping well-organized; easy-to-read notes
- Drawing a final slide
- Developing a good, short summary touching on the most critical points

Mark of a good discussion: Did the student ask probing questions to get all the information from you that you have to offer? Did he have a full understanding of the problem? Did he realize that the demographics of the two sites were very different and Wal-Mart bought this for its technology — the back of the house technology? And, finally; did he draw a final slide?

Tate Pharmaceuticals

Problem Statement

Our client, Tate Pharmaceuticals, produces drugs designed for those who suffer from chronic arthritis. Its most successful drug, RumaX66, is not only the company's most popular product but also the market leader for patients who suffer from a specific type of knee-related arthritis. Tate has seen its market share dominance remain steady, and although sales have been up, profits have been falling slightly. What is the worldwide market size (the US has 20 percent), and what is happening with Tate's profits?

Guidance for the Interviewer

The student should repeat the question to make sure everyone is on the same page, verify the objectives (determine why profits have been falling) and then attempt the market-sizing aspect of the question.

Market-sizing

Since we know that the US makes up 20 percent of this market, the student should figure out what the US market is first, then add 80 percent. Because this is a general population problem, the student might want to draw a chart. The general population of the US is 300 million.

Age	Population	% w/ arthritis	# w/ arthritis
0-20	75m	0%	0
21-40	75m	1%	.75m
41-60	75m	6%	4.5m
61-80	75m	20%	15m
	300m		20.25m

Note: *Regardless of the assumption he makes, use the 20 million number.*

We see that 20 million Americans have this type of arthritis and the US represents 20 percent of the market, 20 million times 5 = 100 million.

This case is designed to test the interviewee's ability to conduct an industry analysis, to determine the industry's competitive dynamics, to evaluate threats and to walk through Tate's options moving forward, either for growth or market exit. (To learn more on market analysis, turn to page 38.) The student will probably fall back on the P&L framework E(P=R-C)M. While this is important for any P&L case, make sure that he just touches on this and spends more of his time coming up with short-term and long-term strategies.

The candidate may ask questions about the size of the company, the market and so forth. For some of these, the answers are listed on the next page; other numbers can be made up by you. Hopefully, you will discuss the following questions:

Data Bank

Ask: Why are profits down? The student should try to determine if this is an industry problem or a Tate problem. All of the pharma companies are seeing their profits dip because of higher costs (e.g., rising costs of ingredients, utilities and other energy). This is an industry problem.

He should ask — if he doesn't, work it into the discussion:

- **Who else makes drugs similar to RumaX66?** There are two main competitors who produce rival drugs: Drug 2 and Drug 3.
- **What part of the revenue stream does each drug represent for its respective company?**
  RumaX66 = 10% of Tate's company sales
  Drug 2 = 20% of its company sales
  Drug 3 = 60% of its company sales (forecasted)
- **What are the differences between RumaX66, Drug 2 and Drug 3?** RumaX66 is currently the cheapest for consumers, at $5 per dose with limited side effects. Drug 2 is more expensive, with only limited side effects (concentrated in males over 50 years old). Drug 3 is currently in the FDA approval process, and industry reports indicate that its company will price it at $2 per dose with no side effects whatsoever.
- **What is Tate's position in the industry?** Tate currently has about one-half of the prescription market for arthritis drugs, with RumaX66 leading the way. The maker of Drug 2 commands one-quarter of the market. Currently there are five other arthritis drugs making up the remaining 25 percent. However, we believe that once Drug 3 enters the market, its company will quickly pick up at least 25 percent of the market, forcing many of the smaller players out and possibly stealing some of our market share. Tell the student that the other competitors' costs are $7 and their drugs have three side effects. As you give this information to the student, look to see if he draws up a chart similar to the one below.

	Cost	Side effects	Mkt share
Tate's RumaX66	$5	2	50%
Drug 2	$5+	1	25%
Others	$7+	3	25%
Drug 3	$2	0	

Tate's options: The basic three options are to keep Drug 3 out, protect market share and get new customers. Some ways to do that are:

Short-term options

- Try to keep Drug 3 out of the market — petition the FDA.
- Protect what's ours, shore up relationships with distributors and doctors, maybe lower the price.

- Increase marketing to the public and to the medical community.
- Increase distribution channels in developing markets. When Drug 3 enters the market, its company is less likely to go after these smaller markets first.
- Buy Drug 3's company.

Long-term options

- Improve RumaX66: reduce costs, reduce side effects.
- Sell the division.

Summary

The interviewee needs to jump right into this without any down time to collect his thoughts. A good summary is about a minute, minute-and-a-half long. It is not a rehash of everything you spoke about; it is a short recap of the problem and two or three main points that the student wants the interviewer to remember.

Did the Interviewee...

- repeat the question, verifying the objective and asking about other objectives?
- make math mistakes?
- touch on the main points of entering a new market and an acquisition?
- determine other considerations like competitive response?
- produce a good, short summary touching on the most critical points?
- have well-organized and easy-to-read notes?

Mark of a Good Case Discussion: A good candidate will set up a matrix or table comparing and contrasting the three drugs against one another in terms of price, efficacy, side effects and other characteristics. Second, a good candidate will conduct a light analysis of the industry; analyze the competition and offer hypotheses of what the client faces down the road. Finally, a good interviewee will walk through Tate's options moving forward, such as whether it should lower its prices, purchase the competitor, do nothing, grow in other markets by increasing channels and advertising or sell the company as a preemptive move. Ultimately, this is a multi-pronged strategy case that should test the candidate's ability to analyze a specific industry, understand the nature of a competitive threat and opine on the costs and benefits of all the options on the company's table. With the student using the few questions and facts above, the rest should flow as a good discussion, which can walk you down any number of paths.

+ Gator Vator

Problem Statement

Our client, Gator Vator, is an American elevator manufacturer. Traditionally, its revenues come mainly from two sources — manufacturing elevators and service contracts to maintain them. Management feels the need to expand across the border into Canada. They have targeted some growth opportunities in Canada. How should Gator Vator go forward thinking about their options?

Guidance for the Interviewer

Make sure that the student summarizes the question and verifies the objectives (should Gator Vator enter the Canadian market; and how?). This case is designed to elicit two things. First, the candidate must walk through the classic entering-a-new-market options for a company looking to expand into Canada. (See page 40 for info on entering a new market.) That is straightforward. Second, a great candidate will also create a sub-framework to analyze whether or not the company should focus on manufacturing elevators, servicing them or both. There is certainly no one correct answer, but based on the information below that you can provide, it should be more than evident what a logical path forward for the company will be.

Data Bank

If prompted by the interviewee, you can offer the following information on the client. If the student asks you a question you don't have the answer for, tell him that either you don't have the information or that his question isn't relevant.

- **What types of elevators does the company make?** Residential and commercial.
- **What types of markets does Gator Vator typically sell into?** Gator Vator has had success in all markets. However, it tends to focus its business in urban centers rather than the suburbs.
- **In the US market, what is the revenue breakdown between elevator sales and service contracts?** The split is roughly 50/50.
- **Which business lines have the higher profit margins?** Service contracts, by a factor of nearly two; however, the company services contracts only for its own elevators.
- **Who typically buys Gator Vator's products?** High-rise apartments and, on the commercial side, office buildings, department stores, factories and other industrial customers. The split here is also 50/50, but in Canada, Gator's management sees more promise in the commercial market.
- **How has the US elevator market been doing?** Over the last decade it has seen growth of between 8 and 12 percent a year. Last year it dropped down to 3 percent.
- **What does the US market look like?** Otis® Elevator Co. has 50 percent, Gator has 20 percent and three other players share the remaining 30 percent.
- **Is the Canadian market competitive?** Not really. In the US, the market is saturated, but there are not any companies of Gator Vator's scale in Canada. The Canadian market

breaks down this way: Otis® (a US company) has a 40 percent market share and three small Canadian companies equally share the remaining 60 percent. The Canadian companies focus on structures less than five stories tall.

Note: You can instruct the candidate to assume that there are no major barriers to entry in the Canadian market, only a small tariff and shipping costs.

Suggested Approach

There are many elements to this case. The student should first build an understanding of the US market and where we sit. Once that is done, he should focus on entering a new market.

- Who are the major players in the Canadian market? What market share do they have? And how do their products and services differ from what we offer?
- What is the customer segmentation?
- Are there any barriers to entry? What about barriers to exit?

The market should look promising. The student now needs to tell you how he plans to enter this market. Each strategy should be accompanied by a cost-benefit analysis.

- Start from scratch: Should the client import into Canada? Do they set up their own factory? Do they just service other companies' elevators?
- Acquisition: Should they buy a Canadian manufacturer?
- Joint venture: Have him discuss the merits.

Chances are the company will want to buy a Canadian manufacturer. If so, what does the company need to consider?

- Why does the company want to buy it? (Make him give you several reasons.)
- Can the company afford to buy it? Do they have to take on much debt? If the economy gets worse can they still make their payments?
- How is the Canadian elevator industry doing? What kind of due diligence should the company be doing?
- How is the real estate market doing?
- How will the competition view this acquisition? What steps might they take? (Competitive response)
- What is the company's exit strategy?

You can always look on page 40 for a more detailed account of an entering-a-new-market case and page 42 for M&A.

Summary

The interviewee needs to jump right into this without any down time to collect his thoughts. A good summary is about a minute, minute-and-a-half long. It is not a rehash of everything you spoke about; it is a short recap of the problem and two or three main points that the student wants the interviewer to remember.

Did the Interviewee...

- repeat the question, verifying the objective and asking about other objectives?
- make math mistakes?
- touch on the main points of entering a new market and an acquisition?
- determine other considerations; like competitive response?
- produce a good short summary touching on the most critical points?
- have well-organized and easy-to-read notes?

Mark of a Good Case Discussion: This is a case that can go one of a hundred ways, but it is also hard to mess up. If the interviewee gets bogged down by asking for hard numbers, you can steer him back on course and remind him that this is about an overall growth strategy for the Canadian market. A good interviewee will make sure to cover the possible growth opportunities in the country, such as mentioning the possibility of acquiring an existing company (both for manufacturing and servicing), setting up a joint venture, initiating a general business expansion and/or hiring away talent from either US-based or Canadian competition. The interviewee should also be touching upon the fact that there could be barriers to entry in the foreign market, even though they are not important in the case itself. An even better candidate will be diving deeper into a framework; to think about how the company should enter the market, and whether Gator Vator should focus on manufacturing, servicing or both. Each of these considerations could be presented with a short cost-benefit analysis per option. This case encompasses growth, entering into a new market and M&A.

✣ STUCK

Problem Statement

Our client is the third largest peanut butter manufacturer in the US. Its brand, "Mickey's," sells 120 million jars of peanut butter a year, but trails behind Skippy® and Jif®. Peter Pan® is in fourth place, but only two market share percentage points behind us, so they are breathing down our necks. Mickey's sells to supermarkets and convenience stores nationwide, which makes up 60 percent of the company's sales volume. Sales to big box stores like Costco and BJ's make up 25 percent, but the biggest customer is Wal-Mart, and Wal-Mart alone makes up the remaining 15 percent.

Our client received some bad news. Wal-Mart is replacing Mickey's with Wal-Mart's private label peanut butter; however, the good news is that Wal-Mart wants Mickey's to produce the chain's private label. They want the same peanut butter, the same jar and cap: everything exactly the same except the label. I want to break this case down into two parts. First, I want you to list the key strategic issues and concerns that Mickey's should be thinking about when deciding whether or not to move ahead with this decision. Second, I want you to run the numbers to see if it makes financial sense.

Guidance for the Interviewer

Two questions the student might ask upfront: (1) What has been the sales trend in peanut butter? It's been flat the last two years and is forecast to be flat the next two years; (2) Why is Wal-Mart taking Mickey's off its shelf? It is part of a larger store trend, to replace the third player in various categories with Wal-Mart's private label.

An impressive MBA student should get six or seven of these issues, and undergrads four or five issues. Discuss with the student the ones she didn't get. Just have a general discussion about each; gauge her thoughts. I'm looking for the student to state the issue first, and then follow it up with a question.

- Profit: Will the new contract be profitable? Wal-Mart is known for squeezing margins.
- Brand image / brand equity: Will our brand take a hit if consumers find out that Mickey's and Wal-Mart's are the same product? How much will it hurt Mickey's when consumers don't see it on Wal-Mart's shelf?
- Capacity: What is the size of the contract and do we have the capacity?
- Cannibalization: Will we be stealing sales from ourselves?
- Market share: Regardless of whether we do this or not, Mickey's will fall to fourth place because they will be losing 15 percent of our volume. Mickey's doesn't get credit for Wal-Mart's label.
- Dependency on Wal-Mart: Currently Wal-Mart makes up 15 percent of our volume. If the volume increases; they could be responsible for up to 20 percent of our volume. And whenever one client has 20 percent of your volume, it's a concern, especially when it is Wal-Mart.

- Private labels for others: If we say yes, we can then make private label for other stores. Will Mickey's get replaced in other stores with a private label?
- Project what happens if we don't accept the contract. Mickey's loses 15 percent of its volume; without much hope of making it up in any other market; and will have to shut down production lines and lay people off.

Data Bank

For the second part of the case, give the following information to the student.

- Skippy, Jif and Peter Pan sell their peanut butter for $3.99 a jar in supermarkets; Mickey's sells for $3.69.
- Total yearly plant capacity is 150 million jars.
- Mickey's makes a per-jar profit in the supermarkets of $1.20, a per-jar profit in the big box stores of $1.00 and a per-jar profit in Wal-Mart of $.50 (selling as Mickey's)
- The new Wal-Mart contract is a one-year deal; calling for 50 million jars with a $0.25 per-jar profit.

Ask: Is this a good deal? Will our client be making more or less money with the new contract? Compare Wal-Mart to Wal-Mart.

Old deal: 120 million x .15 = 18 million x $0.50 = $9 million
New deal: 50 million x $0.25 = $12.5 million

The company makes $3.5 million more in profits; however, the new deal puts our plant into an over-capacity situation by 2 million jars. (120m –18m = 102m +50m = 152m jars) **What do we do? (How quickly did the student realize that there was a capacity issue?)**

These are some of the ideas the student will come up with: (along with your response). As he offers these ideas, keep telling him "no." Even cut him off on one or two to see how he reacts. Does he remain calm? Or does he get upset or try to argue with you? How students react is more important than coming up with the right answer.

- **Mickey's can outsource the 2 million jars.** (No, because the Wal-Mart contract calls for Mickey's to produce the product so we can't outsource and we don't want to outsource Mickey's, it's our main product and we want quality control.)
- **Mickey's can build another production line.** (No, because a new production line is a long-term solution and we don't know if Wal-Mart will extend the contract, plus it is expensive.)
- **Mickey's can add overtime or another shift.** (No, adding overtime would cost too much because we would have to pay the workers time and a half. Besides they are working at full capacity, which means seven days a week, three shifts a day.)
- **Mickey's can acquire a smaller player and run the extra production through the acquisition.** (No, because an acquisition is a long-term solution and we don't know if Wal-Mart will extend the contract, plus it is expensive.)
- **Mickey's can just ship 48 million jars to Wal-Mart.** (No, the contract calls for 50 million jars. If Mickey's can't do it, Wal-Mart will find someone else.)

- **Mickey's can pull 2 million jars from the big box stores.** (No, because that move will cost us $2 **million** in lost profits and we worked hard on the Wal-Mart contract just to make $3.5 million extra profit. It will reduce our Mickey's market share even more. In addition, we want to continue to supply the supermarkets and big box stores with all the peanut butter they need, plus fill the Wal-Mart contract.)

Solution

- Raise your price at supermarkets by $0.20.
- Mickey's price will still be a little less than the competition's while Mickey's will be making $1.40 per jar.
- Higher prices will reduce volume.
- Our analysts projected that volume will drop 10 percent — have the student run the numbers to see if this makes sense.
  - 60% of 120m jars are 72m jars. 72m x 1.20 = $86.4m
  - 72m – 10% or 7.2m jars = 64.8m or 65m jars. 65m x $1.40 = $91m
    We produce about 7 million fewer jars but make about $5 million more.

Summary

The student needs to jump into this without any down time to collect his thoughts. A good summary is about a minute, minute-and-a-half long. It is not a rehash of everything discussed; it is a short recap of the problem and two or three main points that he wants the interview to remember.

Mickey's received notice that they are being replaced in Wal-Mart by a private label; however, Wal-Mart has asked them to manufacture their private label. It is a one-year contract that would require Mickey's to produce 50 million jars at a profit of $0.25 a jar, leading to a $3.5 million increase in profits overall. After reviewing the larger strategic issues like brand equity and market share, Mickey's decided to move ahead. However, the new contract pushes demand 2 million jars over plant capacity. To correct this, Mickey's decided to raise the price of its peanut butter in supermarkets by $0.20, thus reducing demand by 10 percent; or 7 million jars; while making almost $5 million more.

Did the interviewee...

A good interview consists of:

- repeating the question, verifying the objective and asking if there are any other objectives.
- maintaining an even keel as the interviewer rejects the student's ideas.
- coming up with the price increase solution without any help from the interviewer.
- quickly recognizing that there is a capacity issue.
- keeping well-organized, easy-to-read notes. Big points if the student made a chart like the one below.
- developing a good short summary touching on the most critical points, but also bringing up points from both parts of the question.

Store	% of volume	# of jars	Profit/jar	$ profit
Super/conv	60%	72m	$1.20	$86m
Big Box	25%	30m	$1.00	$30m
Wal-Mart	15%	18m	$0.50	$9m
		120m		$125m

Mark of a good case discussion: While this is a first-round case, it is a difficult first-round case because there is only one right answer. I have given this case live more than 200 times and I can tell you that less than 10 percent of the students got the right answer of raising our price in the supermarkets. I look for two other things; (1) how quickly did they pick up on the capacity issue? And (2) how did they react when I cut them off and kept telling them, "No, what else do you have?" To me, this last issue is much more important than coming up with the right answer.

+ Nerves of Steel

Problem Statement

Our client is the second largest maker of steel filing cabinets and desks in the US. It is nearing the end of a four-year rolled-steel contract, which expires at the end of Year 7. Our client signed its steel contract in Year 4.

The CFO wants to know if it makes sense to stockpile two years' worth of steel at the end of the contract at the Year 4 price or sign a new contract at Year 8's price.

You can assume that the company uses 12,000 tons of steel a year and will continue to do so over the next five years.

Guidance for the Interviewer

Make sure that the student summarizes the question and verifies the objective. The student is looking at two options. Option one is to sign a new contract at Year 8 prices. Option two is to stockpile steel for two years, then sign a new contract in Year 10.

Ask the student what he needs to know. He should ask about:

• Cost of steel in Y4 contract	\$600/ton
• Current Y7 cost of steel	\$810/ton
• Amount of steel to stockpile	24,000 tons (12,000/year)
• Time value of money	$FV = PV (1+i)^n$
• Current interest rates	5 percent
• Inventory storage cost	\$50/ton per year paid at the beginning of each year
• Steel price forecast	Economic conditions

While the student may not ask for all this information up front, give him some time to discover what he needs.

Steel Pricing Trends (in dollars per ton)

Y1	Y2	Y3	Y4	Y5	Y6	Y7	Y8
\$263	\$554	\$615	\$600	\$610	\$750	\$810	?

Hand the student this chart. (You can photocopy it from page 225 in the back of this book.) You are looking to see what conclusions the student can derive from this chart — not much. The numbers are all over the place and there is very little consistency. The most it can do is anchor the Year 8 price for him.

Ask him what he thinks the Year 8 price will be. He has a starting point of \$810 (the Year 7 price). He should take into consideration the economic conditions around the world, particularly in the top three industries that use rolled steel: autos, airplanes and appliances (which are tied to housing starts).

Remember that there is no right answer. Students are often reluctant to go out on a limb and give a number, but you need to force your student to come up with a price. (Let's assume he comes up with a Year 8 price of $850 per ton.) Once he comes up with a price for Year 8, look to see what he does with it. Give him big points if he draws up the final slide.

The Final Slide

This is critical. If the student has the foresight to build the final slide, he will stand out from all the other candidates. Whenever you have a case that compares two or more strategies, options or ideas and you are applying the same criteria, you should build "the final slide" almost immediately. As you calculate the numbers, fill them in on the final slide; it keeps all relevant information in one place and makes it easier for the interviewer to follow. Once all the information is filled out, the student turns the final slide toward the interviewer and walks her through it. It is the best summary. It is similar to the final slide of a deck that a consultant would present to a client.

In this case it would look like this (assuming he came up with an Year 8 price of $850 per ton):

	Y8	Y9	Y10	Y11
Option 1 – new contract	$850	$850	$850	$850
Option 2 – stockpiling				

The student should also conclude that he needs to come up with a price for Year 10. If he stockpiles for two years, then the company will have to sign a new contract. Again, he should talk about where he thinks the economy; and those three industries in particular; are headed. Let's say he comes up with a Year 10 price of $900 per ton.

	Y8	Y9	Y10	Y11
Option 1 – new contract	$850	$850	$850	$850
Option 2 – stockpiling			$900	$900

The only two squares left open in the final slide are the stockpiling squares.
They would stockpile 24,000 tons, enough for two years. Because they are stockpiling, they would need to pay for all of it upfront.

Inventory Costs
Inventory costs are paid on a yearly basis at the beginning of each year. When money is laid out at the beginning of the year, you need to figure the "cost of money." Remember: $50 per ton per year.

Year 1 / (24,000 x 50) = 1,200,000
$FV = PV (1+i)^n$ (n = 1)
FV = 1,200,000 x 1.05
FV = 1,260,000 or $1.26m

Year 2 / (12,000 x 50) = 600,000
$FV = PV (1 + i)^n$ (n = 1)
FV = 600,000 x 1.05
FV = 630,000 or $0.63m

Y1 = \$1.26m
Y2 = \$0.63m
Total Storage and Inventory Costs = \$1.89m

Steel Costs

24,000 tons x \$600 = \$14,400,000
Interest rates are at 5%

$FV = PV (1 + i)^n$
$FV = 14,400,000 (1.05)^2$
$FV = 14,400,000 \times (1.10)$
$FV = 15,840,000$ or \$15.84m

Stockpiling = \$15,840,000 + \$1,890,000 (inventory costs)
Stockpiling = \$17,730,000, or round off to \$18,000,000

\$18,000,000 / 24,000 tons = \$750/ton (It always comes out to \$750/ton.)

	Y8	Y9	Y10	Y11
Option 1 – new contract	\$850	\$850	\$850	\$850
Option 2 – stockpiling	\$750	\$750	\$900	\$900

Summary

The interviewee needs to jump right into this without any down time to collect his thoughts. A good summary is about a minute, minute-and-a-half long. It is not a rehash of everything you spoke about; it is a short recap of the problem and two or three main points that the student wants the interviewer to remember.

Did the Interviewee...

- repeat the question, verifying the objective and asking about other objectives?
- make math mistakes?
- design the final slide?
- draw the interviewer into a discussion?
- produce a good, short summary touching on the most critical points?
- have well-organized and easy-to-read notes?

Mark of Good Case Discussion: The key things to look for are the student's knowledge of the current economic conditions, the realization that the company will have to sign another contract two years later if they stockpile and of course the use of the final slide. It is important not only that the slide be filled in, but that the student turn it toward the interviewer and walk through his analysis and decision.

✛ GPS APP

Problem Statement

Our client is a pair of college students who have built an app that will allow customers to download celebrity voices onto their smart phones' GPS systems. The client wants us to determine: the domestic market-size, the breakeven in terms of the number of downloads, the price and estimated profits for the first year.

Guidance for the Interviewer

The student should repeat the question to make sure everyone is on the same page, and he should verify the objectives (market-size, breakeven, price and profits). The student should also ask if there are any other objectives he needs to be concerned with — in this case the answer is no.

Most students will try to determine the market-size first. In this case, you are looking to see if the student first determines the price of the app. He doesn't need to answer the questions in the order that they were given. An exceptional student will determine the price first as well as make a final slide almost immediately. See the next page for an example.

Data Bank

Our client will be first to market; no other app like this exists. There is a patent pending but figure on one year before someone weasels their way around the patent.

Costs: In order to determine the price, the student first must ask about costs. Tell him the fixed costs are $500,000 and the variable costs are: one-third of the price goes to Apple or the other platforms, and a $0.50 per download royalty payment goes to the celebrity.

Price: There are three major ways to determine price: competitive analysis, cost-based pricing and price-based costing.

Competitive analysis: Since we are first to market, there is no real competition. However, given the platform (iTunes, etc.) it is fair to try to compare this to other products being sold, such as songs, ringtones and games. These items range in price from free to $9.99. It is a fair assumption that this product will fall somewhere in that range.

Cost-based pricing: The product's variable cost is one-third of the price plus $0.50 a download. Make sure that all costs are covered.

Price-based costing: What will customers be willing to pay? Will they equate this app to a ringtone? Or something a little more sophisticated?

It is good practice to use numbers that will make your calculations easier. Apple is taking a one-third fee. Songs and ringtones sell for $1.29 each. The student probably wants to use $3 as a sale price. One dollar goes to Apple® Computer, and $.50 goes to the celebrity, which leaves a profit of $1.50 for our client.

Domestic Market size: To determine the market size, the student should calculate the number of cell phones in the US and estimate the percentage that are smartphones. He should also determine who is old enough to drive and most likely to buy celebrity voices (probably 16 to 36-year-olds). Have the student walk you through his thinking for each age group.

Assume a US population of 320 million with an average life expectancy of 80 years, with even numbers of people in each age group. Below is an example. The student's assumptions might be different, which is fine, as long as he can justify them.

	Population	No. of cell phones	No. of smartphones	No. to buy app
0 – 20	80 mil	25m	10m	1m
21 – 40	80 mil	60m	40m	3m
41-60	80 mil	60m	40m	.5m
61-80	80 mil	55m	10m	.5m

He came up with 5 million apps. Also assume that the average person would purchase 2 apps, making the market 10 million apps the first year.

❑ Breakeven:

BE = fixed costs / margin (price – 1/3 price – royalty)

BE = 500,000 / 3 – 1 – 0.5 = 1.5
BE = 500,000 / 1.5 = 333,333 downloads

Profits: If the student assumes that the client will sell 10 million apps the first year, profits would be: 10 million times $1.50 = $15 million minus the start-up costs of $500,000
First-year profits are $14.5 million

Final slide: This simple final slide can be drawn up immediately. Interviewers will watch the order in which the student writes the requests. Did he stick with the order given, or did he realize they were out of order? This final slide acts as a structure, a scorecard (making it easy for the interviewer to keep track of the numbers) and a summary. The student should turn the final slide toward you, the interviewer, and walk you through it.

Price	$3.00
Market size	10m apps
Breakeven	333,000
Est. profits	$14.5 million

Summary

The student needs to jump right into this without any down time to collect his thoughts. If he made the final slide, then that is his summary. He should turn the slide toward the interviewer and walk her through it. If not, a good summary is about a minute, minute-and-a-half long. It is not a rehash of everything you spoke about; it is a short recap of the problem and two or three main points that he wants the interviewer to remember.

We were asked to determine four main factors concerning the GPS app: price, which was determined to be $3; market size, 10 million apps; breakeven in volume, 333,000; and profit the first year; of $14.5 million. If these numbers hold up, this promises to be a very profitable venture.

Did the interviewee...

A good interview consists of:

- repeating the question, verifying the objective and asking about other objectives.
- drawing the final slide.
- making no math mistakes.
- using fair assumptions.
- keeping well-organized and easy-to-read notes.
- developing a good, short summary touching on the most critical points.

Mark of a good discussion: Did the interviewee figure out the price before the market size? Most students that I give this case to do not figure price first; they do market size. This is okay, but you're not going to stand out from the rest of the crowd. Whenever you get a case with a new product, especially when there isn't any direct competition, you should figure price first.

+ Finding Fulfillment

Our client is an online toy store. They ship toys all over the US. Currently, they have one warehouse outside Boston where they receive and then distribute the toys. They ship to the end-user, the parents or the kids through FedEx. The client wants to know if it makes sense to outsource product distribution through a third party like Amazon.com or Danny's. I'd like to break this question down into two parts. What are the pros and cons of outsourcing our distribution and in this case, does it make financial sense to outsource?

Guidance for the interviewer

The student should repeat the question, verify the objective and then ask if there are any other objectives. In this case there are no other objectives. Some students will try to lay out a structure, which is not necessary. The structure is basically a list of pros and cons and a running of the numbers. The candidate should ask for a minute to write down his thoughts and then give you all the pros first, then the cons. If he tries to do it off the top of his head, cut him off in mid-answer and say, "I get it. What else do you have?" How quickly does he move on to the next pro or con? Also, the candidate should realize that because this is a toy store; almost 80 percent of their business takes place in the last two months of the year. So the warehouse sits three-quarters empty for ten months.

Listen to his list, and then go through this list confirming what he said, but mentioning the ideas he might have missed.

Pros of Outsourcing	Cons of Outsourcing
Shutting down the warehouse will save warehouse expenses and labor costs. The warehouse sits ¾ empty for 10 months out of the year.	An outside vendor might be more expensive.
Takes worry and stress out of fulfillment. Allows the client to focus on marketing and selling – what she does best.	Loss of control: can't individualize packages. If the client chooses Amazon everything gets sent out in an Amazon box. Loss of brand recognition.
Outside distributors have multiple warehouses around the country for faster delivery (can shave a day or two off delivery time), lower shipping costs and use less capital if they expand.	What if this fails? The client already closed their warehouse and fired their employees so they'd need to find another vendor and have their entire inventory shipped to another distributor's warehouses. If this occurs during holiday season, they might not be able to find another distributor.
The client doesn't have to ramp up during the busy holiday season by hiring seasonal employees, then lay people off two months later. An accounting and HR nightmare.	Reduces profit (can't make money on shipping). We charge an extra one-dollar per package shipped. This is a handling fee. Look at it as warehouse income.

Data Bank

Client information: Give this information to the student so he can figure out the second half of the question. Tell the student we are going with Danny's. Here are the numbers.

- Currently we ship 250 orders a day, 20 days a month; for 10 months.
- Holidays: They ship 2,000 orders a day, 20 days a month; for 2 months.
- Average toy sells for $20.
- Warehouse rental costs, utilities and equipment cost $75,000 a year.

- Warehouse insurance costs $9,000.
- Yearly labor costs for four full-time employees and benefits totals $200,000.
- Thirty additional holiday employees at $10 per hour, 8 hours a day; for 20 days a month; for two months. No benefits.
- Danny's fulfillment center storage costs are $0.45 per cubic foot (10,000 cubic feet for 10 months, 100,000 cubic feet for two months).
- Restocking fee of $2 per items for any toys that get returned. They have a 3 percent return rate.
- The client pays the distributor a $1 handling fee per package.

Watch to see how well he organizes his notes. He should walk you through his calculations.

Number of packages; revenues and profits
250 orders a day, 20 days a month = 5,000 packages x 10 months equals 50,000 packages
2,000 orders a day times 20 days a month = 40,000 packages x 2 months equals 80,000 packages

Total number packages shipped last year: 130,000

Average revenue is $20 per package x 130,000 = $2.6 million.

In-house Costs
Labor
Full-time = **$200,000**
Part-time = 30em x $10hr x 8hrs = $2,400
$2,400 x 20 days = $48,000 x 2 months = **$96,000**
Warehouse rent and equipment (yearly) = **$75,000**
Warehouse insurance (yearly) = **$9,000**

Warehouse Costs
$200,000 + 96,000 + 75,000 + 9,000 = $380,000

Warehouse income ($1 handling fee per package) = $130,000 (it is important that the student take this into consideration and subtract it from the warehouse costs).

Net Warehouse Costs: $380,000 – 130,000 = **$250,000**

Danny's Fulfillment Center

$0.45 x 10,000 = 4,500 x 10 months = $45,000
$0.45 x 100,000 = 45,000 x 2 months = $90,000

Extra shipping credit = 130,000

3% return rate = 130,000 x .03 = 3,900 x $2 = $7,800

$45,000 + $90,000 + $130,000 + 7,800 = **$272,800**

While the cost of shipping the toys in-house is $22,800 cheaper, the student needs to take other things into consideration and put it into perspective before making a decision.

FORCE THE STUDENT TO MAKE A DECISION

After the student makes his decision; you can say; "Let me tell you why you're wrong!"

If he chooses to keep it in-house; your argument is:

- $22,000 is less than 1 percent of the revenues (22,000/2.6m = .008).
- The company would only need to sell 1,900 more toys (or about 1 percent) to make up the difference. This would free the company up to concentrate on marketing and selling more toys.
- The company could pass Danny's $1 per package handling fee on to the customer as it currently does.
- Shipping costs would be cheaper.
- The industry is headed toward free shipping during the holidays so they would not receive $80,000 out of the $130,000 handling fee.
- If the company is worrying about a bad distributor; they could go with two distributors the first year; then choose one. They might lose some volume discounts; but this strategy would be far less expensive than shipping toys from ten of Danny's warehouses to ten warehouses owned by a new distributor.

If they chooses to outsource distribution; your argument is:

- They would maintain control of their brand and delivery times.
- They have a warehouse sitting ¾ empty ten months out of the year. That is a real opportunity. The company could bring seasonal balance to their warehouse and maybe to their bottom line by generating additional revenues: Since the warehouse sits empty most of the year, the client could rent part of it out, or they could begin to distribute products for other companies. They could expand their website to include things that ship in the spring; like patio furniture, pool equipment or toys.

After you tell the interviewee that he is wrong; and why, does he defend his answer without getting defensive or does he switch to your answer? Did he think through his original answer or shoot from the hip?

Did the interviewee...

A good interview consists of:

- Making no math mistakes.
- Stating fair assumptions.
- Keeping well-organized and easy-to-read notes.
- Turning his notes toward the interviewer to make her feel more like a client and less like an interviewer.
- Developing a well articulated recommendation.
- Defending his recommendation without getting defensive.

A great interview consists of all of the above, plus:

- Putting the $22,800 in perspective.
- Realizing that the handling fee could be passed on to the customer.
- Suggesting that the industry was headed toward free shipping during the holidays and what that would mean for the client.
- Exploring additional revenue opportunities for the warehouse .

Note: Over the past year; I've given this case 200 times. Only one person came up with the dual vendors; only one person suggested that the customers pay the handling fee; only four people came up with additional revenue streams for the warehouse; and **no one** spoke about free shipping.

+ KBO Appliances

Problem Statement

KBO Appliances, a US maker of kitchen appliances, saw its stock price drop from $34 to $30 a share on news that the experts had called the new line of products "pedestrian" — meaning lacking imagination. While the CEO ordered her design team to redesign the major products, she also wants to enter the college market. She wants to know if it makes sense to develop and market a mini-fridge-and-microwave combo.

What is the size of this market? How would you price the product and how much profit could we expect?

Guidance for the Interviewer

The student should summarize the case to make sure everyone is on the same page. She should quantify the change in stock price by percentage (the stock dropped by about 12 percent). She should also inquire as to whether there are any other objectives to be concerned with — in this case, no.

We are looking for several things. What does the student want to know in order to make a decision? Ideally, she would ask about everything listed on the chart on the next page, but that is unlikely. You can give her the information in bold if she asks for it. Whatever she doesn't bring up, question her about it, and then give her the information. You should have time to visit all eight issues. Keep in mind that there is no right answer. You are looking to see how the student thinks and communicates under pressure.

How the student lays out her notes is also very important. Did she set up a chart similar to the one on the next page? This is known as the final slide. The final slide will make it easier for both her and the interviewer to follow the case. As she makes the calculations and thinks about the issues and variables that will come into play, she should fill in the chart. At the end of the case, she should turn the chart toward the interviewer. Her summary is just going through the chart touching on all eight issues and then making her decision. If she doesn't draw a similar chart, show her this one at the end of the interview.

Start off by asking her what she wants to know.

Market-sizing. This is a general population problem. Start with 320 million Americans. Assume that the average life expectancy of an American is 80 years and that there are even numbers of people in each age group. Thus, there are same number of 2-year-olds as 72-year-olds. That means each group has 4 million people. The average age of college students is 18 to 22 — covering five years (my daughter tells me it takes five years to graduate from college now), so that's 20 million Americans of college age. We only care about full-time students, the ones living in a dorm. Assume that 8 million go to college full-time; 2 million are freshman, 2 million are sophomores, etc. Assume that all freshmen live in dorms and that the number of students living in dorms falls off as they go through school. Also, most freshmen have a roommate, so cut the 2 million number in half. That's 1 million freshmen as the market. Assume that all of the others add up to another million, taking into account that students who buy the fridge will hold on to it year after year.

Also assume that the biggest purchasers of these microwave mini-fridges are the universities. They buy them, then rent them out to students. So we'll assume that the market size is 2 million units per year. The student's thought process is more important than the actual number. Regardless of what she comes up with, use 2 million as the market size.

Competition and product differentiation. Tell the student that all of the existing products look the same — white mini-fridge with a microwave screwed on, on top. Ask her how she would differentiate our product, then go with an energy-efficient fridge with a nice cow design.

Data Bank

	Mini-Fridge & Microwave
Market size	2 million units per year
Competition and product differentiation	3 products priced between $300 and $350. Our product will be the fourth and will have a cow design on the outside of the product.
Cost (our manufacturing cost)	$150 per unit
Pricing	In determining the price, the student should take several things into consideration: (1) our costs, (2) competition, (3) what students are willing to pay and (4) the fact that the CEO wants to enter this market.* She should also take into consideration that there is a 20% retail markup. At what price do we sell to the retailer? Can we sell direct to schools and bypass the retailer? If we do that, then follow-up sales will be less since the schools will hang on to them year after year.
Estimated market share	Given the price, the student can now estimate the market share the company can expect. A reasonable number for the first year could be as high as 10%, but no higher.
Profits	Once the student figures out the price and our market share, she should figure out our estimated profits.
Competitive response	How will our competition react? Price war? A tiger design? Get the company's customers to sign a long-term contract?
Other factors	Will we cannibalize our other products? (no) What other markets (e.g., small business, senior housing and hospitals) can we expect to pull from?
Decision	Look for a "go" or "no go" decision.

*The CEO wants to enter the market so she can introduce the quality of her products and brand to students in hopes of having them make bigger purchases as they go through life (think long-term greed). This discovery should lead to pricing the unit on the lower end of the price range — probably the lowest.

Guidance for the Interviewer

The student should have touched on all the issues above in a similar order. Thus, we can't determine the company's estimated market share until we know the price. And we can't calculate profits until we know the estimated market share. Does the student see the big picture? Does she understand how everything is tied together?

Summary

The perfect summary is walking you through the final slide. Don't expect that — very few students ever make the final slide. If the student does it, she is exceptional. That being said, she needs to jump right into the summary without any down time to collect her thoughts. A good summary is about a minute, minute-and-a-half long. It is not a rehash of everything she spoke about; it is a short recap of the problem and two or three main points and a recommendation that she wants the interviewer to remember.

Did the interviewee...

A good interview consists of:

- repeating the question, verifying the objective and asking about other objectives.
- quantifying by percentage the price change in the stock.
- taking into account why the CEO wants to enter this market.
- making no math mistakes.
- keeping well-organized and easy-to-read notes (making of the chart).
- developing a good short summary using the chart and touching on the most critical points.

Mark of a Good Case Discussion: Besides drawing the final slide, did she have everything in the right order? Did she pick up on the fact that the universities are the biggest buyers and that having an energy-efficient model would be the most appealing to them? I also look to see if the student suggests a price war, as a response. If she does, tell her to avoid that option in the future cases if possible. Most firms view it as a knee-jerk reaction.

+ Bulletproof Auto Glass

Problem Statement

Our client is an applied materials manufacturer who wants to enter the bulletproof auto glass industry. They've developed a one-way bullet-resistant glass. Bullets won't come in, but you can fire out. This new glass is lighter and cheaper to manufacture. Word leaked out and their stock jumped from $15 to $18 a share. They want you to calculate the size of the worldwide bulletproof auto glass market, come up with a pricing strategy, determine the plant location and make a decision as to whether to enter this market.

Guidance for the interviewer

Make sure that the student summarizes the case and verifies the objective(s) (calculate market size, come up with a pricing strategy, determine plant location and decide whether to enter the market). When summarizing, he should state that the stock jumped 20 percent, not $3. He should also ask if there are any other objectives about which he should be concerned. In this case the answer is no. After he verifies the objectives; he should take a moment and lay out his structure. Because this is an interviewer-driven case; no hypothesis is needed.

Ideally, his notes should look something like this...

APPLIED MATERIALS MAN

ENTER BULLETPROOF AUTO
INDUSTRY

STOCK $15 > $18
- MKT SIZE
- PRICE
- PLANR LOCATION
- MKT Y / N

ENTER MKT Y / N

ANALYZE COMPANY
- SIZE: REVENUE, BRAND
- OTHER PRODUCTS
- WHAT CONSTITUTES SUCCESS?

ANALYZE MKT
- MAJOR PLAYERS
- BARRIERS
- PROD DIFFERENTIATION
  - FEATURES
    - ONE-WAY MORE OF A DETERRENT
    - CHEAPER & LIGHTER
  - PRICING
    - COMP OBJECTIVE
    - COMPET ANALYSIS
    - COST-BASED PRICING
    - PRICE-BASED COSTING

PLANT LOCATION
- OTHER PLANTS
- LOCATION
- VALUE CHAIN
- RAW MATERIALS
- LABOR
- TRANSPORTATION
- CUSTOMER BASE

Because this is a new product, not only for the company but for the industry as well, the student might want to solve the pricing issue first, before figuring out the market size.

Databank

This information below should help you answer any of the student's questions. If he asks you something you don't know; just state that it's not relevant. If he doesn't ask you about all these areas; turn the question back on him, i.e., "What do you think are some of the barriers to entry?" I look carefully at the structure. Ideally he should lay out his approach in this order: the company, the overall market, pricing, market sizing, plant location and the best way to enter the market. Most students will jump right into the market sizing first, which is okay, but not optimal.

The company

- Size: revenues, brands:
  $15 billion in revenue, all b2b
- Other products? Any in auto industry? No.
  Flat-screen television panels, solar panels, semi-conductors, bulletproof walls and windows for buildings
- Is the product patented?
  Yes
- What constitutes a success?
  10 percent market share within 3 years

The market

- Major players and market share
  Four players, 25 percent each. Two are divisions of larger companies; two are smaller players. Growing by 10 percent a year last five years.
- Product differentiation
  Ours would be lighter, cheaper to manufacture and one-way. No other one-way on the market.
  Disadvantage: Once you fire out, the integrity of the glass is compromised.
- Barriers to entry
  Contracts with OEMs usually take four years to get established
  OEMs make up 80 percent, aftermarket 20 percent

Note: If this company wants 10 percent market share and an OEM contract takes four years; then they need to take market share out of the aftermarket; which means that they need to get 50 percent of the aftermarket — very unlikely without an acquisition.

Pricing

- Company objective: 10 percent market share within 3 years.
- Competitive analysis: Four competitors between $400 and $450 /sq ft.
- Best guess; that it costs them around $300/sq ft to manufacture — figure a standard industry 25 percent margin.
- Cost-based pricing. It costs us $250/sq ft. The average vehicle uses 25 square feet of glass.

- Price-based costing. Do we think that customers would be willing to pay more for our product? Lighter means easier to work with, and saves on gas. But bulletproof glass isn't something that you would try to save money on — you'd want the best. Customers are not price sensitive.

Market-sizing

What is the size of the worldwide bulletproof auto glass market?

Clients that use bulletproof glass are militaries, corporations and government agencies; like the FBI, local police and their counterparts around the globe. Royalty, celebrities, mob bosses, drug lords and armored trucks also use bulletproof glass. Plus; the market needs to broken down into the OEM (original equipment manufacturers) market and the aftermarket.

The best way for the student to solve this is to make some assumptions about the US and extrapolate it out to the world market. Start with assumptions:

1 percent of US vehicles have bulletproof glass.
US vehicles make up 10 percent of the world market.

Next, figure out the number of US cars/vehicles on the road. This is a household problem.

Assume US population is 320 million, 3.2 people per household; or 100 million US households. Next, break this data down by income levels. He should draw this chart and walk you through his thought process for each level.

Income	HH	# Cars / HH	Total cars
High	10m	3	30m
Middle	60m	2	120m
Low	30m	.5	15m

He's calculated 165 million cars owned by households. To that, he should add military vehicles, taxis, rental cars, limos, government cars, university cars, RVs and armored cars. He can bundle all those together in a single number. It makes his calculations easier: in this example say 35 million. Now the total is 200 million vehicles/cars on the road. Assume a car has a life expectancy of 10 years, which means 20 million new cars sold every year.

20 million new cars x .01 = 200,000 new cars with bulletproof glass in the US
180 million used cars x .01 = 1.8 million used cars with bulletproof glass
Total 2 million cars in US have bulletproof glass
The US has 10 percent of market — total market is 20 million cars with bulletproof glass worldwide

Remember, his numbers might be very different; which is okay provided that there were solid assumptions and logic behind his thoughts.

Plant location
He should be asking several questions. Where are the company's other plants? What are the bulletproof glass sales by region? Where are his customers?

Current plants are in Ireland, Germany, Israel, the US and Brazil. The company manufactures bulletproof glass for buildings in their Ireland plant. Other issues to take into consideration are the value chain, raw materials, labor, transportation and customer base. The OEMs are located in Detroit, Tokyo, Berlin and South Carolina.

Another consideration is whether acquiring a smaller player is discussed. If the company acquires a competitor, they may use that company's plant to produce, if they have the capacity.

BPG (auto) market by region and by user

Middle East 35 %
S. America 25%
Asia 20%
US 10%
Other 10%

Entry into the market
What the question is really asking is not only does the company enter this market, but how? What you should be looking for here is for the student to suggest acquiring one of the smaller players; particularly if they have an OEM contract. Remember; it takes four years to get one. This will speed up the process and help the company reach their 10 percent market share in three years since each player represents 25 percent of the market.

Here are five ways for them to enter the market. The student should review these; stating the advantages and disadvantages of each.

- Start producing on their own and try to grow it organically.
- Make an acquisition.
- Sell their technology to another company.
- Produce the glass for all the other companies (private label).
- Do a joint venture.

Final slide: When a student gets a question which asks for "these four things:" he can usually make a final slide on a separate sheet of paper at the start of the case.

This acts as a scorecard as well as his summary. He should fill it out as he goes along and then turn it toward the interviewer and walk him through it.

Below are some answers the student might have come up with different ones, which is fine as long as he used logic and his arguments made sense.

Market Size	20m
Price	$500 / sq ft
Plant location	Ireland
Enter market	Yes

Summary

He needs to jump right into this without any down time to collect his thoughts. A good summary is about 30 seconds to a minute, possibly a minute-and-a-half long at the most. It is not a rehash of everything he spoke about; it is a very short recap of the problem and two or three main "take-a-ways" that he wants the interviewer to remember. If he made the final slide; then that will serve as his summary. He should turn it toward you and walk you through it.

While most students will suggest that the company enter the market, one thing I look for is whether they suggest an acquisition and how they incorporate that into their overall market entry strategy and plant location discussion.

Did the interviewee...

A good interview consists of:

- Repeating the question, verifying the objective and asking about other objectives.
- Laying out a clear structure, starting with the company.
- Asking solid and poignant questions.
- Making no math mistakes.
- Keeping well-organized easy-to-read notes.
- Drawing a final slide.
- Developing a good, short summary touching on the most critical points.

Mark of a good discussion: Did the students ask probing questions to get all the information from you that you have to offer? Did he have a full understanding of the problem? Did he realize that it is not only about entering the market, but how to enter the market? Was he able to determine market size quickly or did he get gummed up on the enormity of the question? And, finally, did he draw a final slide?

+ Statin Blue

Problem Statement

Our client is a large pharma company similar to Johnson & Johnson. It has developed a new cholesterol drug called Statin Blue. Because Statin Blue is on the lower end of the statin chain (meaning that it is weaker than traditional prescription cholesterol drugs), the company has the option of releasing this drug either as an over-the-counter product or prescription drug.

You need to:

- determine which market the company should enter, as a prescription drug or as an over-the-counter product.
- figure the breakeven in terms of the number of customers for both markets.
- calculate the estimated profits for both markets.
- list the pros and cons of entering the prescription market.

Guidance for the Interviewer

Make sure that the student summarizes the question and verifies the objectives (determining which market to enter, figuring the breakeven in terms of customers for both markets, calculating the estimated profits for both markets and listing the pros and cons of entering the prescription market). She should also ask if there are any other objectives she should be concerned with. In this case the answer is no. After the student summarizes the question and verifies the objectives, have her start with the pros and cons.

When she lists the pros and cons, check to see if she asks for a moment to write down her thoughts. By asking for a moment (up to 30 seconds), she can list the pros and cons any way they pop into her head; however, when it comes time to tell them to you, she should list all the pros first, then all the cons. Make sure she doesn't ping-pong back and forth between pros and cons.

Prescription:

+ Price – can charge more
+ Insurance coverage
+ Perceived higher value
+ Good established sales force
– Highly competitive market
– One dominant player (Lipitor with 49 percent of the market)

Over-the-Counter

+ Easy access — don't need to see a doctor
+ High volume
+ Easier to market

Chart 1
Prescription Cholesterol Drug Market

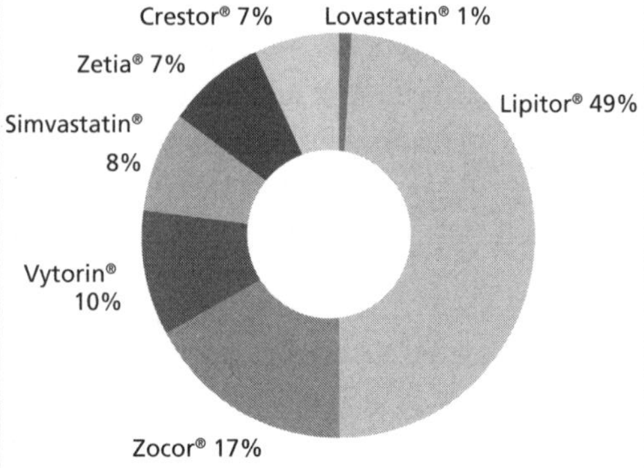

Hand this chart to the student when she asks about the Rx market.

+ Company brand name recognition
+ Potentially huge, untapped market
– Patients in the high-risk category already on prescription drug
– Viewed as less effective (which it is — 10 percent)

❑ **Entering the Market**

After listing the pros and cons, the student should ask about the market. Force her to ask about the prescription market first. What does the student need to know about entering a new market? (For more on entering a new market, turn to page 40.)

Who are the major players?
What market share does the company have?
How do their products differ from those of Statin Blue?

Are there any barriers to entry? (Has the company received FDA approval for both markets?)

Special note — Our company does not produce any of the other Statin products

Data Bank

Our Client

- Large pharma with a large drug portfolio. Fifty percent of its products are over-the-counter and 50 percent are prescription drugs. This should tell the student that our distribution and marketing channels are well established in either market.

Prescription Market (Rx)

- Current market size: 14 million Americans and $14 billion in sales. Hand the student a copy of the donut chart. (Photocopy it from the back of the book. See page 226.)
- If covered by insurance, the patient pays a $15 a month co-pay.

Over-the-Counter Market (OTC)

- No such market exists.
- The OTC version of Statin Blue would cost the consumer $15 for a month's supply.
- No insurance coverage.

Statin Blue

- Think of it as Lipitor Light — it's less effective.
- Similar side effects as with regular Statin drugs, just less intense. Side effects include muscle pain, diarrhea, sexual dysfunction, cognitive impairment and possible liver damage.

Costs

- Costs are $40 million a year. This is the only cost number the student needs to know.

Pricing

- The cost to the end user will be the same regardless of which market we use. By prescription: The patient will pay a $15 a month co-pay. OTC, the patient will pay $15 for a month's supply.

Profits

- The company makes a $20 profit per bottle sold in the prescription market. The patient would use one bottle a month, 12 bottles a year. Yearly profit is $240 per patient per year.
- The company makes a $5 profit per bottle sold in the OTC market. The patient would use one bottle a month, 12 bottles a year. Yearly profit is $60 per patient per year.

❑ **Rx Markets**

Walk the student through a copy of the chart below. Explain that if your cholesterol is less than 180, you are very healthy. If it falls between 180 and 200, the doctor will tell you to exercise more and eat some Honey Nut Cheerios. Patients with cholesterol levels between 200 and 220 are the prime target for Statin Blue. This group makes up 10 percent of the overall prescription market. However, we think that we will be able to get only 4 percent of the overall 14 million-person prescription cholesterol market (which is 560,000 patients). If your cholesterol levels are over 220, then the doctor will prescribe one of the seven drugs in the first chart.

Before there was Statin Blue, if your level was 210 or above, the MD would most likely prescribe one of the seven current drugs; however, you would be over-medicating and at risk for the side effects.

250	Big Trouble (represents 10% of the overall prescription cholesterol market)	
220	Other Prescription Cholesterol Drugs (represents 80% of the overall prescription cholesterol market)	
200	Statin Blue (We believe that the patients whose cholesterol levels fall between 200 and 220 make up 10% of the overall cholesterol market.)	10%
180	Honey Nut Cheerios & Exercise	
<180	Healthy	

❑ **OTC Market**

The market-sizing of the OTC market is the hardest part of the case.

Assumptions:

- There are 300 million Americans.
- There is an 80/20 split between Americans with health insurance (the ones who would have access to the prescription market) and those without health insurance (the ones who wouldn't have access to discounted prescriptions).
- Of the 240 million Americans with health insurance (300 million times 80 percent = 240 million), we know that 14 million or 5 percent have a cholesterol problem (14/240 = 5.8 percent or round-off to 5 percent),

- That leaves an uninsured population of 60 million (300 million x .2 = 60 million). Thus we can assume that at least 5 percent of the uninsured, or 3 million people, have a cholesterol problem (60 million times 20 percent = 3 million). I would add in an extra 1 million because the uninsured don't receive constant health care and have a higher rate of obesity, heart attacks and strokes.
- Out of the 4 million uninsured that likely have a cholesterol problem, we'll assume that 25 percent or 1 million people; would buy this drug. Many have higher priorities (like feeding their families or paying rent) than spending $15 a month on a drug for a problem that they can't see or feel.
- To that 1 million I'd add a group of people ages 20 to 40. These are people who don't have a cholesterol problem, but their parents or relatives do. Since cholesterol levels are tied into genetics, they know that they are on the same path as their parents and may want to take something now to prevent problems later.
  - Three hundred million Americans divided into four even generations of 75 million each: Thus there are 75 million Americans ages 20 to 40.
  - Assume that 5 percent of their parents have a cholesterol problem. Five percent of 75 million is 3.75 million, or 4 million. Out of that 4 million I'll assume 25 percent will take this preventative measure and buy Statin Blue. That equals 1 million preventers.
- Total of 2 million customers for the OTC drug; (This number is not set in stone.) It is not critical that the student use the same assumption numbers, just the same logic — and even then, as long as there is logic to her thoughts, that is fine.

❑ **Breakeven Calculations**
- **Prescription Breakeven**

  $40 million in costs divided by a $20 per-bottle profit equals 2 million bottles divided by 12 months equals 166,667 customers
- **OTC Breakeven**

  $40 million in costs divided by a $5 per-bottle profit equals 8 million bottles, which divided by 12 months equals 667,000 customers.

❑ **Profit Calculations**
- **Prescription:** 560,000 customers x $240 = $134.4 million
- **OTC:** 2 million customers x $60 = $120 million

What would you do?

The Final Slide

This is critical. If the student has the foresight to build the final slide, she will stand out from all the other candidates. Whenever you have a case that compares two or more strategies, options or ideas and you are applying the same criteria to both, you should build the final slide almost immediately. As you calculate the numbers, fill them in on the final slide; it keeps all relevant information in one place and makes it easier for the interviewer to follow. Once all the information is filled out, the student turns the final slide toward the interviewer and walks him through it. It is the best summary. It is also similar to the final slide of a deck that a consultant would present to a client. (Show the student this chart at the end of the case when you are walking through her analysis.)

	Prescription	OTC
Market Size		
Breakeven		
Profit		
Market Choice		
Other Concerns		

Summary

The interviewee needs to jump right into this without any down time to collect her thoughts. A good summary is about a minute, minute-and-a-half long. It is not a rehash of everything you spoke about; it is a short recap of the problem and two or three main points that the student wants the interviewer to remember.

Did the Interviewee...

- repeat the question, verifying the objective and asking about other objectives?
- make math mistakes?
- design the final slide?
- develop a logical and well-thought-out market-sizing process?
- draw the interviewer into a discussion?
- produce a good short summary touching on the most critical points?
- have well-organized and easy-to-read notes?

Mark of a Good Case Discussion: Besides the final slide, students should bring up...

- Competitive response to our entry in either market.
- Entering both markets.
  - Which market would the company enter first? (Prescription)
  - What are some of the pros and cons?

Synergies include a common manufacturing plant. We can also take advantage of already established distribution channels and marketing strategies.

Notes: Make sure the student's notes are neat, well-organized and easy-to-read. At the very least she should have divided her notes into prescription and OTC. Did she draw a line down the middle of her paper? Did she do her prescription and OTC calculations on separate sheets of paper?

✛ Bottled Water

Problem Statement

Last year Americans bought more than 4 billion gallons of bottled drinking water. Our client sold 1 billion bottles of spring water in the .5 liter size. In the past, our client has purchased the empty bottles from a guy named Ed for 5 cents each. These bottles are made from PET (polyethylene terephthalate), which is a combination of natural gas and petroleum.

Ed wants to raise his price by one penny, which would increase the client's costs by $10 million. The client is considering in-house bottle production but currently does not have the resources to do it. The CFO wants you to determine whether this makes sense. The CFO requires a two-year payback (breakeven) on investments and wants to know if the company should in-source the bottle production.

Besides determining whether to in-source bottle production, can you tell me what market share our client has of the US bottled water industry?

Guidance for the Interviewer

Make sure that the student summarizes the question and verifies the objective (determining whether to in-source bottle production) before determining market share. He should also ask if there are any other objectives he should be concerned with. The answer is that there are no other objectives to be concerned about in this case.

How to figure out market share

It needs to be done by volume of water. Tell the student to assume that one pint equals .5 liters.

If he asks (and most students do) ...

2 pints = a quart

4 quarts to the gallon; thus, 8 pints = a gallon

Easiest way is to turn everything into pints;

4 billion gallons = 32 billon pints

1 billion .5 liters = 1 billion pints

1 billion pints / 32 billion pints = about 3% of the market

Ask the student: Before we get into the numbers, just off the top of your head, can you lay out the pros and cons of in-house production?

Pros	Cons
Possible lower price	Added risk
More control over costs in the future	No experience
Produce & sell to competitors	Big investment setup costs
	Economic variables out of our control

If the student misses any from the list above, don't tell him what he missed. He'll figure it out later.

Hand the student this chart. Photocopy it from page 228.

Y1	Ed	Client
COGS	60m	?
Building	N/A	$6m
Equipment	N/A	$4m
Labor	N/A	?
Utilities & Maintenance	N/A	$.04m
Transportation	N/A	?
Admin	N/A	$1m
Cost per bottle	$0.06	?

Explain that the left-hand column represents the costs associated with bottle production. The middle column represents what the client would pay Ed (1 billion bottles times 6 cents each equals $60 million). The right-hand column represents the client. Some of the numbers have been filled in; others are still a mystery and need to be figured out.

Data Bank

COGS — The cost per gallon of PET pellets is $5. It takes 10 gallons to make 1,000 bottles. We want to make a billion bottles.

Answer: $50 / 1,000 = $0.05 per bottle
$0.05 x 1 billion bottles = $50 million

Labor — Twenty people x $4,000 a month each equals $80,000 a month.

Answer: $80,000 x 12 months = $960,000 per year (don't round up).

Transportation — It costs $0.005 to transport one bottle.

Answer: $0.005 x 1 billion = $5 million.

The completed chart should look like this:

Y1	Ed	Client
COGS	$60m	$50m
Building	N/A	$6m
Equipment	N/A	$4m
Labor	N/A	$.96m
Utilities & Maintenance	N/A	$.04m
Transportation	N/A	$5m
Admin	N/A	$1m
Cost per bottle	$0.06	$0.067

$67 million / 1 billion bottles = $0.067 per bottle

Client	$0.067
Outsource	– $0.060

$0.007 x 1 billion bottles = $7 million

The first year, we pay $7 million more than if we had purchased the bottles from Ed.

Tell the student:

For Year 2 — assume that production is up 5 percent to 1.05 billion bottles.
COGS should increase by 5 percent; the building and equipment are one-time charges and can be zeroed out. Labor, utilities and maintenance and administration remain the same, but transportation is up by 5 percent.

The new chart should look like this:

Y2	Ed	Client
COGS	$63m	$52.5m
Building	N/A	N/A
Equipment	N/A	N/A
Labor	N/A	$.96m
Utilities & Maintenance	N/A	$.04m
Transportation	N/A	$5.25m
Admin	N/A	$1m
Cost per bottle	$0.06	$0.056

Have the student come up with the new dollar total, which is $59.75 million.

(52.5 + .96 + .04 + 5.25 +1 = $59.75)

I never make the student divide 59,750,000 by 1,050,000,000; just tell him that it equals around $0.056 per bottle.

Thus $0.06 - $0.056 = $0.004 less than what we would pay Ed.

However, make the student figure out that $0.004 x 1.05 billion = $4.2 million.

To summarize so far:
Year 1: down $7 million
Year 2: up $4.2 million (so we are still down by $2.8 million)

Remember: The CFO wanted a two-year payback.

Tell the student that in Y3 the company will end up with a $3.31 million profit, so we are $510,000 in the black.

What do you tell the CFO?

The student will most likely say that we won't break even in two years; however, if we stay the course, we will become profitable in Year 3.

Tell the student that the CFO wants a two-year payback and that he needs to figure out (1) a way to break even through increasing revenues; and (2) a way to break even by lowering expenses.

Revenues side: Produce more bottles to sell to competitors.

Expense side: Lease the building and equipment.

Summary

The interviewee needs to jump right into this without any down time to collect his thoughts. A good summary is about a minute, minute-and-a-half long. It is not a rehash of everything you spoke about; it is a short recap of the problem and two or three main points that the student wants the interviewer to remember.

Did the Interviewee…

- repeat the question, verifying the objective and asking about other objectives?
- make math mistakes?
- know how to value a company?
- produce a good short summary touching on the most critical points?
- have well-organized and easy-to-read notes?

Mark of a Good Case Discussion: One thing that I look for that the students never do is to stop before they go into the meeting with the CFO and say, "If I go into the meeting now, I will have to tell the CFO that we can't do it in two years. Before I go in, I want to figure out a way to do it in two years. That way I can tell the CFO, yes we can!"

This shows great forethought and a can-do attitude that any consultant would love.

+ Smackdown Rivals*

Problem Statement

Our client, Smackdown Rivals, is a publicly traded sports entertainment company. Smackdown has successfully conceived and developed a very popular genre of wrestling that has cultivated an impassioned international fan base; as it is marketed and distributed globally across live and televised events, digital media platforms and a wide variety of consumer products.

Smackdown had revenues of $526.5 million last year, with an operating profit of $70.3 million and a net profit of $45.4 million. Smackdown has 72.85 million shares outstanding, and it has been paying dividends of $1.44 per share. The company has enjoyed a good growth trajectory and has been expanding internationally. In fact, in the past few years international revenue has been growing at twice the rate of domestic revenue. Smackdown currently employs almost 600 people, not including the approximately 150 wrestlers who are contractors under exclusive agreements with the company.

The COO has asked for your advice. Analysts have praised Smackdown's ability to generate cash, its lack of debt, its healthy revenue trajectory and its generous quarterly dividends. Yet, a few analysts have voiced concerns that costs have been rising out of proportion to growth. In addition to pleasing analysts, the COO knows, the company needs to be as efficient as possible in its operations so it can fuel strategic investments that allow international expansion and other growth possibilities.

The COO wants to keep growing the company aggressively, but he needs to make really solid choices on where and how to grow. If a future creative idea doesn't work out, it could be an expensive loss for the company. On the other hand, if Smackdown is too conservative in its growth investments, its fan base could begin spending its entertainment dollars elsewhere.

I need you to take the following five steps:

1. Determine whether costs are rising out of proportion to growth.
2. Explain whether the analysts have a valid concern about costs.
3. Based on your observations, tell me what you would advise the COO to do, if anything, regarding costs.
4. Give your opinion about how the COO should determine the appropriate cost structure for this business.
5. Give your opinion on Smackdown's recent dividend payments.

Guidance for the Interviewer

- Make sure that the student summarizes the question and verifies the objectives before starting to answer your questions.

*Written by Lynda Knoll Cotter

Questions 1 and 2

1. Calculate whether costs are rising out of proportion to growth.
2. Explain whether the analysts have a valid concern about costs.
   - Give the student Chart 1 (see page 229) and give her time to review the statement.
   - Using Chart 1, the student should be able to calculate the YOY (year over year) growth and cost percentages to answer Question 1.
   - The student might ask for more detailed data. If so, give the student Charts 2 and 3 (profitability ratios and a headcount; on page 230) and Chart 4 (a breakdown of the revenues by business unit on page 230).
   - The student should calculate the YOY percentage growth for revenue and costs as in the table below:

YOY Percentage Growth

Area	2006–7	2007–8
Revenue	17.0%	8.4%
Total Costs	19.6%	8.6%
Cost of Revenue	22.0%	4.4%
Selling/Gen./Admin	13.5%	20.3%

- From the data provided, the student should be able to make the following observations:
  - We have revenue data by line of business but not cost data, so it is difficult to make observations by line of business.
  - At a high level, total costs and revenue are staying roughly in sync. At a more detailed level, SG&A costs just took a big jump, 50 percent+, in proportion to other costs and revenue. **The concern of the analysts appears to be valid.** The student may speculate that some analysts could be worried SG&A costs will continue to rise more quickly than revenue, and the company needs to have plans to ensure that the rising SG&A will not become a trend.
  - The student might point out that the number of employees did not rise in 2008, yet SG&A costs as a percentage of revenue increased by almost 10 percent.
  - The "All Other" bucket of expenses is a high number for a catch-all category, and the student will hopefully ask what is included in the "All Other" expenses. You can tell the student that it's good she asked, but the details are not available.
  - The student should note that there was a dramatic increase in advertising and promotion (over 100 percent) in the last year.
  - Revenue from studios appears to be a new revenue stream, and it is growing the most rapidly, at over 50 percent from 2007–08. The student might hypothesize that the growth in advertising and promotion could possibly be coming from this new venture.
  - The student should comment on the increase in bad debt, and the student may wonder whether credit policies need to be tightened. The student may realize that the increase in bad debt might not be from ignoring credit policies, but instead from paying closer attention and being more aggressive in writing off uncollectible debt.

Question 3

3. Based on your observations, tell me what you would advise the COO to do, if anything, regarding costs.

- It would be difficult for the student to make detailed recommendations on cost-cutting without more detailed information on what the costs represent and how they are allocated to each line of business.
- The student should understand that costs are an investment made to grow the company. The Smackdown leadership team, analysts and investors want to ensure that the company is using its investments in the parts of the business that have the most potential.
- The student should suggest that the COO perform further investigation in the areas where costs have increased the most (i.e., advertising and promotion, bad debt, all others).
- On Chart 2, the student should be able to explain the difference between the two profitability ratios. The definitions are as follows:
  - **Gross Margin:** The percentage of revenue remaining after subtracting the cost of goods sold.
  - **Operating Margin:** The proportion of revenues remaining after taking out costs of goods sold and SG&A expenses.
- The student should be able to explain that the operating margin is going down, presumably due to the increase in SG&A costs.
- It would also be good if the student asked to see the costs of other companies in the industry, to get benchmark information. Although benchmark data is usually fairly easily available, with this particular company you would need to benchmark the different areas of the business separately, so you can tell the student that this information isn't available right now, but benchmarking in general is a good practice to follow.

Question 4

4. Give your opinion about how the COO should determine the appropriate cost structure for this business.

- The student might suggest that Smackdown should control costs differently for a growing part of the business than it does for a non-growing part of the business.
- The student should consider that a new business could require substantial startup costs and may lose money in the first year or two.
- These are good points, but regardless of whether or not a business unit is experiencing growth, the key is to control costs. A business unit leader shouldn't ever have a "no-holds –barred" approach to hiring and other expenditures, regardless of how fast her area is growing.
- The student should suggest that the cost structure for the business be based on the results of ROI analyses for new areas of growth, and that leadership should reduce costs for those lines of business that are not in a growth mode.

Question 5

5. Give your opinion on Smackdown's dividend payments.

- The student should say that Smackdown is currently using all its profits for dividends, which is not a sustainable policy in the long run.
- The student should also mention that growth companies tend not to pay dividends and generally use that money to fuel the growth instead.
- The student should understand that dividends can be a very important part of shareholder value, and she should speculate as to why this company has such a high dividend. The student may surmise that since the company is in a non-traditional business, the dividend could be used as the backbone of its stock valuation.

Data Bank

Smackdown Chart 1

Smackdown Rivals
Trending Schedules
Statement of Operations
($ in millions, unaudited)

	2006	2007	2008
Revenues	**$ 415.3**	**$ 485.7**	**$ 526.5**
Cost of Revenues	244.9	298.8	311.8
SG&A	96.1	109.1	131.3
Dep. & Amortization	8.7	9.4	13.1
Operating Income	**$ 65.6**	**$ 68.4**	**$ 70.3**
Interest and Other, net	9.8	8.0	(1.0)
Income before Taxes	**$ 75.4**	**$ 76.4**	**$ 69.3**
Interest and Other, net	26.6	24.3	23.9
Effective Tax Rate	**35%**	**32%**	**34%**
Income from Continuing Operations	**$ 48.8**	**$ 52.1**	**$ 45.4**
Discontinued Ops			0.0
Net Income	$ 48.8	$ 52.1	$ 45.4
EPS - Continuing Operations	**$0.68**	**$0.72**	**$0.62**
EPS - Net Income	$0.68	$0.72	$0.62
Memo:			
EBIDTA	$ 74.3	77.8	83.4
EBIDTA margin %	18%	16%	16%

Smackdown Chart 2

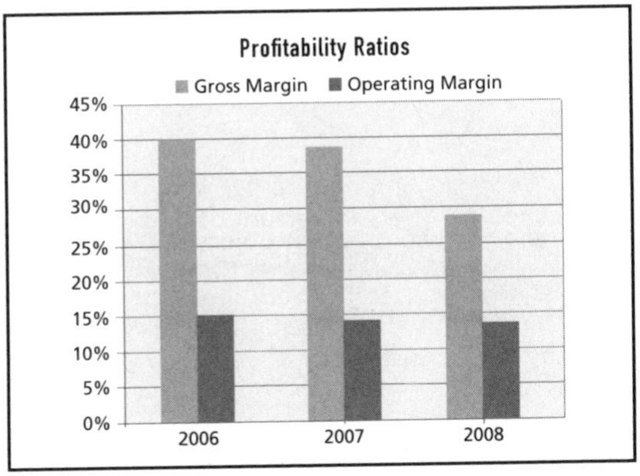

Smackdown Chart 3

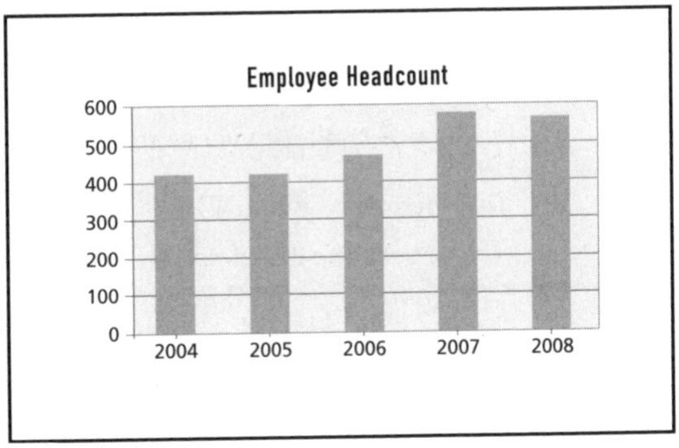

Smackdown Chart 4

	2006	2007	2008
Revenues			
Live & TV entertainment	$292.2	$316.8	$331.5
Consumer products	95.0	118.1	135.7
Digital media	28.1	34.8	34.8
Smackdown Studios	0.0	16.0	224.5
Total revenues	$415.3	$485.7	$526.5

	2006	2007	2008
Staff related	$44.7	$50.3	$55.2
Legal accounting and other professional	10.9	14.0	16.6
Stock compensation	4.7	7.8	8.0
Advertising and promotion	5.2	5.4	11.6
Bad debt	0.5	0.1	2.5
All other	30.1	31.5	37.4
Total SG&A	**$96.1**	**$109.1**	**$131.3**
SG&A as a percentage of revenue	23%	23%	25%

Summary

The interviewee needs to jump right into this without any down time to collect her thoughts. A good summary is about a minute, minute-and-a-half long. It is not a rehash of everything you spoke about; it is a short recap of the problem and two or three main points that the student wants the interviewer to remember.

Did the Interviewee...

- repeat the question, verifying the objective and asking about other objectives?
- quantify her findings?
- make math mistakes?
- produce a good short summary touching on the most critical points?
- have well-organized and easy-to-read notes?

Mark of a Good Case Discussion: This is a tough case. Did the student get rattled by what was asked of her, or did she jump right in? Did she know to ask for more data and what information to pull out? With this case, it is easy to get overwhelmed, so award extra points for staying calm and working through it.

✢ TedEx

Problem Statement

Your client is TedEx (very similar to FedEx). It has annual revenues of $40 billion. It ships 2.5 billion packages a year. The average customer ships five packages per year.

In a survey, its customer service ranked high in all areas except lost package compensation. The complaints included:

- TedEx never tells me when my package is lost.
- Time-consuming, multi-step process that puts the responsibility on the customer.
- Four week payout timetable (takes four weeks to get a check).

What are the lost packages and poor service costing TedEx, and how can it improve its customer service?

Guidance for the Interviewer

The student should repeat the question to make sure everyone is on the same page, and she should verify the objective (How can we improve customer service and increase profits?). She should also ask if there are any other objectives she needs to be concerned with — in this case the answer is no other objectives.

The case should be broken down into two parts, costs and service. On the cost side, we are looking for three numbers: (1) insurance payouts (assume that TedEx pays insurance claims out of its own pocket), (2) business lost because of poor service and (3) the amount spent by TedEx when a package is lost. On the service side, we are looking for ways to streamline the reimbursement process.

Data Bank

Hopefully, the student will ask, how many packages does TedEx lose a year and what does it cost them?

Tell her: TedEx loses 3 percent of its packages, and 80 percent of those lost packages were insured for the minimum $100. This is the group we care about — this 80 percent. We are assuming that every package automatically gets insured for $100 regardless of the contents of the package.

Of the 80 percent of the lost packages with an automatic value of $100, 20 percent of those customers give up on their claim because the process is too cumbersome. Of that 20 percent, 25 percent walk away from TedEx and go to another carrier.

Here are the numbers for you: TedEx loses 3 percent of its packages (75 million: 2.5B x .03 = 75 million) and 80 percent of those (60 million: 75 million x .8 = 60 million) packages were insured for the minimum $100. We are assuming that every package automatically gets insured for $100 regardless of the contents of the package.

Of those 60 million lost packages with an automatic value of $100 (remember, this is the group we care about), 20 percent (12 million: 60 million x .20 = 12 million) of the customers give up on their claim because the process is too cumbersome. **Assume that customers only lose one package, so think of packages and customers as the same.**

TedEx Notes

2.5B x .03 =
75M lost pkgs
↙ ↘
80% Auto-insured for $100
60m pkgs
↙ ↘

20% give up
12m people / pkgs
↙
25% leave = 3m
$40b / 2.5b pkgs = $16/pkgs
3m x ($16 x 5) = $240m

80% successful for $100
48m pkgs
48m x $100 = $4.8b

** Note: How the student lays out her notes becomes very important. The biggest mistakes I see in this case result simply because the student's notes are a mess. If she uses a tree design, then her notes will be clean, and easy to follow and she'll be able to find the information she needs quickly. Ideally, her notes should look like this. If they don't, then at the end of the case show her these notes.*

How much does TedEx lose in future sales?

Twenty-five percent of the 12 million or 3 million (3 million: 12 million x .25 = 3 million) switch to another carrier. If the average revenue per package is $16 ($16: $40 billion/2.5 billion = $16) and if the average customer ships 5 packages a year, that is equal to 15 million (15 million: 3 million x 5 number of average packages sent = $15 million packages a year times the $16 average revenue per package). Thus, TedEx loses $240 million a year due to customers switching after a frustrating experience ($16 x 15 million = $240 million) in future sales.

How much does it cost TedEx to process the lost package claim?

Assume that it costs TedEx $4 per claim when you take into account labor, processing time and overhead. Sixty million packages times $4 equals $240 million.

How much does TedEx pay out in insurance?

Assume that TedEx pays its own insurance. Eighty percent of the 60 million claims are successful, which means TedEx pays $100 each for 48 million packages, or $4.8 billion in claims.

The three numbers we are looking for:

1. $240 million in lost business next year
2. $4.8 billion in insurance payouts (48 million x $100 = $4.8 billion)
3. $240 million in lost package processing costs (60 million x $4 = $240 million)

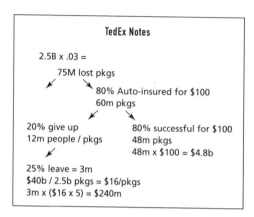

That totals $5.28 billion. **Ask the student what percentage of the total revenues that represents.** Answer: about 13 percent (5.28/40 =13%).

Guidance for the Interviewer

Tell the student that a team down the hall came up with ways to streamline the process. The outcome was the following:

1. The $4 lost package processing fee was reduced to $1 per lost package.
2. The customers who were going to leave TedEx stay.
3. TedEx received very high marks on its customer service.
4. The number of successful claims rose from 80 percent to 100 percent.

Ask: What does this mean for TedEx?

1. The processing fee was reduced to $60 million from $240 million.
2. We don't lose $240 million in defecting customers.
3. TedEx's customer service got high marks, which was one of the objectives.
4. Insurance payouts grew from $4.8 billion to $6 billion! TedEx is paying out $1.2 billion more in insurance claims.

Ask: How can we reduce the amount of money TedEx pays out in claims?

1. Reduce the number of lost packages.
2. Reduce the dollar payout per claim from $100 to $50, which will save $3 billion dollars. Not all packages are worth $100.
3. Instead of paying out cash, TedEx should credit the customer's account or give a TedEx credit. That way...
   a. They keep the customer.
   b. There's no dollar payout.
   c. It might take customers three to six months to use up the credit, or they may never use it.
   d. If the customer does use it and TedEx's margins are 50 percent, then it is only paying out $25 in actual services.

Summary

She needs to jump right into to this without any down time to collect her thoughts. A good summary is about a minute, minute-and-a-half long. It is not a rehash of everything you spoke about; it is a short recap of the problem and two or three main points that she wants the interviewer to remember.

TedEx has received poor marks on customer service relating to lost packages. They are also paying out an extraordinarily high 13 percent of their revenues in lost package expenses. We've worked to streamline the claims process, which resulted in high customer service marks, but also greatly increased the amount of money TedEx pays out in claims. We've come up with three ways to reduce those payouts: reduce the number of lost packages, reduce the dol-

lar amount of an automatic payout to $50 from $100 and credit the claim money to the customer's TedEx account. These three steps should greatly reduce the amount of money TedEx pays out in lost package claims.

Did the interviewee...

A good interview consists of:

- repeating the question, verifying the objective and asking about other objectives.
- making no math mistakes.
- keeping well-organized and easy-to-read notes.
- recognizing quickly that streamlining the process will cost TedEx more in claim payouts.
- realizing that TedEx might have made the process cumbersome on purpose so fewer people will claim the money.
- developing a good short summary touching on the most critical points.

Mark of good discussion: Did the student realize that increasing the successful claims from 80 percent to 100 percent was going to be expensive? Did she recognize that maybe TedEx made the process cumbersome on purpose so fewer people would claim their money (think mail-in rebate)? In addition, the last idea (crediting the customer's TedEx account) is the one idea that very few students ever get. So, if they get it; they deserve big points.

Most of this is psychological. The biggest assets a candidate can bring are a measure of confidence, a perspective of self-worth and a good night's sleep. The interview structure is daunting, the people generally intimidating and the atmosphere tense, but you can slay all these dragons immediately when you choose to arm yourself with a positive self-image. In the end, it's not whether you are right or wrong, it is how you present yourself, your information and your thinking. This is the measure of marketability for the firm and it is what they seek to determine through an imperfect process.

Practice before your interview. No athlete you ever admired stepped up to the plate or went out on the playing field without warming up. You need to do the same thing. You need to get into the right mindset. Log on to CQI and run through some math problems, market-sizing cases or maybe even a full case. It's difficult to walk in off the street and do a case cold. When you did two or three practice cases with your friends, you probably did better on the second or third case than the first, even if the first case was easier. Get into the zone. You don't want the interview to be your first case of the day.

Finally, it's only you against the beast (the case question, not the interviewer). We can't be there with you, but we've given you the tools to feel confident and to have a good time. If you're excited about the challenge and the interview, then you're headed into the right profession. If you dread what's coming, you may want to re-evaluate your career choice. When discussing career choices, Winston Churchill advised his children, "Do what you like, but like what you do." It's all about having fun.

It's easy to forget that the firms know you can do the work — they wouldn't be interviewing you if they didn't think you were smart enough to succeed. Now it's just time to prove them right.

Case closed!

Just in case
If you need more practice, check out CQ Interactive at casequestions.com.

+ Test Prep

Test Prep Chart 1
Hand the student chart 1.

Number of US students getting tutoring assistance (millions)

	Students	Industry Revenue		
Y1	3	$1,210		
Y2	4	$1,375		
Y3	5.5	$1,595		

Test Prep Chart 2
Hand the student Chart 2.

Our Company			
	Revenues	Costs	Profits
Y1	500	450	50
Y2	550	495	55
Y3	600	540	60

Competitor One			
	Revenues	Costs	Profits
Y1	500	450	50
Y2	550	475	75
Y3	600	500	100

Competitor Two (start-up–3 yrs. ago)			
	Revenues	Costs	Profits
Y1	100	90	10
Y2	150	100	50
Y3	250	110	140

+ Online Movies

Hand the student this chart.

US Digital Movie Download Market Share By Downloads

	Market share	Δ in market share
Apple	65.8%	↑ 1%
Microsoft	16.2%	↓ 2%
Wal-Mart	5.3%	↑ 4.3%
Sony	4.47%	↓ 4%
Amazon	4.2%	↑ 2%

+ Nerves of Steel

Hand the student this chart.

Y1	Y2	Y3	Y4	Y5	Y6	Y7	Y8
$263	$554	$615	$600	$610	$750	$810	?

✢ Statin Blue

Statin Blue Chart 1

Hand the student this chart.

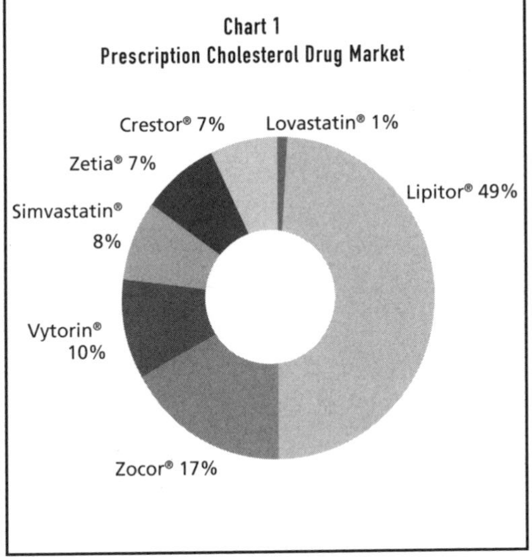

Statin Blue Chart 2

Walk the student through this chart.

250	Big Trouble (represents 10% of the overall prescription cholesterol market)	
220	Other Prescription Cholesterol Drugs (represents 80% of the overall prescription cholesterol market)	
200	Statin Blue (We believe that the patients whose cholesterol levels fall between 200 and 220 make up 10% of the overall cholesterol market.)	10%
180	Honey Nut Cheerios & Exercise	
<180	Healthy	

Statin Blue Chart 3

Show the student this chart during your analysis.

	Prescription	OTC
Market Size		
Breakeven		
Profit		
Market Choice		
Other Concerns		

+ Bottled Water

Bottled Water Chart

Hand the student this chart.

Y1	Ed	Client
COGS	60m	?
Building	N/A	$6m
Equipment	N/A	$4m
Labor	N/A	?
Utilities & Maintenance	N/A	$.04m
Transportation	N/A	?
Admin.	N/A	$1m
Cost per bottle	$0.06	?

+ Smackdown Rivals

Smackdown Chart 1

Smackdown Rivals
Trending Schedules
Statement of Operations
($ in millions, unaudited)

	2006	2007	2008
Revenues	**$ 415.3**	**$ 485.7**	**$ 526.5**
Cost of Revenues	244.9	298.8	311.8
SG&A	96.1	109.1	131.3
Dep. & Amortization	8.7	9.4	13.1
Operating Income	**$ 65.6**	**$ 68.4**	**$ 70.3**
Interest and Other, net	9.8	8.0	(1.0)
Income before Taxes	**$ 75.4**	**$ 76.4**	**$ 69.3**
Interest and Other, net	26.6	24.3	23.9
Effective Tax Rate	**35%**	**32%**	**34%**
Income from Continuing Operations	**$ 48.8**	**$ 52.1**	**$ 45.4**
Discontinued Ops			0.0
Net Income	$ 48.8	$ 52.1	$ 45.4
EPS - Continuing Operations	**$0.68**	**$0.72**	**$0.62**
EPS - Net Income	$0.68	$0.72	$0.62
<u>Memo:</u>			
EBIDTA	$ 74.3	77.8	83.4
EBIDTA margin %	18%	16%	16%

Smackdown Chart 2

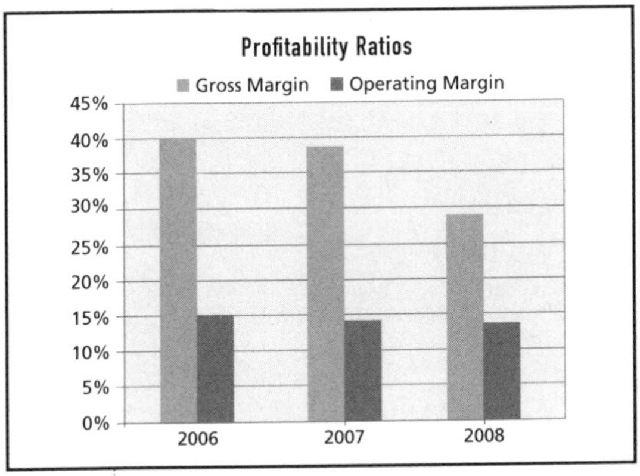

Smackdown Chart 3

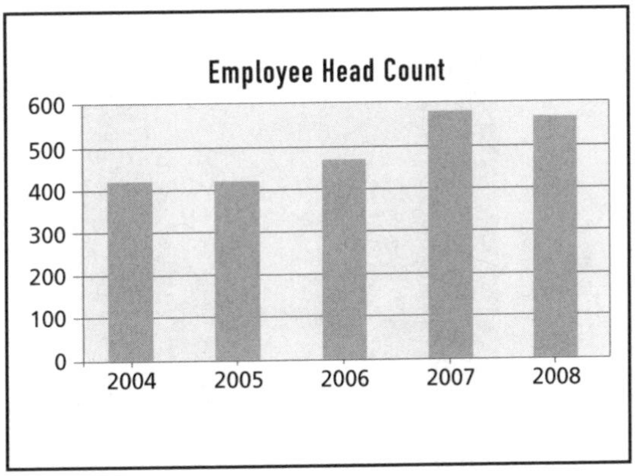

Smackdown Chart 4

	2006	2007	2008
Revenues			
Live & TV entertainment	$292.2	$316.8	$331.5
Consumer products	95.0	118.1	135.7
Digital media	28.1	34.8	34.8
Smackdown Studios	0.0	16.0	224.5
Total revenues	$415.3	$485.7	$526.5

Smackdown Chart 5

	2006	2007	2008
Staff related	$44.7	$50.3	$55.2
Legal accounting and other professional	10.9	14.0	16.6
Stock compensation	4.7	7.8	8.0
Advertising and promotion	5.2	5.4	11.6
Bad debt	0.5	0.1	2.5
All other	30.1	31.5	37.4
Total SG&A	**$96.1**	**$109.1**	**$131.3**
SG&A as a percentage of revenue	23%	23%	25%

Photo: Martha Stewart 2005

About the Author

Cosentino is the CEO of CaseQuestions.com. Over the past 25 years he has advised and coached over 100,000 students and alumni. He has written four books involving cases and consulting. *Case in Point* is now published in four languages and was called the "MBA Bible" by the *Wall Street Journal*. Cosentino has traveled nationwide giving workshops to students at colleges and graduate programs and has held training sessions for career services professionals. He has consulted with and designed cases for private sector firms, government agencies and non-profits.

Cosentino is a graduate of Harvard's Kennedy School, Harvard's Program on Negotiation and the University of Denver.